THE TWO REVOLUTIONS

QUEER / TRANS / DIGITAL

General Editors: Bonnie Ruberg, Amanda Phillips, micha cárdenas

This interdisciplinary series features scholarship that connects queer and transgender issues with digital media and digital technologies. It emphasizes intersectional lenses, foregrounding work that explores topics such as race, disability, and colonialism as co-constituted with gender and sexuality. Across both the humanities and social sciences, contemporary research is increasingly turning to digital media objects and online spaces as key sites for understanding identity and power, both in the present technological moment and across the history of computing. This series embraces this turn by offering a dedicated platform for work that explores the digital in relation to sexuality, gender, desire, and community. Focusing on critical, cultural studies approaches to the social issues that surround technology, this series welcomes work that seeks to understand digital media and digital cultures created about, for, or by queer and transgender people, who are simultaneously working at the forefront of technological innovation and experiencing ongoing and shifting forms of digital oppression.

The Two Revolutions

A History of the Transgender Internet

Avery Dame-Griff

NEW YORK UNIVERSITY PRESS
New York

NEW YORK UNIVERSITY PRESS
New York

www.nyupress.org
© 2023 by New York University
All rights reserved

Please contact the Library of Congress for Cataloging-in-Publication data.
ISBN: 9781479818303 (hardback)
ISBN: 9781479818310 (paperback)
ISBN: 9781479818327 (library ebook)
ISBN: 9781479818341 (consumer ebook)

New York University Press books are printed on acid-free paper, and their binding materials are chosen for strength and durability. We strive to use environmentally responsible suppliers and materials to the greatest extent possible in publishing our books.

Manufactured in the United States of America

10 9 8 7 6 5 4 3 2 1

Also available as an ebook

CONTENTS

Introduction: Laying the Foundations   1

1. Dialing into the Revolution: The Bulletin Board System   29

2. Out of the Cybercloset, Into the Cyberstreets:
   Gender Community Spaces on AOL and Beyond   56

3. Politics and "Petty Useless Bickering":
   Transgender Usenet and the Emergence of "Cisgender"   81

4. Always On: Information, Circulation, and
   the World Wide Web   115

5. Becoming "Obsolete in Your Own Lifetime":
   Membership Declines and Generation Gaps   146

6. Transgender in the Platform Era   174

Conclusion: Owning Our History   201

Acknowledgments   211

Notes   213

Bibliography   233

Index   253

About the Author   265

Introduction

Laying the Foundations

My entire life, I've lived with computers. I can't remember a time when there wasn't one in the house, or when it didn't have an Internet connection. For those like me—middle-class kids who grew up during the Clinton administration's push to get Americans online and the dot-com bubble (and subsequent bust)—the Internet-connected computer became an omnipresent part of our lives, from home to school. Unlike many of my peers, though, there were always two Internet-connected computers in the home: my father's, and my hand-me-downs. Since my father was a systems administrator, maintaining a good Internet connection was essential. I remember a lot of nights with him at work troubleshooting a server on his PC, while I chatted with strangers in any number of web-based fan chat rooms. Despite my seeming computer aptitude, I didn't take to all coding, as I learned during my father's one failed attempt to teach me BASIC. But HTML came more naturally. With the assistance of Frontpage, Microsoft's since-discontinued WYSIWYG (What You See Is What You Get) HTML editor, I created a seemingly endless stream of frames-based fan pages studded with 16-bit animated GIFs and tinny-sounding embedded MIDI files, which then led to eight years of serving as a moderator on midsize message boards.

In every one of these spaces, though, I would always have to eventually "come out," so to speak, as a woman. In a space where users were most commonly identified by usernames and giant robot icons, gender identity was easy to leave unspoken. I never specifically avoided telling people, but I found the presumption of maleness comforting for what were then-nebulous reasons. By the time I identified as trans, I located this habit as part of a larger pattern, enabled by the Internet. My first connections with trans folks came online—a friend of a friend, a German trans man whose writings on his experiences were eerily similar to

Figure I.1. Author's home computer setup in December 1995. Photo courtesy of Michael G. Dame.

my own—and I stayed in contact with trans folks via a state-wide Yahoo Group. Given the risks inherent to being trans in the American South, the Internet was a lifeline for many members. Even after I moved away, it remained a key resource and support system for me. The role of the Internet in my experience was by no means unique. Online, trans youth found and supported each other across a variety of fora, ranging from IRC chat rooms, message boards, home pages, LiveJournal, MySpace, and beyond. For this generation, the Internet was an increasingly quotidian part of their lives. For those who came into their trans identity in the 1970s and 1980s, however, the rise of the desktop computer and the Internet revolutionized not only how they communicated but also the very makeup of what was then known as the "gender community." For these individuals, the Internet ushered in a second revolution: the rise of the term "transgender," which evolved from one self-identity among many to a collective umbrella over the entire community. The contemporary trans movement as we know it now—with all its accomplishments and its failures—could not have come to be without the Internet.

This book chronicles this transformational period, as movement actors launched a national, public-facing agenda under the aegis of a new name: "transgender." Digital communications, including the Internet, were an essential, if often unacknowledged, part of these efforts. Information that had once taken weeks to months to spread widely could circulate within days online, and the limited barriers to publication compared to a print periodical created space for a variety of new voices to enter the conversation. At the same time, the increased corporatization of digital platforms meant that trans users were forced to advocate for themselves, long before more contemporary efforts, like the successful user campaign to get Facebook to add more gender options in 2014. But these revolutions had long-term consequences. Increased reliance on digital platforms, which sometimes required significant access to capital, reinforced existing racial and economic disparities within the movement. Furthermore, trans individuals' preferences for socializing and finding support online weakened the network of local and regional groups who'd built the intracommunity infrastructure that made these revolutions possible. For a generation of trans individuals who'd first come out online, in-person peer groups held far less appeal than an online forum. These changes are reflected in the shifting populations at the center of this book. While much of the first four chapters focuses on the work of transsexual women and heterosexual crossdressers, the final two chapters discuss individuals who, throughout the 1970s and 1980s, were considered by many in the community an "impossible category": out trans youth. Yet, as I discuss in chapter 6, trans youth and adults who are coming out now continue to face challenges online that echo earlier revolutionary struggles.

Beyond just being a social history of trans activism, *The Two Revolutions* is also a net history, which begins not with technology but with users. As media historians Kevin Driscoll and Camille Paloque-Bergès argue, net histories "are concerned with the everyday experience of living and working among computers and networks," covering "any number of systems: a campus network, Usenet, a local BBS, a commercial online service, or some combination of all of them." Ultimately, "the Net arises out of the imaginations of its users."[1] In contrast to existing histories that center great thinkers amid upward progress narratives, net histories reflect the Internet's polymorphic sprawl across geographic and temporal borders, making room for "new origins, side quests, counterfactuals, and net mythologies."[2] For, just as the current trans movement wouldn't exist in its current form without the Internet, the Internet was inescapably shaped by the presence of trans users. In the 1980s and early 1990s, digital platforms struggled with their unclear status in US law: Were they classified as publishers or distributors of content? As publishers, they were liable for content posted to their services, but, if they were seen as distributors, they were not. The presence of trans users, alongside other possibly objectionable populations, forced companies to grapple with what they defined as "obscene" content and how they would manage it on their platform. In the early 2000s and beyond, trans people would again pose challenges for platforms that sought to tie users' Internet presence to their supposed "real names."

This history of the transgender net, then, focuses on a group of users ranging from professional programmers and long-time hobbyists to total newbies who first connected to the Internet when they plugged an AOL floppy into their A: drive. As such, it primarily takes the perspective of consumers, who had limited access to the technical aspects of a platform's infrastructure and little say in the policies that governed them. When safe space online wasn't granted to them, these users made space for themselves through obfuscation and elision, manipulating existing infrastructure to meet their needs, using techniques they'd already perfected over a long history of silencing and oppression.

A Brief History of Transgender Movement Building

For trans people in the United States, the 1970s were a particularly turbulent time. The decade began with increasing visibility, activism, and organizing, only to see most of these efforts challenged or halted by its end. In the late 1960s, a new network of university-supported trans care clinics had begun to emerge, offering transition-related care to a select number of patients who met clinicians' criteria. Alongside them arose a burgeoning social movement, driven not only by groups like the Erikson Education Foundation (EEF), which engaged in institutional advocacy, but also radical liberation groups such as the Street Transvestite Action Revolutionaries (STAR), founded by Sylvia Rivera and Marsha P. Johnson, and the Queens' Liberation Front (QLF). These groups, drawing inspiration and energy from the gay liberation movement, focused on direct action and providing mutual aid for other trans people. At the same time, heterosexual crossdressers were building their own national network through the work of Virginia Prince, publisher of *Transvestia*, one of the first periodicals focused on cross-dressing, and founder of Phi Pi Epsilon, or the Foundation for Personality Expression (FPE), a chapter-based organization that sponsored support groups and social outings for members. In 1976, FPE merged with a similar organization, Mamselle, founded by Carol Beecroft, to become the Society for the Second Self (more commonly known as Tri-Ess), headed by Beecroft. Structurally, Tri-Ess was inspired by college sororities, wherein a national branch oversaw a variety of smaller, regional sororities, all of which use Greek letter naming conventions. Unlike other movement groups, most crossdressers involved in Tri-Ess saw their cross-dressing not as a shared identity but as a private practice, and group membership offered them a social outlet. Moreover, Tri-Ess's emphasis on members' middle-class respectability severely limited qualification for membership—centering members who had little reason to risk said middle-class status by engaging in activism.[3]

As transgender historian Susan Stryker chronicles in her *Transgender History*, much of this progress was halted or undone as a result of multiple social factors, from the defunding of university-based clinics serving trans individuals to the emergence of anti-trans radical feminism, which sought to restrict trans individuals' access to medical care and functionally expel them from public life. As a result, by the early 1980s, most of the surviving community groups and events had shifted their attention away from public advocacy to intracommunity development.[4] These groups formed the core of what was then known as the "gender community," a term signaling community members' shared gender-related interests. One of the most notable of these early groups was the Human Outreach and Achievement Institute (later renamed the Outreach Institute for Gender Studies), founded in 1975 by Ariadne Kane. The institute was heavily involved in both educational outreach to medical professionals and also running the annual Fantasia Fair conference in Provincetown, Massachusetts. However, its higher public profile was unusual for the time, as most other active groups operated on a relatively small scale and focused on offering support and socializing in monthly meetings mixed with occasional outings to friendly local restaurants, clubs, or bars. Generally, these groups concentrated on the needs of middle-class individuals, though the makeup of their membership varied: while the Tiffany Club (later the Tiffany Club of New England, or TCNE) and the Golden Gate Girls/Guys (later renamed the Gateway Gender Alliance or GGA) had a mixed membership, allowing both transsexuals and crossdressers, Tri-Ess restricted their membership to heterosexual male crossdressers. Notably, the GGA was one of the few organizations to include trans men and trans masculine individuals, who lacked a national presence until Lou Sullivan founded FTM, a peer support group, in 1986, which would eventually become FTM International.

By the late 1980s, however, increasing interest in political advocacy drove the founding of several prominent national level groups specifically focused on outreach and public education. The first (and largest) of these organizations was the International Foundation for Gender Education (IFGE), founded in 1987 by TCNE president Merissa Lynn Sherrill. That same year, the IFGE held its first major conference, "Coming Together, Working Together," where attendees from a variety of smaller groups assembled for movement building. These discussions continued in IFGE's magazine, *TV-TS Tapestry* (renamed *Transgender Tapestry* in 1995), which for many years was the most widely circulated English-language trans-related periodical. That same year, JoAnn Roberts, Alison Laing, Angela Gardner, Trudy Henry, and Melanie Bryan cofounded the Philadelphia-based Renaissance Education Association (later renamed the Renaissance Transgender Association). Like Tri-Ess, the group operated via a chapter system, but was open to both transsexuals and crossdressers. Roberts and Laing would go on to have long careers with trans activism; Roberts would be involved in several different political groups, while Laing would for many years serve as an IFGE board member, including a two-year stint as executive director. Even before founding Renaissance, Roberts was involved in the community through the publishing house she founded in 1985, Creative Design Services (CDS). Throughout the 1980s and 1990s, CDS published a variety of informational and educational materials, such as *LadyLike Magazine, International TranScript, Renaissance News & Views* (later *Transgender Community News & Views*), as well as maintaining the first large trans community website (which is still active today), Transgender Forum (TGForum).

Groups would continue to emerge throughout the 1990s, only beginning to slow down at the start of the 2000s.⁵ In 1990, Atlanta-based activist Dallas Denny founded American Educational Gender Information Service (AEGIS), which offered a variety of informational pamphlets, as well as publishing the *Chrysalis Quarterly* journal. Three years later, Riki Wilchins and Denise Norris founded direct action group Transexual Menace (later renamed Transgender Menace) and achieved public visibility for their protests and vigils related to the murder of Brandon Teena. In 1995, Wilchins would be named executive director of the first trans-specific political action committee, GenderPAC, which advocated around issues of gender stereotyping and discrimination and sponsored an annual National Gender Lobbying Day.⁶

Such rapid growth wouldn't have been possible without the movement's sizable and active network of publications, which ranged from the magazines and journals mentioned above to numerous smaller group newsletters published with some regularity by local and regional support groups. Compared to *Tapestry*, *LadyLike*, *Chrysalis*, or the *Femme Mirror* (Tri-Ess's national journal), these newsletters were much more modest, often focused on group news, events, and local issues. However, they also provided a forum for group members to discuss the major community issues of the day, and a lifeline for those who weren't able to attend in-person meetings. Collectively, these publications formed the underlying infrastructure of the increasingly interconnected gender community. As media scholar Cait McKinney notes in their analysis of lesbian media technologies, this "everyday work" of maintaining information infrastructure "provides crucial support for the high-stakes goals that drive social movements in the first place."⁷ For the lesbian archivists, historians, indexers, and catalogers, among many others, that McKinney studied, this work was a form of "information activism," providing the "basic support and care that makes living a lesbian life possible."⁸ In a similar vein, gender community members relied on these publications as a safe space where their cross-gender interests were not just accepted but celebrated. They were also the main venue for community discourse, including one increasingly prominent debate throughout the 1990s: What should we be called?

What's In a Name?

Developing community-specific terminology for gender nonconformity had long been a goal for members. Though their etymology vary, new terms' shared primary objective was better describing individuals' experience of gender in ways that didn't forefront pathology or deviancy. One of the first efforts was spearheaded by Virginia Prince in 1961. In her role as head of FPE, Prince pushed to replace the terms "transvestite" and "transvestitism," which she felt were closely associated with sexual deviancy, with what she considered the more desexualized "feminiphilia," "feminiphile," "femmephile," and "femmepersonation"—all of which terms remained largely unused beyond Prince herself.[9] Once Prince began living full-time as a woman in 1968, she would coin (and then abandon) the term "transgenderal" to differentiate herself from transsexuals, eventually adopting the term "transgenderist" in 1978 to describe those who lived as their identified gender but didn't seek surgical intervention. Notably, all three of these categories (transsexual, transvestite or crossdresser, and transgenderist) reflected dominant understandings of gender as a binary, be it crossed full or part time. Those who felt they were not on one side or the other, however, sought out terminology to describe this "other" experience. One popular choice was "androgyne," which had roots in classical writing and psychoanalysis, and its adopters included Ariadne Kane. Others used the term "bigender" (as well as variants like "bigendered" and "bigenderist"), which appeared in the *Journal for the International Alliance for Male Feminism* as early as 1979.[10] A list of relevant terms and the definitions commonly used for them within the gender community in the 1980s and 1990s can be found in table 1.1; note that some of these definitions, as well as the language used, may differ from the way these terms are currently defined.

This community-specific lexicon, in the view of community members and leaders, served an important role in not only building commonality between individuals and groups but also challenging the dominant, clinical understandings of cross-gender interests. Periodicals ran glossaries of relevant terms, or articles explaining these terms and the reason their use mattered, and they developed pamphlets for distribution at professional conferences with allied medical professionals.[11] The Outreach Institute framed their pamphlet, *A New Glossary for Better Understanding*,

Table 1.1. Definitions for terms common in the gender community during the 1980s.

Term	Definition
Transsexual (TS)	An individual who does not identify with the gender or sex assigned at birth and, as a result, pursues related medical care, including hormone replacement therapy (HRT) and sex reassignment surgery.
Transvestite (TV)	An individual who enjoys regularly wearing clothing associated with their opposite gender. Unlike the associated psychological diagnosis that uses the same term, their dressing may or may not have an erotic component.
Crossdresser (CD)	Has the same definition as TV, but became the preferred term within the community in the 1980s.
Transgenderist (TG)	An individual who permanently lives as a gender different from the one assigned at birth. May pursue hormone replacement therapy, but does not seek gender-related surgical care.
Androgyne	A person who might comfortably express their gender in either binary role in social settings. Some definitions include bigenderist as a subcategory of androgyne.

as bridging "the gap between outmoded and misused terminology which has been used by professional people and the general public" and promoting "improved clarity and better communications and understanding."[12] Though organizations advocated for professionals and the public to adopt in-community terminology, community members remained ambivalent about the boundaries between terms like "transsexual," "crossdresser," and "transgenderist." Some would experiment with inventing new terms, like "transvitate," "contragender," "gender ambiguous," and "gender transient," though none of them would see much use beyond their inventors.[13] It's worth noting that, according to the archival record, in-community terminology discussions are centered almost entirely around the concerns of trans women, transgenderists, and heterosexual crossdressers; until the early 1990s, trans men are largely absent.

Other advocates focused on changing terminology and definitions in educational or reference texts. In the early 1990s, Tri-Ess president Carol Beecroft led a campaign to urge authors of college-level psychology textbooks to change how they defined and discussed cross-dressing, while Billie Jean Jones, an active member of California-based ETVC and editor of independent newsletter *TV Guise* (later renamed *GenderFlex*), proposed a "Dictionary Project" to lobby major dictionaries and lexicographers to remove associations between biological sex and gender in their definitions of "transsexual" and "transvestite."[14] In the mid-1990s, Transexual Menace founder Riki Wilchins would make a similar effort at redefinition by using the single-s spelling of "transexual." According to Wilchins, changing the spelling would allow trans individuals to "[take] back a little power over what we were called," since, "if the entire community started spelling it this way, sooner or later the Powers That Be would have to accept it."[15] While this alternative spelling never caught on, the implication was clear: self-definition was a first step to community pride and activism.

This same impetus underlay efforts emerging in the early 1990s to replace "gender," which had always been relatively nonspecific, with "transgender" as the chosen term for the community. Part of this nonspecificity was related to the two largest subgroups that made up the so-named gender community: heterosexual crossdressers and transsexuals. Heterosexual crossdressers who followed the party line of Tri-Ess distanced themselves from transsexuals for fear that the association would make others, particularly spouses, assume their cross-dressing was a "first step" to transition. In contrast, transsexual individuals emphasized an innate "female" gender and built in-group boundaries around their identity by going "full time" and passing, as opposed to the "fantasy" of the transvestite.[16] Developing a shared political consciousness within the community, then, would require a shared term not merely to unite the "fractured" groups featured in figure 1.2, but to adequately describe the lived experience of their constituent members. These terminological turf wars were so omnipresent that they inspired several satirical takes: a "Gender Terms Mix-N-Match" activity reprinted in the September 1992 issue of community periodical *Cross-Talk* (fig. 1.3), and a proposed list of new community terminology (reprinted in the April 1993 issue of *Cross-Talk*) that was, according to author Sarah, more in keeping with "the New Wave culture." Entries ranged wildly from "Heels on wheels: CD who sneaks out to drive the car" and "Fembot: CD who talks computers" to "Sears towers: Tall CD in high heels."[17]

Several different collective umbrella terms were proposed, including "bigenderal" by Virginia Prince and "conscious gender community" by Adriane Kane.[18] Ultimately, though, repurposing "transgender" as an umbrella term—early on often in the adjectival form "transgendered"—would find the most early advocates, who highlighted transgender's

Figure 1.2. This play on the famous "Join, or Die" political cartoon was first printed on the cover of Tri-Ess's quarterly newsletter, the *Femme Mirror* (Winter 1993). Each section of the snake is labeled for a prominent group within the gender community. Courtesy of the National Transgender Library and Archive, Labadie Archive, University of Michigan.

GENDER TERMS MIX-N-MATCH
by Justine Sahnjay

This contest challenges you to invent the best new mix-n-match term to describe ourselves. The most original entry wins the eternal devotion of the community for giving us the word to describe ourselves.
NOTE: Virginia Prince, Merissa S. Lynn, and Kym Richards can't enter because they are "professional termsters", and the idea of trying to invent the best terms is only for amateurs!

Bi	self
Fem	genderist
Cross	ophile
Trans	dresser
She	vestite
Mo	ronic
Eo	vert
Per	nist
Closet	dysphoric
Gender	queen
Drag	male
Homo	phobia

I thought of Bidysphoric, Femovestite, and Closetophile. But you have your own fun ... send in your terms with an explanation of how you arrived at them!

[Reprinted from "GirlTalk", Powder Puffs of Orange County, Yorba Linda CA.]

Figure 1.3. This satirical "activity," reprinted in the September 1992 issue of *Cross-Talk*, references the various debates over what the "appropriate" new term for the "gender community" would be. From *Cross-Talk: The Gender Community's News & Information Monthly* #38 (1992), courtesy of the Digital Transgender Archive.

extensive possibilities. In her 1991 article "The Transgender Alternative," Holly Boswell offered "transgender" as a term to encompass an "entire spectrum" of identities, including not only the "crossdresser to transsexual person" but also those who fell outside these two categories.[19] Leslie Feinberg, in hir 1993 pamphlet "Transgender Liberation," highlighted the political possibilities of this expansive definition. In advocating for "transgender," Feinberg argued that zie and others were "trying to find words, however inadequate, that can connect us, that can capture what is similar about the oppression we endure."[20] It's important to note that Boswell and Feinberg's uses of the term were far more expansive than modern iterations of "transgender," including any individuals who transgressed gender norms, such as drag queens, butch women, and femme men. The influence of the movement to adopt "transgender" was most immediately apparent in publication, organization, and event names. When Phyllis Randolph Frye, already active for many years as an activist and lawyer for trans causes, hosted the first conference on trans legal and policy concerns in 1992, she titled it the International Conference on Transgender Law and Employment Policy (ICTLEP). Similarly, when activist Anne Ogborn split with direct action AIDS group Queer Nation due to transphobia within the organization, she named her group Transgender Nation. And the IFGE's national "alliance" of trans organizations, the Congress of Representatives, would in the early 1990s split off from IFGE and change their name to the Congress of Transgender Organizations.[21] Most notably, in 1995, the IFGE's long-running flagship publication, *TV-TS Tapestry*, switched their title to *Transgender Tapestry*. Accompanying this flurry of renaming was material that sociologist Laurel Westbrook terms "teaching transgender articles," which defined and naturalized the term for an in-community audience.[22] Only once "transgender" had found wide acceptance among community members was the term deployed as a political tactic in other arenas, helping it to enter common usage. It's also important to note that "transgender" wasn't the only new term emerging during this period: rising visibility and acceptance of gender nonconformity led to the emergence of new terms like "genderqueer" and "intergender." However, within trans periodicals, "genderqueer" (the only of these terms to really see frequent use) had an inverse trajectory compared to "transgender," moving from a collective term inherently critiquing gender policing to an individualized identity.²³

Alongside this growing emphasis on a shared collective identity came a new focus on public, and at times confrontational, political action. Inspired by AIDS activism, groups like Transgender Nation and Transexual Menace (later Transgender Menace) picketed and held protests challenging social and governmental indifference to transphobic violence. Transexual Menace's confrontational style was visually embodied by their iconic T-shirt design: the group's name depicted in dripping blood in the style of the logo of *The Rocky Horror Picture Show*. Wilchins summarized this new approach to political organizing in the first issue of the community bulletin of political actions she edited, aptly titled *In Your Face*: "The fight against gender oppression has been joined for centuries, perhaps millennia. What's new today, is that it's moving into the arena of open *political* activism. . . . These pages are only going to grow. We're not invisible anymore. We're not well behaved. And we're not going away. Political activism is here to stay."²⁴ In the group photo taken during the first National Gender Lobbying Day in 1995, participants held a banner declaring in bold, all-caps lettering, "transgendered & proud! and we vote!" By the late 1990s, the community had a well-developed movement infrastructure and a recognizable identity—"transgender." As community member and activist Gwendolyn Ann Smith put it in 1999, "In just a few short years we've been able to put the word 'transgender' on the floor of Congress and in the pages of *Time* magazine."²⁵ Yet none of these changes would have been possible at such a rapid pace without one key element: the Internet.

Logging On

Though computers are now ubiquitous, they remained largely specialized technical objects throughout the 1980s until their domestication in the mid-1990s. In population surveys conducted by the US Census Bureau, home PC ownership increased gradually throughout the 1980s and began accelerating in the 1990s.²⁶ As marketing scholar Alladi Venkatesh argues, this increase is likely tied to the shifting perception of personal computers as solely a job-related technology to a domestic technology.²⁷ In the mid-1980s, white-collar male workers were perceived as the "model" user for the home PC, which they likely chose to purchase because they had become familiar with it through work.²⁸ And though it was possible to communicate using computers, the practice was largely restricted to bulletin board systems (or BBSes) and commercial platforms, at the time mainly called "videotex" services, and the audience for both of these technologies was relatively limited. In 1987, the Videotex Industry Association estimated the total membership of the forty existing videotex services, which included Compuserve Information Service (sometimes abbreviated as CIS) and General Electric's GEnie, was just 750,000 subscribers.²⁹ Notably, unlike contemporary Internet platforms, users of a given service were locked into a closed ecosystem, often limited to communicating with only other subscribers to that service. BBSes, in contrast, did offer system intercommunication, but their membership skewed toward the technically savvy. As a technology, the social and commercial possibilities of digital communication were clearly present from the earliest days of the BBS. As media scholar Althea Delwiche notes in her history of the BBS scene, public discussion about BBSes included themes that would become commonplace in coverage of later communication technologies: concerns about teenage use, the disruption of existing business models, long-distance romances, utopian visions of a freer digital future, and (of course) pornography.³⁰ In many ways, the BBS represents the earliest predecessor to digital social media platforms, as users and sysops grappled with questions of "anonymity, identity, privacy, sexuality, and trust," in the process establishing values and norms replicated on later platforms.³¹

By the mid-1990s in the United States, home computer ownership was beginning to grow exponentially. In 1993, competition between PC makers pushed the cost of a home system below $2,000, while relatively speedy modems were becoming increasingly affordable and commonplace, often as part of a home PC bundle or in a commercial service's "start-up kit."³² In 1994, a National Telecommunications and Information Administration (NTIA) survey found 50 percent of households that were making at least $50,000 (roughly $94,000 in 2021) had a computer and modem at home, and by 1997 that figure had jumped to 60 percent.³³ Part of this significant increase was connected to a "new wave" of computer owners who'd bought a computer for personal use within the last two years.³⁴ Now the entire household was using the computer—especially children, often as part of their schoolwork.³⁵ For some families, educational use was their stated primary reason for purchasing a home computer, even if, in practice, it was used mostly for entertainment.³⁶ Increasing demand for PCs drove the growing direct-to-consumer market, led by Dell and Gateway 2000 (who would drop the 2000 in 1998), with its iconic cow-print branded boxes. Whereas 76 percent of all PCs shipped in 1995 went to retailers before being sold to consumers, by 2005 "nearly 55 percent" of all PCs shipped were sold directly to the consumer.³⁷ Instead of focusing on technical specifications, these companies framed the PC as a customizable appliance that could either be purchased outright or, similar to a comparable home appliance or furniture purchase, financed through the company and paid off in monthly installments. Rising computer ownership was also no doubt influenced by the Clinton administration's "New Economy" logic, which posited information technology—computers and digital communications in particular—as the key to American economic success. Access to a computer and modem, they argued, were the "keys to the vault" of the "Information Age," and those without them were at risk of being left on the wrong side of the "digital divide."³⁸ And although computers were becoming increasingly affordable during this period, computer ownership continued to be generally correlated with education and income. In different surveys conducted in 1995 and 1997, over half of all home PC owners reported both earning an income of at least $50,000 or more a year and having completed a college or graduate degree. Notably, one of these surveys found that, while the proportion of white home PC owners was relatively more spread out across various income brackets, home PC ownership among people of color was far more concentrated in the upper income brackets.³⁹

One of the largest drivers of this home computer boom? The increased importance of the computer as a communication tool. The rise of the World Wide Web marked a particular moment in popular culture, as network fever overtook media. Just as the 1983 film *War Games* offered an aesthetically persuasive vision of computer communication's possibilities and risks—enough to convince then-president Ronald Reagan to pursue cybersecurity legislation—films from this era such as *Hackers* (1995) and *The Net* (1995) presented audiences with a (highly visual and stylized) vision of the possibilities of the new electronic frontier. Browsers like Netscape Navigator, also launched in 1995, made many of these features accessible to the wider population. Rhetoric of the period encouraged users to see themselves as "homesteaders," exploring new vistas and eventually staking their claims via personal home pages. The development of web design as a field was an essential part of making this rhetoric coherent. As media scholar Megan Ankerson argues, "Collective imagination yoke[d] together discourses of what cyberspace means, how it looks and feels, how it is experienced on a daily basis, and what the future portends; within this organized field of social practice, speculation meets web design."[40] The number of folks online rose steadily throughout the 1990s. By 1998, a Pew study found that 41 percent of all adult respondents were using the Internet, up from 36 percent in 1997 and 23 percent in 1996.[41] These users consistently skewed younger as well: 70 percent of eighteen- to twenty-nine-year-olds surveyed said they were regular Internet users, though thirty- to forty-nine-year-olds weren't far behind, at 61 percent. By 2005, these numbers had increased to 83 percent and 79 percent, respectively. However, this access remained concentrated among upper income brackets.[42]

All of these changes were mirrored in the US-based gender community, which was, according to author Stephanie Rose, "in the midst of two revolutions." Writing in *Chrysalis Quarterly*'s inaugural 1991 issue, Rose contrasted the overt revolution in the gender community's growing shared political consciousness around the umbrella identity of "transgender" with their more "covert . . . computer revolution," from which the community "[stood] to gain more from than any other social groups out there."[43] Rose's article was just one of many in publications both alternative and mainstream extolling the virtues of communicating via computer. Based on the amount and variety of community newsletters produced in word processors and prepackaged layout software, a not-insubstantial portion of the gender community were active computer users. Some, like programmer and artist Jamie Faye Fenton, were involved in both the San Francisco tech scene and gender community groups.[44] However, it's more likely that they used computers as part of their white-collar day jobs, while a smaller proportion may have been hobbyists on the side. Though specific details about rank-and-file community members' occupations and daily lives are limited, over half of respondents to surveys of the community conducted during the early 1990s said they had worked in white-collar professions.[45] Several notable figures held positions at corporations with major investments in hardware and software: community publisher and activist JoAnn Roberts worked at NASA in an unspecified role prior to founding Creative Design Services; longtime FTMI head Jamison Green was employed by Sun Microsystems in the late 1980s; and, prior to founding the Transsexual Menace, Riki Wilchins worked as a computer programmer and consultant on Wall Street.[46]

In this way, the gender community was primed for communicating via computer not because of a widespread community inclination to programming and tech wizardry, but due to familiarity with the mundane realities of business computing: databases, spreadsheets, and word processing. Thus, a significant part of the gender community, already within the model demographic for home computer users of the 1980s, were more likely to be able to access a computer and modem, as well as afford the phone bills associated with dialing in. The online forums they created existed in parallel to in-person community groups and at times structurally mirrored them, with registered membership, regular "meetings," and shared resource libraries. For some individuals, participation online led to becoming involved in and attending in-person group meetings. These spaces would be the primary fora for the gender community until the late 1990s and early to mid-2000s, when shifting attitudes toward the home PC and increasing rates of Internet access accompanied a generational shift within what was now called the "transgender community." The domestication of the home computer, particularly as an educational tool, made it a fixture of many middle-class American homes. No longer just for working adults, the home PC had become the primary hub of Internet-based communication for the family—particularly once the rise of the World Wide Web cemented an industry-wide shift to monthly pricing schemes, making regular Internet use more affordable. The children of these families spent at least part of their days online, and Internet use played a key role in their wider social lives. For trans and questioning youth, then, the Internet became a source of community and support. However, the community spaces they frequented were often predominantly created by and for youth, producing a wider generational shift away from existing infrastructure that mirrored the gender community makeup of the 1980s and 1990s. Though many of these earlier spaces continued to remain active, they often struggled to achieve the levels of activity they'd seen though the mid-1990s. In contrast, in the contemporary platform-defined era, earlier community-specific spaces have given way to the trans individual as a platform user. On these platforms, trans users are guided to fit their understanding of transness within the platform's defined affordances and infrastructure, instead of having a space designed for them. Yet, in making their self-identity platform ready, their understanding of said identity reflects the modular logic of the database—the identity as classifiable data, able to be easily defined, linked, and recalled. This shift, I argue, has very real consequences not only for trans individuals, especially those just coming out, but also the development of sustainable community infrastructure.

Each step of the way in the history of the computer communication, then, trans people have been there. Initially, they entered via fake doors, used coded language and passwords, wrote extended private message exchanges, or applied for membership in safe "closed" communities. Later on, they would be able to join open communities under names they chose, be they femme or self-assigned, and find social support and strength there. As server space grew less precious, and home connections increased in speed, they shared photos of themselves, created stylized home pages, joined community-specific message boards, and publicly journaled about their experiences. Like many users, they'd eventually leave their home pages, forums, and journals behind and focus their energy on contemporary social media platforms. Each successive generation of trans people have often unknowingly come out in an environment defined by those that came before. Trans youth on Instagram adopt photo sharing practices inherited from trans users of Internet yore, as far back as the BBS and its lo-fi .GIF library—users whose practices in turn arose from print magazines and their "cover girl" photo spreads. The history of trans life online is one of sedimentation, with each subsequent change leaving its remains behind to settle and eventually solidify into a mass of images, text, and memory on which new communities are built.

On Writing (Trans) Web Histories

The task of *The Two Revolutions*, therefore, is to study the fine particles and from them identify the outline of the trans Net. The reality of web archiving leaves behind a necessarily incomplete picture; part of each of the platforms discussed has already been lost. By design, many early BBS software regularly kept only a small archive of recent messages, while decentralized networks like FidoNet and early Usenet had, as Kevin Driscoll frames it, an "anti-memory design," surviving in dispersed "bits and pieces."[47] Communities hosted on corporate platforms like CompuServe, Prodigy, or America Online (AOL), who had commercial incentives to keep their content from being reproduced on the wider Web, vanished almost entirely when companies pulled the plug or were sold. A website, far from being just the visible document, encompasses a set of strata, including individual elements like images and text, page layout, the interconnected pages that make up the site, the sites that are connected via links to that site, and the wider Web at the moment of that site's creation.[48] Though projects such as the Internet Archive and the Archives Unleashed Project do excellent work, they cannot always capture every element. Website preservation is further complicated by formats like Flash, whose proprietary status makes it very difficult—if not impossible—to archive.[49] Lastly, modern contemporaries of early walled gardens, such as Yahoo! Groups and Tumblr, have little financial incentive to maintain services or posts whose existence adversely impacts their bottom line.

Ultimately, the primary sources for much of this book, particularly the first half, are not born-digital files but print. As noted earlier, the community for many years had a highly active newsletter exchange network, and the growing presence of digital communications and the Internet was often referenced in these publications. Beyond authors writing about their experiences, newsletters are often the only remaining sources of writing about and documentation of early BBSes and trans spaces on commercial platforms. Newsletter editors, who regularly found themselves scrambling for content to fill each month's issue, reprinted columns, news pieces, chain letters, lists of "cool" website addresses, and all manner of other writing posted online. In effect, they were "printing the network" for those members who didn't have access to the trans Net.[50] These newsletters were then preserved in various archives, including the National Transgender Library and Archives, part of the Labadie Collection at the University of Michigan (a key source for this project), as well as digitized documents hosted by the Digital Transgender Archive. Beyond these more traditional archives, however, many of the sources I draw upon weren't preserved out of any archival impulse, but as part of early efforts to commercialize certain aspects of digital communications, like freeware and document sharing (shareware CDs), Usenet (the Dejanews archive), or the many Internet "how to" books that flooded the market in the mid-1990s. In the case of Usenet, these same money-making motivations limit contemporary access to the archives, at times shutting off access entirely.[51] Access to these resources also informed the topical foci of this work; technologies such as email listservs and databases that have limited archival records, both in terms of primary sources and secondary discussion, are discussed, but aren't the subject of substantial analysis.

For a history that spends so much time on the decisions of technical and corporate actors, very few of these sources come from those actors. Instead, *The Two Revolutions* centers the perspective of trans consumers, who often felt they were interacting with what was, at best, a series of faceless corporate entities for whom trans folks were one of the many problematic user populations they had to manage. Furthermore, the realities of rapid change and turnover during this period meant that identifying who made these decisions may be impossible. On AOL, for example, day-to-day content moderation was left to a largely unpaid contract workforce, over whom corporate officials had limited oversight. Within the realm of community publications, there were similar limitations. While some publications did run full-length articles on computer communication, many of the references come in small single news items, or asides within larger columns. The evolving nature of digital communications also meant that, in the 1980s, authors would often refer primarily to BBSes or commercial services only by name or acronym. Later, authors would adopt a wide variety of referential terms present in discourse, including various permutations of "Web," "Net," "information highway," "Internet," and any number of terms prefixed with that omnipresent marker of 1990s cool, "cyber." When transgender topics were mentioned in mainstream and noncommunity publications, they were often as part of one-off special-topics articles that were rarely ever referenced again. My research method, then, could often be described as "rabbit-holing": following a single name, reference, or phone number across different archives in search of more detail. Having access to digitized indexed archival documents through the Digital Transgender Archive was an invaluable resource, as were the many popular press texts held in the Internet Archive. In research, one source could lead to another and another, creating a bridge between archives. At times, sources emerged from bits of Web detritus, abandoned web pages and unsecured FTP servers that had since been indexed by search engines, offering addresses that could be retrieved from the Internet Archive's Wayback Machine.

As a history, then, *The Two Revolutions* spans the gap not just between two generations of the community, but two archive eras: physical material and born-digital multimedia documents. The former are contained within formal archives and collections, and their amount and content reflect the number of individuals and groups who could produce such materials during the 1980s and 1990s. Yet, as more of trans life moved online, beginning in the late 1990s, born-digital documents became the dominant format, of which many more were produced at a far greater scale. As historian Ian Milligan argues, studying such born-digital materials requires a strong sense for understanding their context within Web archives, for "the mere fact of something existing–or even hundreds of something existing–may not signify something significant." For these materials, distant reading methods and computational analysis are key methods for getting "a sense of what was being created and talked about, and what mattered to people, at scale."[52] Given the size of Usenet newsgroup archives, which number in the tens of thousands of messages, network visualization and descriptive statistics were essential for identifying "what mattered" to regular posters.

Beyond their material differences, born-digital documents and their online persistence point to the ways that the Internet has changed perceptions of time. "Internet time" may be best understood not as a single homogenous chronology, but as an assemblage of interconnected timings understood in relation to the different elements that comprise them.[53] In other words, the Internet changes trans individuals' experiences of their community history, particularly when that historical content is not clearly designated as "archival." A contemporary profile may live alongside an older web page, with little clear designation of their difference; historical choices and narratives bleed into the present moment. As such, these contemporary topics also require methods focused on capturing the present, such as the ethnographic interview. This coexistence additionally raises serious questions about anonymity and privacy. Born-digital documents' metadata can include a variety of identifying and compromising information, from legal full names and employer emails, while evolving norms around giving out information online means that some archived home pages include not just names but home telephone numbers. In this book, I've taken several steps to maintain authors' privacy. For authors writing on a widely published platform, such as Usenet or TGForum, I use names and personal pronouns as provided by the author. When quoting the creators of trans home pages, however, I use only first names, even when other identifying information is available. In screenshots, I've blurred out or redacted any faces, middle or last names, or hometowns that appear. Furthermore, citations to individual archived home pages are not included. While this information is technically still available via the Wayback Machine, not including these citations limits the overall visibility of these pages.

This history is shaped not only by questions of anonymity and privacy but also the limitations of its archival sources. Reflecting the demographic realities of the movement until the late 1990s, early chapters overwhelmingly focus on the experiences of trans women and heterosexual crossdressers. Cross-dressing groups in particular maintained a robust newsletter network for many years throughout the 1980s and 1990s, making up a significant portion of the existing archive. These individuals were also a sizable proportion of periodicals' consumer base—for example, in a 1998 editorial in the Powder Puffs of California (PPOC)'s newsletter, Joan complained that the summer 1998 issue of *Tapestry* had little material of interest to "their subscription base (read that to mean male crossdressers)," and exhorted the editorial staff not to forget "who brought you to the dance and where your financial base is located."[54] Yet, despite their archival dominance, many authors in the 1980s and 1990s offered only limited detail on other parts of their lives beyond their community activity. This absence likely results from a combination of community norms and publication audience: first, the high value placed on maintaining anonymity and privacy, and, second, the assumption of a known audience. Except for notable individuals, most writing in newsletters was printed under pseudonyms or an author's first name, for crossdressers often their "femme" name. Any personal details not specifically related to community activities, if included at all, were often obscured through vague references to "work," "the office," or "the family." This practice allowed authors to maintain their privacy, since their audience could fill in these details through existing contextual knowledge. As such, information about community demographics regarding race and class during this period come from two large-scale community surveys conducted during the early 1990s. Lastly, trans men and masculine individuals don't appear as a significant proportion of computer users in the archive until the late 1990s and early 2000s. For example, in the February 1994 newsletter of FTM International (FTMI), the largest trans male and trans masculine-specific organization throughout this period, one letter writer to their "Networking" section bemoans that, "surely, it cannot be true that I am the only techno-geek in the FTM world. Why is it, then, that I can find nobody of a like mind on the internet?"[55] Moreover, FTMI maintained a limited Web presence and purposely focused on developing their newsletter as a physical document throughout the 1990s due to concerns regarding a divide in Internet access among members.[56]

Crossdressers' high level of visibility and activity during this period contrasts sharply with their presence within contemporary trans communities, where they've largely faded from view.[57] In 2018, Miqqi Alicia Gilbert, a crossdresser and long-time trans activist, described her experience of "being a crossdresser in a modern trans community" as "strange, let me tell you." Crossdressers, in her view, are often placed near the bottom of the community hierarchy, "the bratty little sisters that nobody really wants around."[58] Some within the community have argued that they don't qualify as trans, due their perceived "choice" to crossdress or lack of gender dysphoria or expressed euphoria.[59] But such a relatively limited and binary understanding of cross-dressing, I argue, flattens the vast spectrum of ways in which crossdressers during the period this book covers experienced and expressed their gender. Part of this flattening results from the long shadow cast by Virginia Prince and Tri-Ess, whose approach to cross-dressing centered both the heterosexual male crossdresser and a femme self who embodied a desexualized, idealized femininity necessarily kept largely separate from one's male identity.

However, in their daily lives, crossdressers expressed their gender and sexuality in a variety of ways that frequently blurred the male/female binary, such as perming their hair or getting regular clear-coat manicures—even as they limited their time in full femme to community events and club meetings. In their conversations, particularly in early email listservs (briefly discussed in chapter 1), self-identified crossdressers discuss their experience of gender in ways that have far more in common with contemporary understandings of gender as a spectrum of experience. Finally, any historical consideration of the "crossdresser" must locate the category within its particular context: the community of the 1980s to the late 1990s was constructed around not only the gender binary but also a very clear crossdresser/transsexual binary, with "crossdresser" effectively functioning as the default category for all individuals who didn't wish to pursue gender-related surgical procedures—even those who identified with terms like "transgenderist," like Prince, and "androgyne," like Kane.

The writing and work of both Prince and Kane also contributed to one of the book's and the wider archive's notable limitations: the influence of respectability politics. Respectability politics has long been a unifying theme of middle-class trans activism, and both the activists discussed above (among many others) argued that societal acceptance of cross-gender behavior hinged on cross-gendered individuals' respectability in the eyes of the mainstream public. Much as Kane did in her early advertisements for Fantasia Fair, discussion of trans life online, as well as online trans forums and websites' own mission statements, claimed education and self-empowerment as their primary goals—a move that allowed them to use the discourse of respectability to claim membership within the wider digital public while deflecting any association with pornography or deviancy.[60] Beyond in-community attitudes toward pornography, commercial platforms maintained strict policies against hosting such content, further limiting its mainstream visibility. Trans erotica was available on BBSes and Usenet, but they had a relatively limited reach in comparison to such big commercial players as AOL or CompuServe.

Despite this larger desire to disassociate the community from pornography, individuals within the community both produced and consumed erotica with cross-gender themes, and some publications ran ads for publishers and authors.[61] Community norms, however, actively discouraged members from discussing their reading habits "on the record," so there's limited documentation of just how many community members regularly read these stories. Nevertheless, some authors did discuss how computer communication allowed them to explore the erotic aspects of their identities in a relatively low-risk environment—simply put, being hit on in a text-only chat room was less risky than a night *en femme* at a club, where an individual might be easily outed if the space wasn't community friendly. Once the World Wide Web replaced corporate walled gardens, trans-themed erotic content became increasingly visible and accessible. Moreover, as I will discuss in chapter 4, home pages allowed their creators total control over their self-representation, giving them space to embrace the erotic aspects of self-fashioning. Some of that material has been preserved in the GeoCities archive, but, as with earlier commercial platforms, the service's restrictions on hosting erotic content means that, at times, only traces are left. As a result, discussion in this book of trans porn and erotica is largely restricted to examining these traces and the surrounding discussion, and what they suggest about attitudes toward trans porn and erotica online.

The simultaneous focus on respectability and dissociation from pornography also speaks to a larger underlying issue within gender community spaces in the 1980s and 1990s: the predominance of whiteness as a baseline for community norms. While crossdressers and trans women of color, like Tennessee-based activist Marisa Richmond, were present and active within the community, community norms of pseudonymity and privacy largely obscure their presence within the archive. Thus, while *The Two Revolutions* highlights voices of color when they are preserved, this history is almost entirely told from the perspective of those who had the racial and economic privilege necessary to access digital communications. For though writing pseudonymously did protect authors' privacy, it functionally obscured other aspects of their identity, such as class and race. Absent this information, the pervasive whiteness in so much of the gender community during this period has become an entrenched, if unrecognized, aspect of the archive. Finally, it must be noted that this book presents a distinctly American history. Though digital communications increased transnational communication among trans individuals, American issues are the primary reference point for all conversations, and English functioned as the lingua franca among Internet users.

Chapter Outline

Chapters are organized in a loosely chronological order, based on the point when each platform hit the apex of its popularity, both within the wider user base and among trans users. However, these dividing lines are inexact, since platforms often lingered after their peak as users migrated from one to the other for a variety of reasons. Chapter 1 considers how the first digital platform, the BBS, began transforming the trans community. It starts by studying how trans individuals communicated and sought out information prior to the advent of digital communication. Using the group newsletter, group library, and hotline, members first came into contact with others like them and learned what resources were locally available. Yet, while these methods kept users informed and fostered group identity, they were at best inconsistently available, and they presented the risk of being outed at different points. The BBS, in contrast, offered these same features with greater consistency and other affordances, such as asynchronous messaging. Most importantly, though, it offered users a space to more regularly embody their gender identity outside of the physical peer group meeting. The BBS was a relatively technical and niche platform compared to the commercial "walled garden," the focus of chapter 2, which explores how the gender community created space for themselves on platforms such as Prodigy, CompuServe Information Service (CIS), and AOL. As in wider American culture, community interest in the Internet grew rapidly in the mid-1990s. Many of these new, often less tech-savvy users opted to join an existing commercial platform like AOL. Platforms' existing rules, however, often banned or limited the visibility of gender community spaces, drawing implicit or explicit connections between gender content and pornography. Trans users' increasing visibility therefore threatened to undermine platforms' family-friendly image. On AOL, which outright banned use of the terms "transsexual" and "transvestite," gender community users launched a concerted campaign to change these rules, using the logic of capitalism to frame their presence as a viable consumer demographic rather than a problem to be removed.

Chapter 3 shifts focus to a platform whose public profile rose rapidly around the same time, much to long-time users' chagrin: Usenet. Prior to the World Wide Web, transgender-themed newsgroups were the only cross-platform discussion space available to most users and played a key role in popularizing the neologism "cisgender." Though the term's current ubiquity would suggest a trajectory of increasing adoption, for many years "cisgender" and "cisgendered" appeared only on Usenet. Studying posts held in the platform's archive, I argue the infrastructure and affordances of Usenet—lack of content moderation, widespread readership, imbalanced poster to reader ratio, extensive use of quoting, and platform agnostic design—allowed the term's advocates, a small but vocal subset of regular posters, to give it far greater visibility than its use in print periodicals would suggest. However, their definition had key differences from contemporary usage that reflect advocates' outsider status within transgender politics at large. The term would have likely been unable to gain such wide adoption without the platform at the center of chapter 4: the World Wide Web. In an information landscape based primarily on print books and file servers, the website represented a radical shift in information access and delivery. Where previously individuals needed to make contact with knowledgeable community members or allies to find and access information, websites made this information available to anyone with the site address. More importantly, it opened up publication to a far wider swath of the community. On their home pages, trans individuals could freely represent themselves using all the technical and graphical affordances of the new medium. These pages served as a transitional medium, germinating representational norms now commonplace on social media sites.

Chapter 5 steps away from individual platforms to consider the Internet's role in two parallel but interconnected shifts within the trans community throughout the late 1990s into the early 2000s: first, increasing concern about the long-term future of transgender periodicals and offline social groups, and, second, an emerging new transgender "generation." As in-home Internet access became an increasingly common middle-class norm, questioning individuals found new ways to connect with each other and build community online. Though some local and regional groups did see membership growth from their Web presences, others struggled to stay afloat. Their struggles were compounded by the fact a substantial portion of the new transgender generation were youth, whom groups were wholly unprepared to serve, having historically avoided youth outreach for fear of legal action by concerned parents. More modern efforts during this period either remained fairly hands-off, funneling support toward groups like PFLAG, or took a paternalistic view of trans youth as victims in need of saving. In contrast, youth who did reach out found most trans groups unprepared or uninterested in addressing their concerns. Online, however, they developed youth-centered spaces and groups.

Chapter 6 tackles the longer impact of these shifts in the contemporary Internet environment by considering two of the biggest technological innovations of the last fifteen years: the search algorithm, and social tagging. In different ways, each of these affordances has shaped the way users understand "transgender" as an identity and concept. As part of my analysis, I contextualize them within the longer history of trans information-seeking and self-definition. In both cases, "transgender" has become enmeshed in and defined by the very infrastructure through which trans users learn about themselves, severely limiting users' agency to shape definitions or terminology. In the conclusion, I turn from the past and present to consider possible futures for the trans Net. If the very idea of "transgender" has become inseparable from the systems by which we understand it, what might alternatives look like? How could a platform meaningfully center and support user agency?

1

Dialing into the Revolution

The Bulletin Board System

In his March 1985 *Playboy* article on erotic resources online, "Type Dirty To Me," author Robert E. Carr reports that he had the chance to "witness an incredible statistic": multiple transsexuals in one place. The place? GenderNet, a bulletin board system (BBS) billing itself as an "information source for the transvestite, transsexual, spouse and support professional." To Carr, GenderNet presented an irresistible opportunity. "After all," he notes, "how many transsexuals do you know who own computers? One, two, three at the most, right?" Either way, "there still don't seem to be enough transvestite/sexuals *cum* computers to support such a data base."[1] Unbeknownst to Carr, however, quite a few not only owned computers but were also using them to communicate and network nationwide.

Nationwide communication didn't begin with the BBS, however. Gender community–specific periodicals had been in circulation throughout the 1960s and 1970s, and an extensive national newsletter exchange network emerged in the mid-1980s. While some individuals did subscribe to national periodicals, local group newsletters were more often readers' most immediate connection to the gender community. These newsletters were the communicative heart of a group; they kept members informed of recent changes and upcoming events, and they fostered readers' social identity as gender community members. The newsletter was an "enclave sphere" where members could safely discuss relevant issues: for crossdressers, their *en femme* persona and its cross-gender desires; for transsexuals, their struggles with gender dysphoria and skeptical medical authorities.[2] When members felt isolated by their life *en drab*, the newsletter served as a lifeline to others who "truly" understood them. However, creating a newsletter could require a sizable time commitment for the uncompensated volunteer—one editor estimated a newsletter took, on average, "100 to 250 combined hours" to complete—leading to a variety of production delays.[3] Moreover, the act of discussing and reading about one's desires, be it through postal mail or on the phone, could be a risky proposition for those not out to their spouses or children.

On a BBS, gender community members were able to not only replicate core features of the "group and newsletter" format but also to expand upon them in important ways. As this chapter shows, BBS advocates within the gender community envisioned digital communications, often in especially cyberutopian terms, as the cornerstone of a new social and political movement. On the BBS, users could anonymously present *en femme* without the risk of harassment or unwanted social exposure. For questioning individuals, socializing on a BBS was a low-risk, low-investment alternative to a social club or support group, while still offering some of the same benefits. Beyond the social aspects, the BBS could host digital versions of a variety of previously print-only texts, making them available at a theoretically international level. Moreover, the BBS provided all of these benefits with far greater speed than conventional postal systems. Though the BBS and similar commercial platforms would eventually be supplanted by the World Wide Web (as discussed in chapters 4 and 5), gender community users would judge future platforms' suitability based on whether they included these core affordances: relative anonymity, rapid asynchronous communication, and file sharing.

Making a World to Fit the Words

Shared print documents have long been key to strengthening bonds and building a sense of shared identity among members of marginalized communities.[4] Virginia Prince began publishing the first periodical aimed specifically for the gender community, *Transvestia*, in 1960, and other periodicals, such as the short-lived *Turnabout: A Magazine of Transvestism*, would soon follow. Through *Transvestia*, Prince sought to transform cross-dressing from a private practice into a shared social identity, in part by deemphasizing its erotic aspects in favor of a respectable, nonthreatening image.[5] For readers, having safe places where they could publicly discuss desires and experiences that often went unexpressed in their daily life was transformative. In their letters and articles, authors made a world that "fit the words," where cross-gender desires could be explored and celebrated.[6] As Prince well knew, however, publication didn't come without risk: from 1961 to 1962, she was the target of an obscenity case related to a letter she had sent to another crossdresser.[7] Moreover, publication was an expensive business, and only the largest national and regional organizations, such as the Society for the Second Self (Tri-Ess), the Erikson Educational Foundation (EEF), and the Tiffany Club of New England (TCNE) could afford to produce their own periodicals. With modern technological innovations such as the Xerox machine and the electric typewriter in the 1980s, however, these smaller groups could now produce and distribute their own regular newsletters. By 1987, there were so many periodicals available that, according to Prince, "no cross-dresser anywhere need be without at least correspondent contacts even if she lives in the middle of the badlands of the Dakotas."[8] Presenters at the first annual IFGE conference in 1987, Coming Together, Working Together (CTWT), repeatedly emphasized the newsletter's importance to keeping members informed and involved. Via the newsletter, members were able to keep up with meeting minutes; exchange makeup, dress, and presentation tips; recount gender-related experiences; and learn about upcoming meetings and outings. Befitting the conference's title, newsletters were also a key avenue of intragroup communication, often via exchange networks. Some groups reported receiving between twenty to sixty newsletters on a semiregular basis.[9]

Most importantly, however, was the development of the newsletter into a site of shared social identity. Editors looked for ways to make it a document that readers would not just read, but use and interact with in their daily life. With the introduction of personal puzzle-generating software, such as Crossword Magic for the Apple II, editors could even add topically relevant puzzles. The Educational TV Channel (ETVC) March/April 1986 newsletter word search had readers hunting for "Avon," "Eyeliner," and "Rouge," among other related terms. Newsletters also occasionally ran serialized stories featuring cross-dressing protagonists, leaving readers eagerly awaiting the next installment. In some cases, these stories combined authors' cross-dressing interests with their fannish passions: *Petticoat Junction*, newsletter of the West Texas Gender Alliance (WTGA), published several installments of the Star Trek fan fiction "Rising of the Moons," wherein Kirk and crew encounter the Genderoids, an "enlightened" alien race whose male members resemble cross-dressers. In order to avoid a confrontation with a Klingon landing party, the crew hides crossdressed among them. Kirk is so taken with the experience he begins to present as Jane T. Kirk, a change that results in him "[maxing] out his Intergalactic Charge card at the dress and wig shops on Gamma 7."[10]

As apparent in the prior example, many authors and editors relied on topical humor to foster a sense of community in readers. "A little bit of humor helps some people to deal with their situation," Renee Chevalier, newsletter editor for The Transgender Independence Club in Albany, New York, told attendees at a CTWT panel on forming an organization. "People get turned off to pushing and shoving against their will."[11] Republished newspaper cartoons, especially those that referenced cross-dressing or gender differences, were a favorite of many editors, and the same cartoon often appeared across multiple different newsletters within months of their initial publication. At least four newsletters reproduced a *Far Side* cartoon (originally published January 15, 1990) featuring a snake cross-dressing in his wife's nylon, as well as a cartoon featuring a besuited office worker wearing a single heel captioned: "The doctor says it's transvestitism, but it's a very mild case." Editors also used built-in graphical software to make their own gender community–specific comics (fig. 1.1), or ran strips by community members like *The Adventures of Karen* by Karen Ann Michaels. These comics played off the quotidian experiences of gender community members or shared community knowledge, such as the main character confusing one IFGE for another in figure 1.1.

As word processors and desktop publishing software replaced the electric typewriter as the dominant medium in the 1990s, editors' use of preinstalled, premade imagery increased exponentially. Especially for newsletter editors who lacked content to fill their pages—a never-ending struggle, according to their columns—clip art allowed them to fill blank space with a variety of topically or seasonally appropriate graphics, such as comical turkeys in pilgrim gear in November and smatterings of snowflakes in December and January. Illustration choices are particularly representative of the era, featuring metaphorical human caricatures rendered in color-blocked, thick-thin lines. Many editors accompanied

Figure 1.1. Using preinstalled graphic software and clip art, gender community members could create art and comics around shared community knowledge. From *TV-TS Tapestry*, no. 53 (1989), courtesy of the Digital Transgender Archive.

their monthly columns with clip art of professional women using desktop computers (for a contemporary representation, see fig. 1.2).

Generally, such prepackaged clip art reinforced existing gender norms. In her analysis of four popular collections of the time, communication scholar Marilyn Dyrud found that men were represented as active, involved leaders, while women were often in secondary roles as service workers or secretaries. While men are represented as "blue Bart Simpsons" whose hair stands on end when they're "locked in combat with machines" in clip art libraries, women appear to be "content at the keyboard. Corel's 'computer' file, for example, depicts women merrily typing away, their technology world apparently in order."[12] For newsletter editors, however, they could draw on the commonsense iconographic meaning of prepackaged clip art to further represent themselves

Figure 1.2. Contemporary representation of clip art that newsletter editors often used to represent themselves. Public domain image, courtesy of WPClipart.

as put-together, collected, and well-coiffed women of the 1990s, even if they limited their femme self-expression to the meeting space.[13]

Making First Contact

However, even communicating one's internal desires around gender—much less attending a group meeting and subscribing to a newsletter—could seem insurmountable to some. By far, overcoming one's internal sense of isolation and reaching out to support groups or social clubs were the biggest initial challenges for many within the gender community. Individuals would recount their experience of making "first contact" with a group as a transformative first step toward self-acceptance. In reflecting on the growth of their Tri-Ess chapter, one anonymous author reminds readers of their duty to "the shakey [sic] voice on the phone or the confusion and hope written between the lines in letters of the solitary, reaching out, reminds us of our own thoughts not so long ago. We must continue to be a beacon of light, beckoning the unsure to cast off their guilt and know their potential, and lighting a path of acceptance in the community."[14] To light this path, many groups maintained two main avenues of contact: postal letters and telephone hotlines, where those were struggling could call in, get information about the organization, and, possibly, speak to a group member. In both methods, confidentiality was strictly enforced, given the risk of social censure from violating gender norms; however, neither was entirely secure. Mail could be opened by the wrong recipient, as in Jackie's cautionary tale "So You Think You Don't Need a Post Office Box." In her account, a questioning individual had recently reached out, via mail, to a local cross-dressing organization, using her home as the return address. By the time the organization replied, the individual had moved. Her mail still got to her, though—forwarded by the new owner in an envelope addressed to the individual's clueless wife. The marriage survived, but "just barely."[15] P.O. boxes offered individuals some privacy, but any items sent through the mail could still serve as physical evidence of one's desires. On the hotline, callers could call in and listen to an answering machine message without necessarily expecting a response.[16] In fact, according to Kymberleigh Richards, a prominent community member and editor of community magazine *Cross-Talk*, this contrast led to hotline volunteers' number-one complaint: although individuals called in seeking help and support, they wouldn't allow the organization to mail them information, for fear of being outed.[17]

Even so, the hotline wasn't entirely confidential. Functionally, it was an asynchronous mode of communication, since most calls went straight to the answering machine. One individual described calling a hotline twenty-one times before connecting with a live volunteer.[18] Calls were returned when a volunteer was available, but those times could be rare indeed. For example, the hotline for the Boulton and Park Society, a prominent San Antonio-based cross-dressing organization, was only staffed by live volunteers on Tuesdays after 7 p.m. Moreover, the phone presented its own privacy concerns, especially for individuals calling in via home lines accessible to spouses or children unaware of the caller's anxieties. Return messages left on home answering machines could be heard by anyone with access to them, and a changed home phone number after the initial phone call could inadvertently out the intended recipient of the message.[19] Beyond initial contact, transsexual individuals faced an additional risk if they sought the ultimate goal of transition, according to the medical model at the time: the total erasure of one's prior experience living as a different gender, alternately known as being "stealth" or "woodworking" (as in fading into the woodwork). Evidence of past or current membership in a gender community–related group, then, risked outing via association.

Getting the Bulletin

Given these concerns, the BBS seemed the ideal platform for private, anonymous communication. As its name implies, the bulletin board system was initially modeled after the community bulletin board commonly found in cafés, houses of worship, supermarkets, and community centers: a collective shared space where individuals could post queries or information, communicating asynchronously via their postings. In this way, the BBS represented a traditional "hub and spokes" network, where all discussion was centralized around one hub, with each user representing a spoke.[20] With a BBS, one computer served as the "server," or core "hub" BBS server, which other users dialed into via modem. Though the first BBS, the Computerized Hobbyists Bulletin Board System (CBBS), was founded in 1978, software and BBSes emerged en masse in the mid-1980s, following the development of technical standards that allowed cross-platform communication.[21] BBSes were maintained by a single sysop (or system operator), who handled not only technical issues but also social disputes and group governance. Given the amount of work the position, most sysops were altruistic individuals with a deep investment in the BBS community.[22] If a user had to be disciplined or banned, that decision was made by the sysop, who likely lived driving distance from that user, since most board regulars were located within the same area code. Since users had to dial into a BBS via modem, making repeat long-distance calls could get quite expensive; some users described amassing sizable phone bills as a result of regular BBSing.[23] As BBS technology further developed, BBSes became interconnected via worldwide networks such as FidoNet. Founded in 1984 by queer activist Tom Jennings, FidoNet used a "store and forward network" structure to affordably share messages and content with BBSes beyond one's local area code.[24]

While the technical specs, topical focus, and social structure varied from board to board, all BBSes offered three core functions for their users: messaging, file sharing, and remote computing.[25] On January 1, 1984, the first BBS for the gender community, GenderNet, went live. In their official launch announcement, GenderNet's sponsoring organization, the California-based Gateway Gender Alliance (GGA), emphasized the board's messaging features and file hosting capabilities. Within its first thirteen days, the board had received 207 calls from as far away as Massachusetts.[26] Callers were initially restricted to just thirty minutes of use, lest anyone was tempted to be a "time hog." Though GenderNet did not offer a mail function, it did provide a variety of information, including a digital version of GGA's Correspondence Directory. Similar to a newsletter, the BBS also featured several regular advice columns (modeled after the Dear Abby format) such as "Dear Counselor" and "Dear Mistress." While anyone who dialed in could read some free content, GenderNet required membership to post messages and contribute content.[27] Due to the financial strain of

Figure 1.3. Initial advertisement for GenderNet, published in *TV-TS Tapestry*, no. 42 (1985), courtesy of the Digital Transgender Archive.

hosting the BBS, GenderNet would eventually implement a member fee to cover its operating costs.

Given the newness of the technology, the GGA sent out a "road map" to their members on how to use the board and find information. By 1985, the GGA proudly claimed to have "more [calls] than we ever anticipated. Last month we said there had been 3,000 calls as of the end of August. As of the 15th of September the number has increased to 3,402. Quite a few in a 15 day period."[28] Though GenderNet would close shop with the 1986 dissolution of the Gateway Gender Alliance, its success served as proof of concept for a variety of individuals within the gender community.

Throughout the late 1980s, more BBSes specifically targeted toward the gender community would launch: the trans-specific portion of the Jersey Shore System in Trenton, New Jersey; Passing Fancy, out of Alexandria, Virginia; TerraNet in San Juan Capistrano, California; Carolyn's Closet in of Minneapolis, Minnesota; Puss n Boots in Grand Prairie, Texas; and Feminet in Monterey Bay, California, among many others. By 1991, at least two gender community–specific international networks existed: a GENDER echo, or discussion forum, running on the FidoNet backbone, with approximately sixty nodes, or member BBSes; and TransgenderNet (TGNet), a FidoNet-style network, hosted by the Feminet BBS, with eight community-specific echoes and thirty-nine nodes. By 1994, TGNet had grown to ninety-seven nodes. For those who didn't have a gender community BBS within their area code, these networks allowed them to stay connected to the wider gender community, if they could convince the BBS sysop to carry them—not always an easy task. Listings for trans-specific BBSes begin regularly appearing in *TV-TS Tapestry*'s Directory of Organizations and Services as early as 1987 and would receive their own section by 1990. These listings emphasized the social aspects of boards, such as email, messaging, and file libraries. At the same time, activists began to increasingly express interest in the BBS as a tool for political organizing.

"Uniting Ourselves in One of the Most Important Causes in Our Lives"

Politically minded BBS users of all stripes had, by the mid-1980s, begun to tap into boards' activist and organizing potential. These varied from small-scale projects, including Dave Hughes's use of his Old Colorado City Electronic College BBS to organize residents to protest a proposed local ordinance, and wider organizational networks such as the Institute for Global Communications (IGC), maintained by antiwar activists and computer professionals Scott Weikart and Mark Graham. The IGC created an international network supporting organizations dedicated to a variety of progressive political causes, from disarmament to labor organizing.[29] Beyond such formal political advocacy organizations, special interest groups whose ideas or practices were excluded from mainstream media saw a clear opportunity in BBSes. White supremacists were one of the first groups to receive popular attention for their use. In 1984, two different white supremacist BBSes, Info. International Network and Aryan Liberty Net, launched, offering discussion boards, various "enemies lists," and digital copies of racist and anti-Semitic literature. The last point was particularly important, as it allowed white supremacists and neo-Nazi groups to circumvent Canadian Customs' ban on importing "hate literature."[30] To demonstrate the ease by which this literature could be downloaded and disseminated, Chip Berlet, a researcher at progressive organization Political Research Associates, often brought a portable "briefcase-sized" printer/terminal, acoustic coupler (an early modem), and "100 feet of telephone wire" to his speeches on racist organizing and recruitment. As he later recounted, "the printer would be spewing out a continuous roll of thermal paper filled with anti-Semitic and racist text being downloaded in real time" while he was speaking. At the end of his speeches, he "would invite the audience to tear off several feet and bring it home to read and discuss with their children. People were amazed."[31] As Berlet's printer activity amply demonstrated, white supremacists and neo-Nazis quickly recognized the power of computer networking for organizing those excluded from the political mainstream. Those who logged onto Aryan Liberty Net in 1985 were greeted with this message from the sysop (originally published in all caps):

> FINALLY, WE ARE ALL GOING TO BE LINKED TOGETHER AT ONE POINT IN TIME. IMAGINE IF YOU WILL, ALL OF THE GREAT MINDS OF THE PATRIOTIC CHRISTIAN MOVEMENT LINKED TOGETHER AND JOINED INTO ONE COMPUTER. ALL THE YEARS OF COMBINED EXPERIENCE AVAILABLE TO THE MOVEMENT. NOW IMAGINE ANY PATRIOT IN THE COUNTRY BEING ABLE TO

CALL UP AND ACCESS THOSE MINDS, TO DEAL WITH THE PROBLEMS AND ISSUES THAT AFFECT HIM. YOU ARE ON LINE WITH THE ARYAN NATIONS BRAIN TRUST. IT IS HERE TO SERVE THE FOLK.[32]

The force of calls like these, as well as growing white supremacist BBS use, would inspire Berlet to found AMNET BBS, "the first BBS devoted exclusively to challenging the right," in 1985.[33]

However, hate groups were not the only ones using BBSes to spread information and make connections. A 1984 *Advocate* article estimated that there were "just under two dozen" exclusively gay-themed BBSes, some of their names tinged with innuendo: The Backroom, Micro Smut, Joystick, and Kinky Komputor. However, their content ranged widely, including personal ads, chat conferences, AIDS-related health articles, and advice columns.[34] The number of boards would grow over the next five years: the first edition of the Gay and Lesbian BBS Listin, first published on August 20, 1989 and circulated monthly until 1999 via BBS networks and Usenet, included 199 boards.[35] One of the most popular, the Gay and Lesbian Information Bureau (GLIB) in Arlington, Virginia, was voted among the top five BBSes in North America by *Boardwatch* readers in 1993—quite a feat, given its fellow boards were "'monster BBSes' . . . with dozens of incoming lines, exclusive shareware, and commercial support."[36] Beyond general gay and lesbian boards, BBSes were vital sources of accurate information and support for PWAs (People With AIDS) and the wider HIV/AIDS movement.[37] Given the sparse amount of treatment information available, the BBS allowed for the rapid dissemination of news, medical studies, and other important material. The anonymity of communicating via BBS allowed PWAs, often the subject of much public stigma, to seek support and discuss their struggles. The Backroom BBS for several years hosted a discussion forum entitled "Survivors" for PWAs and their family, friends, and significant others.[38] Recognizing the importance of BBSes in treatment, in 1985 the state of California allocated funds to support the creation of the Computerized AIDS Information Network (CAIN), which allowed users—especially those in smaller towns who lacked specialized medical care—to access treatment information, medical documents, and conference (or chat) with other users.[39] One of the more prominent HIV/AIDS boards, the AIDS Education Global Information System (AEGIS), originally began life as gender community BBS TerraNet. The importance of information circulation was well known to TerraNet's sysop, Sister Mary Elizabeth, one of two founders of J2CP Information Services, an information clearinghouse for medical providers and general gender community members that built on the earlier work of the Erickson Educational Foundation. Following an encounter with PWAs in rural Missouri, she converted TerraNet's focus to providing HIV/AIDS information to callers and initially renamed it the HIV/AIDS Info BBS before adopting the name AEGIS.[40]

In the gender community, the first seeds of the BBS as a site for activist networking were planted in 1987, when several attendees at a Coming Together-Working Together session on organizational networking raised the prospect of using BBSes to more effectively connect small organizations and share information.[41] In a 1989 column in *LadyLike*, editor JoAnn Roberts (also owner of influential trans-specific publishing house Creative Design Services), presented a "little wish list," her "Future View of where we could be and should be going," which included a desire for a "gender-oriented BBS with a 1–800 toll free number."[42] In 1989, Jennifer Wells, moderator of the GenderLine board on CompuServe Information Service noted in a letter to *Tapestry* that, while BBSes were "a dramatically successful and growing part of our community's communication link," "for numerous reasons all the current systems have shortcomings." Wells saw an opportunity for national-level organizations, such as the IFGE, to support a "project for our future"—"an international computerized gender data base and bulletin board or networking system," accessible via local access points or a toll-free 1-800 number. Wells ended her letter with a call to action, urging interested readers to get in contact.[43] Wells submitted a slightly reworded version of her appeal in the next issue of *Tapestry*, but no further developments related to the project appear in the archives. In their appeals, these early advocates primarily understood the BBS as a tool to support movement organizing by groups. They were well aware that the BBS could empower individuals but failed to articulate a connection between the individual user's experience and formal groups' more bureaucratic technology needs, such as word processing, data storage, and information sharing.

Over time, advocates' appeals shifted to reflect the increasing cultural influence of digital utopians espousing a new form of sociality: the "virtual community." Digital utopians—also sometimes called "cyberutopians"—

emphasized the personal computer as a (if not the) preeminent tool for personal and political liberation.[44] They envisioned "cyberspace" as a place where disembodied, autonomous individuals, liberated from offline social constraints, could engage in truly egalitarian discourse.[45] Feminist digital utopians in particular considered cyberspace a safe locale for experimenting with and subverting gender, as well as escaping the constraints of binary social norms. In the process, they embraced a Cartesian body/mind dualism, where the mind, in cyberspace, is "freed" of the gendered body's limitations.[46] Once gathered together, these autonomous users would form nonhierarchical "[communities] of shared consciousness."[47] The Whole Earth 'Lectric Link (WELL), a subscription-only BBS founded in 1985, was often cited as the model for this idealized community. Users understood the WELL as "a community held together by talk, the textual mirror of a physically dispersed tribe that felt itself linked by a shared invisible energy."[48] BBS advocates in the gender community relied on similar imagery to attract their readers. The Sunday Society, an offshoot of the Chicago Gender Society, founded in 1988, to specifically serve the needs of transsexuals, was one of the earliest organizations to present digital communication as imbued with utopian possibility. The group was itself founded with fairly grand ambitions: its founding announcement, published in *Tapestry*, outlines a broad agenda, from financial and social support to "[educating] society as to our condition and our needs through any available media, [assisting] in the formation of a consumer 'watchdog' agency, and [working] closely with other TS organizations in an effort to strengthen and unify us in our cause."[49] A centerpiece of their unification efforts was the United Sisterhood of Transsexual Outreach Organizations (US TOO) network. Initially conceived as a network of home terminals connected via modem à la FidoNet, US TOO later transitioned to a BBS in November 1989. In their inaugural newsletter, an unnamed author (likely one of the group's two founders) presented the US TOO network as a way to overcome technology's limitations and unite users as part of a larger movement. Compared to the existing information "grapevine," where information and support were spread unevenly among its many branches, a computer network was a far more sustainable distribution system, where information could be quickly and evenly spread among its many nodes.[50] When promoting the project to other groups (see fig. 1.4), the organization urged readers to imagine a future where they could

> communicate with other TS organizations across the country in a way never possible before! Think of the limitless possibilities of enhancing your newsletters and other publications by tapping a vast nationwide resource of knowledge from our community! Realize the potential for reporting up to the minute news, articles, or anything of interest to our community! But most of all, enjoy the benefit of the strength that comes from uniting ourselves in one of the most important causes in our lives!

In her October 1989 column, Sunday Society cofounder Louise L. Raeder leaned heavily on technoutopian rhetoric to emphasize US TOO's revolutionary possibilities and encourage reader involvement. She compared US TOO to the first Saturn V launch, that moment when "science fiction became science fact and fantasy became reality" through the hard work of "many years of planning, experimenting, and testing by many sincerely dedicated individuals." Now, "some 20 years later, a new mission is under way," and, like the Saturn V launch, launching US TOO, she said, would be an equally difficult but rewarding endeavor. Using language from the quintessentially technoutopian franchise *Star Trek*, Raeder framed transsexuals seeking transition as explorers of the "Final Frontier," the "ultimate congruity" of post-transition life, "where no man (or woman) has gone before." For these explorers, US TOO was an opportunity to not only "solve one of our greatest obstacles, the communication gap within our community," but also to "make history and forever change the way our community is considered by others." She ended her column with a challenge to readers: "Whether we have a smooth liftoff or blow up on the pad will be up to all of us. All systems are go on this end! How about you?"[51]

However, at this point, the "you" Raeder is addressing in this column remains unclear. While the US TOO network was to be made of linked "personal computers," the authors implicitly assume most network members would not be acting as independent individuals but as representatives of existing organizations—thus their ad's emphasis on communicating with "other TS organizations." Two factors led Raeder to shift her target audience to the empowered individual. First, US TOO

A new way to unify our community

Imagine being able to communicate with other TS organizations across the country in a way never possible before!
Think of the limitless possibilities of enhancing your newsletters and other publications by tapping a vast nation wide resource of knowledge from our community!
Realize the potential for reporting up to the minute news, articles, or anything of interest to our community!
But most of all, enjoy the benefit of the strength that comes from uniting ourselves in one of the most important causes in our lives!

The United Sisterhood of Transsexual Outreach Organizations (US TOO) is a project being introduced by THE SUNDAY SOCIETY in an effort to end the communication gap in our community once and for all. It will be a network using personal computers linked by modems to transmit and receive data anywhere telephone service is available.
The requirements for participation in this project are:
1. any personal computer
2. a modem with a rate of 300, 1200, or 2400 baud (with the appropriate communication software)
3. a single telephone line (not a party line)
4. a serious desire to help our community
That's all there is to it!, about as easy as calling someone on the phone except that now, the possibilities for growth of our community will become virtually unlimited.
We would like to see as many groups participating in this project as possible.
For further information, call or write:
THE SUNDAY SOCIETY
2511 N. St. Louis Av.
Chicago, IL 60647
(312)-486-3125

Figure 1.4. Promotional advertisement for US TOO network, published in the July 1989 issue of *Twenty Minutes*, the newsletter of the XX (Twenty) Club. Courtesy of the Digital Transgender Archive.

transitioned to a BBS in November 1989, meaning that the project had to be reconceptualized not as a network of interconnected independent nodes but as a centralized hub and spokes, which would primarily focus on an audience of largely unknown individuals. Second, recent political developments required not just collective but individual action: the then-recent addition of Senate Amendment 722 to the Americans with Disabilities Act (ADA). S.772, cosponsored by senators William L. Armstrong and Orrin Hatch, barred "homosexuality," "bisexuality," "transvestism," "transsexualism," and "gender identity disorders," among others, from being considered disabilities—preemptively excluding these individuals from being able to claim accommodations under the ADA.[52] Introduced in September 1989, the amendment was intended, according to Hatch, to forestall "all kinds of misunderstandings with regard to rather sweeping language of this bill."[53] However, these "misunderstandings" were merely a cover, scholar Ruth Cokler argues, for legislators' deep-seated prejudice against transgender individuals.[54] Beyond the amendment's discriminatory intent, however, Raeder was "shocked" by how the community of "at least 80,000" first learned of the amendment's passage: activist Sister Mary Elizabeth's chance recognition of the word "transsexual" over a friend's shoulder while they were reading the newspaper. In order to prevent future missteps, Raeder argued, individuals must get involved, and those with access to modems and computers had a special duty to call in to share information, because "the computer is a powerful tool and our enemies know it when they use them to their advantage. We can also make them work for US TOO!"[55] Beyond just information sharing, Raeder contended, BBS technology enabled transsexual activists to "speak back" to those in power, such as medical gatekeepers who control access to necessary care. As evidence of the BBS's efficacy, she cited efforts to form a "Gender Identity Disorder" area on DocTalk, the official BBS of the American Medical Students Association.[56] Having a GID area on DocTalk, sponsored by large pharmaceutical companies such as Merrell-Dow, Eli Lilly and Company, and Wyeth-Ayerst Laboratories (producers of Premarin, the brand name estrogen prescribed to many trans women) gave transsexual users a chance "[play] ball" in the "big leagues" and talk back to "the helping professionals of the very near future waiting to hear what WE have to say about ourselves, our community, and our condition." Transsexual individuals had it "in our power to determine our future," but achieving this future required, Raeder emphasized, "actually participating in the task at hand, in this case by simply logging on and letting everyone know how you feel and what you think."⁵⁷ In both cases, Raeder appealed directly to the individual whose empowerment lay tantalizingly within reach; all it required was a computer, a modem, and a desire to make a difference.

Talk among Yourselves: Claiming a "Transgender" Identity Online

However, Raeder implicitly assumes her user has *already* accepted themselves as transsexual, whatever their stage in the transition process. For Raeder, the problem was not personal empowerment by accepting one's transsexual status, but political empowerment to claim transsexuality as an identity worth advocating for. Given the then-current medical model's (over)emphasis on living "stealth" as the ultimate goal of transition, Raeder knew her target demographic was already predisposed to "dropping out" of the community once they felt they'd completed transition.⁵⁸ As the idea of a shared transgender identity began to gain traction, advocates shifted attention to technology as a site of personal empowerment first, with political empowerment to follow. Writing in the inaugural spring 1991 issue of *Chrysalis Quarterly*, Stephanie Rose noted that "the gender community [was] in the midst of two revolutions": the overt development of a shared political consciousness later labeled "transgender," and the covert "computer revolution," from which they "[stood] to gain more from than any other social groups out there."⁵⁹ These benefits, as Rose and others argued, replicated and expanded upon some of the social club or support group's core features: offering space for safe, confidential self-expression; providing support from and fostering relationships with other community members; and accessing community-specific information.

Compared to earlier methods of contact—postal mail and the hotline—the BBS allowed users to maintain far more privacy. Like a hotline, a user had to dial in via modem to the BBS. But, unlike the hotline, boards didn't need to be staffed by a live sysop in order to keep user information secure. In some cases, a generic-sounding name could be enough to deter gawkers, as BBS directories often included little more than a name, a phone number, and which baud modem you could use to connect. GenderNet's somewhat opaque name led Carr to assume that the board was "just what I was looking for: a B.B.S. specifically for the netting of the opposite gender."[60] Many of the BBSes that came after GenderNet employed a variety of gatekeeping methods to protect users, including passwords, passcode sequences, and "false fronts," such as fake login pages. Feminet had two layers of security: once dialed in, users were initially presented with a public BBS, "Digicomputronica," after which they had to use a secret key press ("P") and password sequence ("KEY") for access. Sysops also limited publication of BBS numbers and login sequences to group newsletters or community publications like *Cross-Talk* or *Tapestry*. Gender community BBS phone numbers were not published in either popular BBS "trade" magazines like *Computer Shopper* or *Boardwatch* or the Gay and Lesbian BBS Listing; at any given time, only four to five boards offering TV/TS content appeared on a list of roughly one hundred boards.

Beyond gatekeeping, the BBS's registration-based architecture meant that users could maintain anonymity via a self-selected handle, which could serve as a whole new mode of self-representation, entirely unrelated their identity outside the BBS. Name selection has a long history as a practice by trans individuals. For transsexuals, a new name represented a moment of "rebirth," while members of cross-dressing groups often used self-selected femme names to emphasize the difference between their male and female aspects.[61] For some, the pressure to maintain a gendered "guise" could remain, though. In a short autobiographical essay, Paula Keiser, sysop of the Jersey Shore System (JSS), describes her internal agony in picking a name when she was finally ready to register for GenderNet after weeks of anonymous reading:

> Finally I got up enough nerve to actually join GenderNet. The first item I was asked for was, of course, my name. oh, no! I wasn't about to use my real name or location. Thinking fast, but insanely, I thought, "What name couldn't possibly be connected with me." I thought through my relatives' and friends' names, and chose the first name of my favorite cousin, Paul Williams, Jr. Okay, my first name was Paul. . . . The last name was obvious,

then. What more obscure a last name can there be than "Rupp,: Paul's middle name? So, On GenderNet, I became known as "Paul Rupp."[62]

Even when anonymous, Keiser felt she had to maintain the guise of a "sympathetic non-trans person" on GenderNet before she was ready to come out as Paula on JSS in late 1984.[63] Once logged in, users could communicate in several different ways, depending on the BBS software: some boards only supported asynchronous public postings, while others allowed users to send private messages or engage in synchronous chat. Even when faced with software limitations, sysops did their best to foster communication: when GenderNet's server lacked the hard drive space to support a mail function, the sysop worked around this limitation by hosting a copy of the Correspondents Directory, allowing interested users to keep the conversation going outside the BBS.[64]

As in the newsletter, through their conversation BBS users constructed a world centering around their interests, concerns, and desires. "Finding and talking to others like ourselves gives us strength," Rose argued. "We feel more comfortable when we know we are not alone. The message sections of BBSes give us that sense of community."[65] Robert Carr's description of his experience in *Playboy* points to the world-making power of the BBS. As someone who was "quite happy with both my sex and my clothing," reading GenderNet left Carr feeling "a little like Kevin McCarthy in *Invasion of the Body Snatchers*," surrounded by a world where the "normal" order of gender has been replaced with something entirely different. While it's unclear what Carr expected to find there, it was clearly *not* a world wherein gender nonconformity was not only embraced but celebrated. Unlike McCarthy's Dr. Miles Bennell, however, Carr doesn't run into the proverbial street, warning of an impending invasion. Instead, he concludes that "apparently a real need is being served here. After all, before GENDERNET, there was no place a computing cross dresser could turn for advice—and certainly his long-suffering wife was up the creek. The brave new world of computerized sexual frankness has opened electronic inroads to all sorts of communities."[66]

For advocates, one the BBS's greatest appeals was the ability to be frank about one's cross-gender desires without fear of social repercussions. According to Tri-Ess BBS sysops Rachel and Kathy Cummins, members of the board "averted several suicides" and "helped many come to an acceptance of their cross-dressing behavior and have counselled wives of crossdressers."[67] In her 1999 memoir *Crossing*, economist Deirdre McCloskey recounts how BBSes facilitated her own coming out a trans woman. Though McCloskey long sought out resources with information on "gender crossing," she avoided purchasing or checking out books with "an obviously crossgender theme" because "the moment of acknowledgment, eye-to-eye" with the clerk or librarian "would have been too much."[68] The BBS, in contrast, allowed her to read materials and anonymously converse with "a half dozen or so Chicagoland crossdressers and gender crossers" using the handle "Jane Austen."[69] When her then-wife confronted McCloskey with the mounting telephone bills following hours of long-distance BBSing, McCloskey argued her BBS use as a kind of "therapy, considering what the BBSers talked about."[70] McCloskey's choice of analogy positions the BBS as a kind of self-help group where she, as "Jane Austen," could find relief from the isolation of her day-to-day life. In a 1991 column on the importance of support groups, Tere Fredrickson, then–newsletter editor for San Antonio-based group Boulton & Park, emphasized the BBS's self-help aspects. When first struggling with her transgender identity in 1986, BBSes served as her "own little life raft in the maelstrom" on her journey to self-acceptance. She assured readers that their greatest support would come not from medical authorities or academic researchers, but "from your sisters—they truly understand you!"[71] In their advertising, the TCNE BBS (sponsored by the Tiffany Club of New England) played up the sisterhood angle in their slogan: "For Our Sisters and Our Community." Similarly, ads for gender community BBS Cross Connection also leaned heavily on the sisterhood theme, briefly adopting the cyberutopian tagline "We would all be just the same if there were no crossings." Embedded within these slogans was the belief that, without the limitations of gendered embodiment, BBS users share a core "sameness," uniting them as a community. This experience of sharing with others, Rose argued, built these sisterly bonds. On the BBS "you see and learn about others just like yourself. You see the problems they are facing, the successes they have had, and what special people they are." Some of these people may come to "know you better than your non-gender friends," because the anonymity of the BBS handle allows used to feel "free to be yourself."[72] Part of this freedom came not only in expressing desires but also (virtually) living them out.

Being Yourself Online: Disembodiment and Experimentation

As a primarily text-based medium, BBS users were able to experiment with self-presentation beyond their current embodiment. In text, users could present idealized versions of themselves, imaginatively performing their inner selves for a supportive audience. Allucquère Rosanne (Sandy) Stone, whose 1987 essay "The Empire Strikes Back: A Posttranssexual Manifesto" is now a foundational text in transgender studies, presented these behaviors as "computer crossdressing": "On the nets, where warranting or grounding, a persona in a physical body, is meaningless, men routinely use female personae whenever they choose, and vice versa." This online persona can take on "a kind of quasi life of its own, separate from the person's embodied life in the 'real' world"—even taking over their offline life entirely.[73] For cross-dressing users, especially closeted ones, their BBS use often represented literal "computer crossdressing": the BBS might be *the only place* where they could safely crossdress and explore their femme persona. On a BBS, they could imagine owning and using material objects like dresses, wigs, and makeup, through these imaginings envisioning what they'd look like as their femme self. For those possibly interested in partial or full social and/or medical transition, they could explore issues around gender identity in a supportive social space.

Moreover, users' online forays could lead to offline expression and participation in local gender community groups. McCloskey's offline explorations began at home, dressing as "Jane" while messaging others via BBS. Over time, these online connections evolved into offline friendships and involvement in wider gender community groups in Iowa and Chicago.[74] One of the more touching descriptions of this shift came in a 1988 letter from Kimberly N., recounting how her life had been enriched by becoming involved in the gender community. Before attending her first meeting of the Rainbow Gender Association, a California-based group founded by former GGA members, she described spending "sleepless nights like a child in nervous anticipation, pouring over GenderNet printouts." Using GenderNet gave her the courage to become involved offline, and "the process unleashed what I have always suppressed, spilling it over into my male, and turning him around completely. Now I am content with my outgoing self regardless of which gender I choose to assume."⁷⁵ Beyond merely serving as an example of the BBS as a catalyst for personal acceptance, Kimberly's story—specifically, her reference to "GenderNet printouts"—also draws attention to one of the most transformative aspects of the BBS: the ability to host, download, and print files.

Sharing the Lore

Though by no means the most futuristic or exciting aspect of the BBS, being able to remotely access and download information via BBS allowed users to circumvent what had once been a sometimes long and drawn-out process. Pre-Internet, most information seekers began their search at the nearest sizable information hub: the local library. However, the information they found there—if they found anything at all—usually came from medical studies and textbooks, whose clinical tone failed to reassure already anxious readers. And, in some cases, all books related to cross-dressing and transsexual issues had been stolen and not replaced.⁷⁶ Alternately, seekers might fear the potential exposure that came with checking out a book: when using the library, Deirdre McCloskey differentiated between books whose obscure titles meant they could safely be checked out, like Nancy Hunt's *Mirror Image*, and "library-only" reads, such as Renee Richards' *Second Serve*.⁷⁷ Recognizing the importance of the library as an information source, Tri-Ess maintained an extensive library card placement program: each member was mailed five cards to be placed in the card catalog of nearby public and university libraries, with the ultimate goal of placing cards "into a thousand libraries."⁷⁸ These cards, according to a sample set published in a 1990 issue of Tri-Ess's newsletter the *Femme Mirror*, contained a dictionary-style definition of either "Transvestitism," "Crossdressing," or "Eonism" (a term coined by sexologist Havelock Ellis), a note to contact Tri-Ess for more information, and Tri-Ess's mailing address. According to the CTWT presenter, Tri-Ess received "quite a large [public] response" from this system but had difficulty keeping the cards from being removed.⁷⁹ Given this challenge, Marlene in California described in a 1990 letter to the *Femme Mirror* a somewhat elaborate placement process. Instead of merely inserting a handwritten card, Marlene recreated an imitation catalog card, including sticky label, placed it in the catalog's "transsexuality" file, then located books with any mention of "crossdressing" and taped a dated card in the back. According to her, this process could be repeated every few months, as needed. At the end of her letter, Marlene acknowledged that, while it was unclear if this method was "legal, illegal, or even safe . . . over the years a whole lot of sisters have found us because the first place they look is the public library."[80] However, libraries' increasing shift away from physical and toward digital catalogs threatened to undermine not only Marlene's method but also Tri-Ess's library card system entirely. As a self-contained, nonphysical artifact, the digital catalog didn't allow users to challenge the catalog's "authoritative" representations. In response, Tri-Ess shifted to offering stickers that could be placed in the back of books. Beyond libraries, the adult bookstore was the other first stop for many information seekers. Given cross-dressing's sexualized connotations within the popular imagination, stores often did stock erotic periodicals alongside more social publications like *LadyLike* and *TV-TS Tapestry*. However, the adult bookstore's uncomfortable social connotations could deter some information seekers.

Whatever their method for making contact, individuals' information options increased exponentially once they connected to the gender community. As a member, they gained access to what ethnographer Anne Bolin terms the "transsexual lore" (and, I would add, cross-dressing lore) amassed by community members over the years, including libraries of documents maintained by support groups. For transsexual members, these documents included necessary information like "recipes" on successfully getting adequate care from medical authorities.[81] Access to information via the group library, however, still didn't resolve the closeted individual's dilemma: What happens if someone stumbles onto the book or newsletter? What if someone else pops in the wrong VHS tape? Information in a digital format, though structurally reflecting print norms, greatly reduced one's risk of discovery. Instead of living in a locked trunk or a secret suitcase, files could be renamed and hidden deep within the OS's hierarchical file structure. Those who feared, as McCloskey did, "the moment of acknowledgment, eye-to-eye" with a librarian or bookstore clerk now faced only their computer screen. Furthermore, BBSes dramatically increased documents' delivery speed and reach. Assuming the BBS didn't require a subscription, access to hosted files was limited merely by the speed of one's connection and software compatibility. Texts that would take weeks to arrive via mail could be downloaded within minutes from a BBS. Furthermore, FidoNet's echomail system let users distribute files to others on the network, allowing documents to spread well beyond the confines of one BBS. Not unlike Berlet's printer, wheeling out foot upon foot of white supremacist texts as he spoke, gender community BBS users could print out page upon page of information—though for a far less hateful cause. They could also easily make and share their own text, as creating a textfile required "no special software or technical skills," and they could be transferred "between otherwise-incompatible platforms" with relative ease.[82]

The content of the files hosted in a BBS's library varied widely. Informational texts, ranging from listings of support groups and community-oriented retailers to makeup and fashion tips, were a common staple.[83] Some hosted essays and columns penned by the sysop or other users. Jersey Shore System sysop Paula Keiser, for example, published regularly to JSS on a range of trans-adjacent issues. These latter documents reflect the popularity of textfiles in BBSing circles at large. Textfiles, according to media historian Kevin Driscoll, "were the broadsides of the modem world, an ephemeral street literature for the information superhighway."[84] Beyond information, many libraries included collections of trans-themed fiction, including erotic or forced feminization stories. However, the most popular section was usually the GIF library, which included graphics from any number of sources. According to authors, BBS users voraciously consumed these images, and they likely posted some of their own photos.[85] Having their photos taken was a passion for many cross-dressers in particular, and groups sometimes sponsored studio sessions with a friendly photographer during their regular meeting times. Some in particular embraced the "high femme" aesthetic of that seemingly ubiquitous fixture of 1990s American shopping malls, Glamour Shots. For their part, select Glamour Shots franchises seem to have deliberately courted this association; a local Atlanta Glamour Shots was one of five commercial vendors at the 1995 IFGE convention.[86] Given this highly visual culture, the GIF library offered BBS users an even wider platform to share and circulate their photos.

Once posted to a BBS, a file could then travel even further offline via "chains of access," a strategy wherein, according to ethnographer Elisabeth Jay Friedman, one individual with access to a communication medium (in this case, the BBS) reproduces content in a more accessible medium, such as in print or over the phone.[87] Media scholar Cait McKinney, in their analysis of the HIV/AIDS organization Critical Path's newsletter and BBS, demonstrates how early BBS users "printed the net" for wider circulation via their newsletter.[88] Gender community groups engaged in a similar practice. Prior to the BBS, it was not uncommon for newsletter editors to reproduce content from other groups' newsletters and include an attribution to the original author and source. The practice was so common, some newsletters included reproduction policies in their editorial masthead. Editors repeated these practices with BBS content: essays and articles ran with either an introduction or conclusion noting the source, BBS phone number, and other access information. For example, JoAnn Roberts, in her capacity as editor of *Renaissance News*, regularly published columns originally posted to the Jersey Shore System BBS by sysop Paula Keiser. Once published, this content would then circulate through the existing newsletter network, reaching groups across the United States and beyond.[89]

Content reproduction wasn't limited to moving from digital to print media, however. Four years after GenderNet first came online, community members launched the first trans-specific email list, CDForum, which was published as an anonymized, semiregular digest. Much like a BBS, members used CDForum to discuss their personal cross-gender experiences, find support, share information, and discuss major issues of the day within the community. The listserv was also an excellent platform for sharing printed content, since it could easily be copied and reshared elsewhere. However, their audience was relatively limited in the listserv's early years, since access to an email address was largely restricted to individuals who worked at universities or corporations connected to ARPANet, though access to email via BBS would begin to see an uptick in the early 1990s.

All of this advocacy, though, didn't immediately translate into widespread audience adoption. While the BBS set the standard for what users might expect from digital communications, their user base made up a relatively small portion of the wider gender community. Outside of articles by advocates, computer-based communication was often framed as a "technical" endeavor for the "computer literate" who "[knew] the lingo"—or, in one evocative turn of phrase, "the 'hackers' in our community."[90] As with the rest of America, however, the "computer illiterate" of the gender community would ride the dotcom bubble to a place branding itself as "the Internet and a whole lot more": America Online.

2

Out of the Cybercloset, Into the Cyberstreets

Gender Community Spaces on AOL and Beyond

Few items are more emblematic of a specific moment in Web history than the free America Online (AOL) trial CD. For those over a certain age in the mid-1990s, these discs were ubiquitous, offered with everything from breakfast cereal and Blockbuster videocassettes to Omaha Steaks.[1] By design, they reduced the seemingly complicated and technical process of "getting online" to a plug-n-play experience requiring little more than the disc and a phone line—a physical embodiment of AOL's latter 1990s slogan "So easy to use, no wonder it's #1." Though they're now largely emblematic of the dot-com boom feeding frenzy of the 1990s, the CDs were key to AOL's commercial success, according to AOL marketer Jan Brandt, turning it from an also-ran behind CompuServe and Prodigy into the most widely used digital communications platform (and, later, service provider) in America.[2]

By 1997, AOL had reached 10 million subscribers, estimated at the time as around half of all households online in the United States.[3] In their branding, AOL emphasized the breadth of their base with ads centered around frenetic jump cuts between users—all notably diverse, if vaguely middle class—extolling AOL's accessibility and ease of use. Included in this diverse user base, though never featured, were cross-dressing, transsexual, gender nonconforming, and questioning users, who "got wired" alongside the wider population. Compared to the BBS, commercial services' increased focus on reducing technical barriers, alongside the rising domesticization of the personal computer, made digital communications accessible to a far wider potion of the community.[4] Community publications also fostered growing reader interest in the nascent "Net" though a variety of community-specific informative articles and "how to" guides.

Nevertheless, commercial services remained ambivalent toward this portion of their user base, whose very existence appeared to some to undermine services' "family-friendly" image. As trans users' presence grew, though, so did their sense of autonomy as well as their ownership of the platform, and "their" spaces in particular. When confronted with discrimination, these users strategically used the logic of capitalism to frame their presence as a viable consumer demographic, not a problem to be removed. This move toward collective and capitalist subjectivity mirrored current trends in what was now framed as LGBT politics: first, toward the use of "transgender" as a collective identity term, which would then be folded into the GLBT/LGBT initialism; and, second, marketers' increasing interest in reaching the "gay market."[5] By the late 1990s, trans users were firmly among those included in services' target "LGBT market." However, these spaces would ultimately be done in by changing economic trends, which incentivized building an ever-increasing audience share over maintaining a loyal user base.

A New Technology for the Home

In the early 1990s, a variety of different proprietary communication services existed alongside smaller independent BBSes, the four largest being America Online (AOL), CompuServe Information Service (often referred to as just CompuServe or CIS), Prodigy, and GEnie (General Electric Network for Information Exchange). Service subscribers paid an initial flat fee for a set number of hours (with an added fee for each hour over the limit) for access to a variety of services, such as forums, private messaging/email, and file and game libraries. Each service also had their own unique selling point, such as online shopping (Prodigy), exclusive access to certain publications (CompuServe), or community and chat (AOL). Effectively, these services were "walled gardens": easy to enter and use, but with few avenues beyond their walls. While some offered limited Internet capabilities early on, many would not convert to being full Internet service providers (ISPs) until the late 1990s—if they even survived that long. As this chapter will discuss, the existential crisis these services faced following the emergence of the Internet was a key factor not only in their corporate decisions but also in their approach to content moderation.

Excitement and interest around this new medium drove popular media coverage, such as Bryant Gumbel's now-iconic 1994 inquiry to his skeptical *Today Show* cohosts, "What is the Internet, anyway?"[6] Had Gumbel been at a bookstore, he could have gotten an answer from any number of instructional books and videos filling the shelves with titles like *Internet Starter Kit*, *Traveler's Guide to the Information Highway*, or *Internet for Dummies*. Some texts like the (now widely parodied) *What the Heck's the Net?* offered advice on possible uses for the Internet within the family and domestic life. More commonly known as *Moms on the Net*, this twenty-five-minute instructional video taught "ordinary moms" how to "tap into the power" of the Internet to complete a variety of "average" Mom tasks: finding kid-approved recipes, planning craft projects, and collecting information for their schoolwork.[7] In their print and television advertising, commercial services placed a similar emphasis on the domestic sphere. Commercials featured smiling middle-class professionals and their families happily using their computers to read the news, chat with friends, make travel arrangements, and shop—all from the comfort of home. Prodigy's in-house promotional materials, for example, highlighted the service as the "ultimate time saver" for busy American families, many of whom were investing in their first PC.[8] More importantly, these ads emphasized that their services were for the entire family, offering glimpses of stylish middle- and high-school-age teens happily tapping away at their keyboards to get help with homework, IM with friends, or play interactive games. In these ads, youth are almost exclusively using the services' "kid's areas," with their bright day-glo colors and playful typography.

Though seemingly absent in their ads, users within the gender community were equally present and prevalent on these services. From 1994 to 1997, a number of gender community publications ran articles introducing readers to the Internet and the "information superhighway," while national trans-specific conferences such as Fantasia Fair and Southern Comfort began running workshops on computers and the World Wide Web. The longest-running of these series appeared in *Cross-Talk*, which ran an eleven-article series from June 1994 to April 1995 entitled "The Information Highway and You." Much like mainstream publications, the authors of these articles imagined their audience as computer novices, framing them as falling behind the "techno-snobs" or "virgin[s]" in need of their "first kiss"— "the kiss of communication."[9] While some authors were long-time users, others were new adopters themselves whose initial interest had been sparked by the dot-com boom. Writing in *Powder & Pearls* (newsletter of the Tennessee-based Memphis TransGendered Alliance), author Rose described how the Internet's omnipresence in print and television ads spurred her to become a regular user, while author Linda, writing in the *Cross-Port InnerView* (newsletter for Ohio-based gender community group Cross-Port), reported buying a Prodigy subscription as a "Christmas present for the family." Novice authors at times offered their own inexperience as proof that anyone could use the Internet.[10] In her article "Computer Chronicles: Surfing Through The TG BBs," author Brenda Thomas told her *Tapestry* readers, "I KNOW NOTHING ABOUT COMPUTERS.... I can load a program and read instructions, and that is about as good as it gets.... So you do not need to be a guru to be able to access boards and have a lot of fun."[11]

Author expertise also shaped article content: experts focused on the technical aspects of Internet access, such as appropriate hardware and software, while novices offered "reports from the field" on their own Internet experiences, highlighting the social benefits of digital communication. In a 1995 column, editor Alicia of *Transmission Line* (newsletter of the Gulf Coast Transgender Community group in Houston, Texas) described how getting online via AOL's free trial transformed her life. Online, she was able to access information and find support. For her, talking on AOL was "like going over to a friend's house" where there would always be a sympathetic ear. Only once she had the support of her online friends did Alicia feel comfortable disclosing to her wife for the first time, but also going out in public as "Alicia."[12] Like Alicia, Kiki Carmichael's first experience with the online gender community came via AOL, when she finally subscribing after receiving "as least 10" discs. Writing in the March 1996 issue of the *Chi Tribune* (newsletter of the Chicago-based Chi Chapter of Tri-Ess), she described her first forays online as Kiki. Assumed to be a voyeur when going by her "male" name online, visiting gender community-specific AOL chat room "TV Chat" as Kiki led to something unexpected—"being hit on!"[13] For some users, just being able to communicate online allowed them to feel comfortable *en femme*: author Anya told her *Powder & Pearls* readers that she sometimes wore a dress and pumps while chatting on AOL, because "computers and the internet allow me to experience some of these things" without having to go outside, where she was much more likely to face scrutiny.[14]

Unsurprisingly, novices and experts diverged in their opinions about what kind of service their readers should use. In contrast to experts' preference for BBSes and independent local ISPs, novices recommended popular commercial services like AOL or CompuServe. They valued the accessibility of these services, but experts were skeptical. Author Jenifer, writing in the March 1995 issue of *Devil Woman* (newsletter of the Diablo Valley Girls in California) compared using a commercial service to "going to Paris and saying that you've seen Europe; yes, you've seen a piece of Europe, but you missed a great deal."[15] Experts also worried that their audiences' inexperience could inadvertently put their privacy and security at risk. Whereas the one-to-one, direct-dial model of the BBS offered security—a local phone call listed on your bill said nothing about the content of your conversation—one's activities on a commercial service or a work-based Internet account could not only be tracked; they were also attached to one's legal name (as the name on record of the account). In a 1996 column in *Renaissance News*, author Angela Gardner warned her readers against using their work computer to discuss trans issues online, since "somewhere, in the electronic bowels of the company computer there lurks a ghost of *every word you've ever written* . . . any message you send/receive via the net thru your company's email system is now—potentially—in the hands of your boss."[16] This concern drove Jenifer, writing in the May 1995 issue of *Devil Woman*, to finally subscribe to the Internet from home, freeing her from the fear that her employer might discover her trans identity. Whereas her privacy practices on her work computer were meticulous—files were always ambiguously named, encrypted, and stored on a hidden, password-protected, unmounted partition, all online communication anonymized through spoofing or remailers—on her home PC she could write whatever she wished, leaving her "in absolute heaven!" As her comfort level grew, she began taking risks, like hosting a website for the Diablo Valley Girls through her at-home service provider. Though she risked realizing her "worst fear" (having her service provider discover her gender community activity), she reasoned that they'd be "far too busy to care about this

[site]." They did notice, however, letting her know that they'd made her home page Web-accessible, and that they'd be willing to register the dvg .org domain for it as a "community service."[17] Though Jenifer's experience came to a happy ending, authors (Jenifer included) offered readers a variety of advice on keeping their communications, particularly their "femail," private via careful selection of email address (no full femme names, to prevent inadvertent "outing") and use of Web-based email services (which left no trace after logout) like Hotmail, Excite, and Net@ddress.

Growing public interest in the Internet didn't go unnoticed by BBS sysops, who saw value in grabbing the attention of potential future subscribers. Cross Connection, which remained one of the most prominent transgender BBSes throughout the 1990s, purposely altered its advertising strategy between 1994 and 1995, reframing its capabilities in more familiar social terminology. In early 1994, their advertising language (see fig. 2.1) highlights specific technical benefits: shareware libraries, a technical forum, GIF files, and Usenet access. A year later, (see fig. 2.2) forums and Usenet newsgroups were "discussion and roundtables," GIF files were presented as "picture libraries," and new mention of a "shopping mall" suggested the act of social consumption. And, as noted in chapter 1, users were now cast as members of a shared collective, a group of trans "sisters" who belonged to the "cybergender movement." Their new tagline—"We would all be just the same if there were no crossings"—encapsulated their shared social experience of sisterhood via digital communication.

Nevertheless, users primarily gravitated not to BBSes but commercial services, AOL in particular, as indicated by the email addresses published in newsletters and national publications. Though their structure and social norms varied, all of these services had spaces where gender community members could meet.[18] On CompuServe, trans users could either gather in CB Simulator (an early text chat) Channel 13, also known as "Gender Alternatives," or Forum 9/HSX-200, more commonly known as "GenderLine," in the Human Sexuality Forum. While Gender Alternatives was a publicly accessible channel, GenderLine was a more private forum overseen by sexologist Roger Peo, a well-known ally and regular contributor to the *Femme Mirror* and *Tapestry*. A fairly active space, GenderLine received an estimated one hundred notes (or

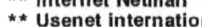

Figure 2.1 and 2.2. The shift in rhetoric regarding transgender community online is apparent in the two ads for the Cross Connection BBS service. The first (fig. 2.1) appeared in the January 1994 issue of *Cross-Talk*, while the second (fig. 2.2) appeared in the January 1995 issue. Figure 2.1 from *Cross-Talk: The Gender Community's News & Information Monthly* #51, and Figure 2.2 from *Cross-Talk: The Gender Community's News & Information Monthly* #63, both courtesy of the Digital Transgender Archive.

posts) a day and was the second-most-visited area of HSX.[19] According to user Terri Main, GenderLine offered a supportive, welcoming space. In her essay "A Girl at Heart," published in 1991 as part of *CompuServe Magazine*'s Member Essay Contest, she described finding "people who understood how I felt, because they had felt the same things. They provided encouragement, support, advice, friendship, even a shoulder to cry on occasionally."[20] Their support was crucial to her own personal transition: at their urging, she got in touch with a counselor and started planning for sex reassignment surgery. For Main, being able to chat with other members and use the GenderLine's files made a "significant difference" in her life: "It sounds strange to talk about electronic impulses this way, but I could feel love radiating from the computer screen. Sometimes when you live in the twilight region between genders you just need a hug from someone who cares. The conferences were like a big worldwide electronic hug."[21] Her essay is accompanied by a photo of a smiling Main, fingers perched above the keyboard of an early model laptop, as if she'd been caught a second before logging on to GenderLine. In contrast, trans users on Prodigy lacked a permanent area until late 1993, instead gathering in the "adults-only" Frank Discussions forum. Following Prodigy's closure of the forum, trans users were first given a "CD" area within the Fashion section (itself a subforum of the HomeLife forum), and by 1995 it had a Gender Issues area within the Support Groups Bulletin Board. On GEnie, trans topics were placed under the Family RoundTable, or forum, in Category 48. Given GEnie's struggles to attract users, the Transgender Community, otherwise known as the "GEnie Girls," was far smaller, averaging around thirty to forty users. In her comparison of AOL, CIS, and GEnie, author Marla Louise found GEnie to be the "friendliest and most caring" of the three areas.[22] The "Girls" hosted events such as their annual "Best Legs" contest, where users competed for the coveted title via submitted photos of their legs *en femme*.[23] Gender community spaces on AOL had by far the most transient existence. For many years, gender community users met primarily in unsanctioned member-created public chat rooms, eventually receiving space and support from the Gay and Lesbian Community Forum (GLCF), the "sanctioned" gay and lesbian space on AOL. Of all the nationwide commercial services, only the short-lived Millennium Online (active from 1993 to 1994) specifically billed itself as "gay-friendly." Not only did Millennium offer an official gay and lesbian forum, but they also hosted a gay and lesbian business directory, provided free advertising to non-profit AIDS organizations, and distributed condoms packaged to look like floppy disks at promotional events and trade shows.[24]

Yet while trans individuals found social support and camaraderie online, commercial services were grappling with their own role as hosts of material that some in the public deemed to be less than family-friendly, and social anxieties around just what children could access online drove services' content moderation policies. During this period, online services' legal status within the United States as it related to the First Amendment was still unclear: if they were classified as publishers, their responsibility for what users posted was far higher than if they were classified as carriers, like a telephone service. Moreover, there was little guidance on how to define "community standards" as they related to determining obscenity online. Emerging legal precedent, however, only addressed services' liability regarding defamatory speech, not obscenity.[25] What counted as "obscene" and how such content was moderated varied from service to service. In 1986, Commodore-specific service Quantum Link (which would eventually become part of America Online) initially stopped promoting and later disbanded their officially approved GLB club, Alternative Lifestyles, following pressure from Protecto, a "Christian-owned" mail-order computer company that had a sizable financial stake in Commodore. Even before the club's closure, Quantum Link's management was already leery of possible "sexualized" associations, having vetoed the founders' initial proposal to call their chat room a "Gay Bar."[26] CompuServe's highly structured forum format allowed them to restrict minors from accessing spaces intended for "inappropriate" or "adult" topics, such as the Human Sexuality section. However, the medicalized associations of the section also implicitly reinforced existing associations between LGBT individuals and psychological disorder and deviancy. Both Prodigy and GEnie employed human screeners to monitor postings in specific fora; Prodigy in particular branded itself as a family-friendly service, and its screening policies were thorough, with screeners reviewing and at times removing an estimated one hundred thousand messages a week, including a number of LGBT messages, which were considered "not an appropriate subject for a family bulletin board."[27] Prodigy's solution embodied the contradictory realities of content moderation. Following user complaints of inappropriate content on boards like the family-friendly HomeLife section, the service created the Frank Discussions forum in 1992 as an alternative adults-only section for users. However, the section was buried within the service, according to author Orlando Outland: "To ensure that junior doesn't stumble upon subjects like 'Oral—Penis Now!!' or 'Back Door Action' while researching his 9th grade science paper, users must jump through a series of hoops. First, they must transfer into the bulletin board section, which includes innocuous topics like 'Arts,' 'Computers,' or 'Homelife' (a sort of Regis and Kathie Lee online, often joked about by Frank Discussion users)."[28]

Despite this seemingly safe space, gay and lesbian users would complain of encountering persistent homophobia on the service, notwithstanding Prodigy's warning that "personal insults and bashing notes will not be tolerated." Within a year of its opening, Prodigy would close Frank Discussions without warning, citing issues with the frankness—so to speak—of user discussions.[29] In several cases, frustrated gay ex-Prodigy users proclaimed in no uncertain terms their preference for another service: America Online.

This choice made sense, given AOL's branding in the early 1990s, which emphasized fostering user community through forums and synchronous chat, as well as a seemingly more relaxed approach to content management. In 1991, CEO Steve Case presented AOL as a "town square, where people can stand on their soap box and make their opinions known," and further asserted that AOL "rarely deletes messages—about once a year."[30] However, many users were using the service not as a soapbox but for discussions of a more erotic nature: a sizable portion of AOL's chat rooms were "sex-oriented." The presence of these chats put AOL in a contradictory position: while they attracted users and kept them online (increasing their monthly bills), the content of these chats ran counter to AOL's own content moderation policies, which included a clearly defined list of "vulgar" language that members could not use in public settings.[31] This list included a variety of sexual terminology, such as "penis," "clit," "twat," and "slut," alongside identity terms whose use was being increasingly reclaimed, like "queers," "fags," and "dykes." Most importantly for the gender community, "transsexual" and "transvestite" were classified as vulgar terms, while "ts" and "cross dressing" were banned in the titles of public chat rooms. Although "tv" was accepted, rooms using it were still at risk of being made private, should a guide enter and read the chat contents.[32] Policing these chats for terms of service (TOS) violations was the task of volunteer moderators—"guides," in company parlance. AOL used a three-strike system: a reminder to start, then a stern warning, and, finally, account suspension for six months. In contrast, public chat rooms that violated the terms of service in their name were frequently converted into private rooms, making them inaccessible to anyone who wasn't already there.[33] In many cases, gay and lesbian users found the GLCF a far more welcoming space than the general People Connection chat, since it was maintained not by AOL corporate but an independent contractor, QView, which was far less invested in enforcing the TOS. QView also had a monetary incentive to keep members online, as their income was based on "churn" rates—that is, how many users stayed logged onto AOL in their area instead of logging off, or "churning."[34]

In this environment, trans individuals occupied a precarious position. Cross-gender activity's cultural associations with pornographic and adult topics made users and their spaces vulnerable to policing and condemnation, even as trans users implicitly or explicitly discouraged public discussion of adult topics in their chat rooms. This informal ban had long been part of a larger push by trans organizations, and cross-dressing organizations in particular, to gain mainstream respectability. As noted in the introduction, Virginia Prince spent most of her career working to reduce the stigma of "sexual deviancy" associated with cross-dressing, instead presenting it as a "harmless gender variation."[35] Despite users' attempts to counteract these associations, they easily transferred over from print to computer-based communication. Though Robert Carr may have been disappointed at GenderNet's decidedly nonsexual content, his *Playboy* article (and the sexual connotations of the magazine itself) would lead to the first mention of a gender community–specific online forum in a government document, a one-sentence reference to GenderNet as one of several "sexually oriented" BBSes in the Meese Commission's final 1986 report.[36]

As parental concern over the accessibility of adult material online mounted throughout the 1990s, discussions of gender community–related issues were increasingly cited as evidence that perversion was creeping into the public sphere. Reader response to Main's essay on GenderLine, for example, ran the gamut: one letter writer praised it as "both well-written and moving," while another complained that CompuServe displayed "poor taste" in publishing it and "[bringing] what the general population considers perverted into respectability."[37] A similar theme underlay a 1993 syndicated *Washington Post* article on the risks of online usage, entitled "Caution: Children at Play on Information Highway." In it, author John Schwartz began with an evocative story: an innocent eight-year-old girl, "seemingly safe at home," "playing with her favorite $2,000 toy, her computer," innocently enters a room on AOL called "TV Chat." What she does not know is that the chat's audience is not discussing television, but a topic much more "adult": transvestitism. The girl is rescued by Massachusetts grandmother and "self-appointed crossing guard on the information highway" Genevieve Kazdin, who says of the girl, "She was thinking in all innocence, 'We're going to talk about Barney.'"[38] For Schwartz, this was just one example of how children could now be exposed to "some of the raunchier aspects of human life."[39]

Nevertheless, no gender community authors reported repeat content moderation of gender community content on CompuServe, Prodigy, or Genie, all three of which offered some form of stable gender community–specific area. AOL, in contrast, was notoriously stringent in policing and removing trans-related content. In their official policy, AOL made clear associations between transness and perversity, functionally banning all discussion of trans-rated topics. AOL users in the gender community developed workarounds, like coded terminology, for each successive ban, but these were temporary solutions. In practice, this policy made discussion of trans and trans-adjacent topics a bannable offense and isolated questioning users unfamiliar with these coded terms. As member subscriptions to AOL steadily grew throughout the mid-1990s, existing trans users knew that they needed not merely a permanent home, but a change in policy legitimizing their presence on the service.

America, Online

Even before AOL became AOL, members of the gender community were present, if not particularly visible, on its service.[40] In her autobiographical writings, America Online Gender Group founder Melanie Anne Phillips describes firing up her 300-baud modem and Commodore 64 to access Quantum Link (also known as Q-Link) and connecting with the service's "small, clandestine gender community."[41] At the time, the technical limitations of Q-Link would lead Phillips to abandon it for the relatively greener pastures of Prodigy and trans BBSes like the Jersey Shore System, only to return in 1991. By then, Q-Link's parent company, Quantum Computer Services, had rebranded another of their Link-themed services, the failed AppleLink Personal Edition, as America Online and now offered access via both Mac and PC. As part of their relaunch, AOL had also partnered with small firms, commonly known as "content developers," to provide and maintain content for topic-specific areas, including the GLCF.

As Phillips found, however, the gender community had no such home on AOL, even within the GLCF. As she recounts it, she "couldn't believe that in a community so large as AOL, there wasn't a single public message from anyone regarding gender issues."[42] Following a few targeted postings, Phillips hosted a private "Gender" chat, which rapidly grew from a gathering of three initial attendees to a public room that regularly maxed out its twenty-four-member cap. Out of this room emerged the America Online Gender Group (AOLGG), a loosely affiliated organization that published a weekly newsletter and logs of the "Gender" chat. At some point in 1992, the GLCF volunteered its forty-eight-person conference room for the group to use once a week—again, regularly at capacity. The following year, Phillips would ask the GLCF to approach AOL about adding a "Gender Issues" folder to their library.[43] Within a few months of its creation, the resulting folder would hold "approximately 200 files" and have "well over 25,000 downloads." Throughout this period, AOLGG membership grew rapidly, with an estimated "10–20 new member[s]" joining each month, leading Phillips to project that group membership would grow to "almost 600 members" by the end of 1994.[44] Alongside the weekly conference chat, users also began creating a regular public room under a variety of aliases: "TV Chat," as noted above, or other coded language such as references to Christine Jorgensen, one of the most famous trans women of the twentieth century, or "Friends of Virginia," a play on the in-group gay term "Friends of Dorothy," but instead referencing Virginia Prince. But these were only temporary solutions, and chats were frequently closed or converted once a guide entered the room.⁴⁵

By late 1993, Phillips began seeking a permanent space, to be housed within the GLCF, for the rapidly expanding AOLGG, as well as a keyword, "Gender," that would take users directly to this forum. This process exposed the contradictory nature of the AOLGG's relationship to its namesake. Though their use of GLCF's conference room seemed, to Phillips, a form of "tacit" approval of the AOLGG, its public nature meant that participants were still technically barred from using language that accurately described their identities and experiences. Even as the chat room formed a "'safe haven from sexual harassment'... the one place online that a body could go to discuss the gentle, peaceful, issues of self-discovery—not just another gathering place for self-gratification," AOL construed self-gratification as the inherent purpose of all trans topics.⁴⁶ The AOL TOS served as, according to Gwendolyn Ann Smith (who would go on to moderate the AOLGG's second incarnation, the Transgender Community Forum), a form of "erasure," and that it was "delegitimizing, as if to say that the only reason one would need to talk about trans issues was for a sexually deviant reason.... We were not seen as humans who simply wanted to come together to discuss our interests, no matter how mundane they might be."⁴⁷ Moreover, any new expansion required the backing of GLCF management, who were still beholden to AOL not only for their paychecks, but also for support and access to resources for the very forum that paid their bills.⁴⁸

Around the same time, AOLGG members saw an increase in the closure of their public room for using vulgar language in its name. This closure inspired AOLGG members, including Smith, to begin a letter-writing campaign protesting what they saw as direct harassment and asking AOL to reconsider their classification of trans terminology as "vulgar" language.⁴⁹ Many users wrote letters, and one user visited AOL headquarters in Vienna, Virginia.⁵⁰ In an anonymous letter, one writer reports that AOL's initial response to the letter campaign was to increase their monitoring, closing or converting public gender community rooms "even more frequently—sometimes as often as 10x/hour." Some gender community users also received account termination warnings addressed to their screen names but using their legal names (under which their AOL accounts were registered) in the body text, which "frightened the entire community, because their careers [and] lives could be ruined if their gender orientation was made public knowledge." Since members did not know moderators could access this information, the unnamed writer argued, "using their real names could only be construed as a tactic of intimidation."[51] Moreover, most of AOL's moderators were, despite their internal categorization as "remote staff," volunteers with limited day-to-day oversight from paid AOL employees. As such, moderators had substantial leeway in the actual practice of TOS enforcement. Thus, even if corporate employees overseeing TOS issues had not requested increased surveillance of TV Chat, select volunteer moderators could have chosen, of their own volition, to overemphasize trans-related TOS violations.

For AOL TOS management, however, these two campaigns could not have come at a less convenient time. Right as both efforts were getting off the ground, AOL was seeing explosive membership growth, thanks to the mid-1993 launch of its infamous "Free Trial CD" direct marketing campaign, leading to one million new members by August 1994.[52] Though the demographic makeup of these new members is unknown, AOL's campaign was aimed directly at possibly-less-tech-savvy middle-class families, who were looking for an easy-to-install, easy-to-use service. To these new members, a visible "gender community" would have clashed with AOL's family-friendly image. In order for these campaigns to be successful, Phillips and letter writers had to change not only how AOL understood their community, but also how they understood themselves as a collective bloc with social and economic power.

"A bunch of girls who'd just gone shopping"

From the outset, Phillips recognized that, for the gender community, AOL's "family orientation" was a "strength and weakness of AOL at this time." As a service that sought to "appeal to middle America and "[seem] much more accessible to the novice user," it brought in many "mainstream people with gender problems who make their first contact with others like them here on a family oriented board." However, that same family orientation meant that there was "a lot of resistance to 'coming out' of our section," the GLCF, and being visible as part of the wider AOL community.[53] Phillips and campaigners, then, had to reframe the gender community as a respectable, nonsexual group unlikely to challenge AOL's public branding. In her initial email to the head of AOL's Lifestyles and Interests (who managed AOL's forums) about creating a more permanent space for the AOLGG, Phillips opened her letter emphasizing the difference between gay and lesbian individuals and "crossdressers and transsexuals who are trying to come to terms with their gender, which is completely different from their sexuality." Not only does "gender (masculine and feminine) [have] no direct tie to being male or female nor to one's sexual preferences," Phillips argued, but also "95% of all crossdressers are straight, and half are happily married, most with children." By focusing on AOLGG members' normality, Phillips preemptively countered corporate perceptions of AOLGG members as vulgar deviants. She returned to this theme at the close of her letter, following her request for a gender-specific space. Since she didn't know if the unnamed reader knew any gender community members, she described herself: a "technical consultant and manager of a major R&D program," married with two kids, a Girl Scout and a Sea Cadet contemplating a Navy career, both in advanced placement classes. However, she emphasized, she was by no means an outlier, as many AOLGG members had respectable positions in society—"the head of a major psychology school, an air traffic controller, and MD." Phillips, like many trans women, was "generally wholly integrated into society" and "no one knows about our past unless we choose to share it." Should her reader doubt the veracity of this claim, she pointed to a copy of her photo as evidence. As it showed, AOLGG members "are not a 'wild and crazy' group of men dancing around in skirts. In fact, we are a responsible group of transgendered individuals seeking enlightenment, information, understanding and support."[54]

A 1994 *Philadelphia Daily News* column about the TOS change campaign echoed this focus on members' social respectability outside of their cross-gender interests and identities. Reporting back on his experience in the "TV and CD Chat," author Mabarak Dahir described talk in the room as "far from sexual": friendly greetings, shared exchanges of social support, and complaints about AOL's closure of the chat, but not one "mention of sex." According to one member quoted by Dahir, "If you looked at our conversation, most of the time you'd think it was a bunch of girls who'd just gone shopping."[55] Dahir reinforced this sense of normality by emphasizing members' heterosexual masculinity outside of the chat, noting that "all of the guys I talked to were married with children. One is an aerospace engineer; he'd played college football and served in the Marines. Another did two tours in Vietnam, was on the police force for 15 years, and is now a private investigator."[56]

However, this "bunch of girls" were seriously divided within. While they shared some mutual topics of interest, transsexual and cross-dressing individuals at the time largely understood themselves as separate groups joined together by their cross-gender interests and shared oppressions. However, their relationship was fraught, and which group received the most attention, energy, and support was often a topic of discussion in "shared" groups like the AOLGG and publications such as *Tapestry*. Within the AOLGG, the group's increasingly close association with the GLCF was a particular point of contention. Though the GLCF's independence gave the AOLGG more freedom, some members were adamant that any association with gay and lesbian organizations would reinforce wider social preconceptions around sexuality and cross-dressing, and some had initially opposed holding a weekly chat in the GLCF's conference room.[57] Though Phillips recognized these users' discomfort, the GLCF was, in her view, the best venue for any new gender community–specific space. The proposed "Gender" keyword offered one compromise: instead of having to enter via the GLCF, using "Gender" would send users directly to the Gender Forum, allowing the group to simultaneously "[maintain] our political protection and [add] to the clout of our hosts at the GLCF by still being part of their area" while permitting concerned users to "enter the Gender Forum with no reference to the GLCF." Unlike the GLCF, the focus of the Gender Forum would be "all gender issues," which should reassure "those who are troubled by too close an association."[58]

However, Phillips urged readers to think of gay and lesbian individuals not as threats to their self-identity but as allies in a shared cause. This move mirrored contemporaneous trends in wider gay and lesbian politics, as embodied by the emergent initialism GLBT (later LGBT), though the place of the "T" remained controversial within the gender community.[59] In a letter to Phillips' e-zine, *The Subversive*, DawnSEL declared that she "cannot accept or in any way support the AOL mandatory characterization of what we loosely call the 'gender community' as Gay/Lesbian/Homosexual. Whatever my own sexual orientation may be, I cannot and will not allow AOL to rule that I MUST be G/L/H if I am TV/CD. I commented long ago, and repeat now, that the urgency of our crusade for a forum had us put expediency before principle. [Please note that I said AOL, not GLCF.]" In her response, Phillips reminded Dawn that "AOL never offered us anyplace to be," and that their current space existed "because the GLCF OFFERED the room to us, without even being asked." The gesture, to Phillips, was a signal that the GLCF will be a gender community ally: "They offered the hand of friendship, not to say we are gay—they KNOW we are not!—but to help another minority that is oppressed by traditional societal roles. I, for one, welcome the opportunity to join with others against the common oppressor, for in unity there is strength." She also presented the GLCF as a model for the AOLGG's ambitions. Special interest groups like gay and lesbian users, she argued, used their "niche" to grow and lobby for "a home of their own" once they were "a large enough force online."⁶⁰ Much like the AOLGG, the GLCF was founded following member activism, including a 1989 letter-writing campaign, lobbying AOL for a gay and lesbian specific space.⁶¹ Given the AOLGG's rapid growth since its founding, the best method for receiving a Gender Forum would be to "keep adding services for our increasing membership until we, too, are a force big enough to be recognized." Phillips closed her letter by urging "everyone in the gender community to spend at least some of their online time here, thereby contributing to our political clout and ultimately to a forum of our own."⁶² This call to "spend time there" was, in essence, a request for AOLGG members to understand themselves as not only a group united by shared interests but also a valuable portion of AOL's consumer base whose needs deserved to be met. In particular, Phillips encouraged readers to exploit AOL's existing interest in cultivating content and services to keep users from "churning." In an early letter about her efforts to get a "Gender" keyword, Phillips told readers that "the increasing numbers of our membership DO carry weight with the AOL management. But they are MOST impressed by attendance to forum functions, since that is how they judge how much money our special interest group represents."⁶³ From the corporate perspective, those hours regular members spent attending AOLGG functions could add up quickly, particularly since attendees were likely to use up their five prepaid hours within just a few weeks, leaving them to pay $3.50/hour (lowered to $2.95 in 1994; $5.67

adjusted for inflation) for the rest of the month. In her communications with AOL, Phillips made a point of emphasizing that prospective AOL users within the gender community were choosing, despite their expressed dissatisfaction, to stick with services like CompuServe and GEnie because they offered gender community–specific forums. By the start of 1995, members' consistent lobbying, as well as their use of the service, would begin to see dividends.

A Changing Relationship

The first major change came in early 1994, when AOL contacted campaigners to let them know that the TOS would be updated to allow TV Chat as well as all gender community terminology.[64] The campaign's success increased users' sense of autonomy and ownership of their presence on AOL. Throughout 1994, the gender community became an increasingly visible part of the GLCF, adding a cross-dresser-specific conference, Alpha Omega Lambda, that previously met in a member-created chat room, as well as a gender-specific message board. Increasingly, well-known figures within the trans community, such as Kate Bornstein (who used the AOL handle OutlawGal), were also extolling the virtues of the gender community on AOL.[65] In January 1995, the GLCF was finally cleared to host the long-sought Gender Forum, overseen by Gwendolyn Ann Smith, as Phillips had largely stepped back from leadership of the AOLGG. Now named the Transgender Community Forum (TCF), the TCF would host a variety of gender community resources, including its own conferences, chat room (the Gazebo), several message boards, and an extensive file library of user-contributed content ranging from makeup and binding tips to personal coming-out stories. The forum also came with accompanying keywords, such as "Gender," "Transsexual," and "Transgender," for easy user access. In a 1997 article on the TCF, one user described how a simple keyword search for "Transgender" allowed her to find resources after only ten minutes on AOL.[66]

The Gazebo in particular became a key resource for both average AOL users and prominent trans activists such as Mara Keeling and Phyllis R. Frye.[67] The chat room's name, according to Smith, was meant to invoke "a place where everyone can come together and gather, and relax, and enjoy each other's company on an endless summer's day."[68]

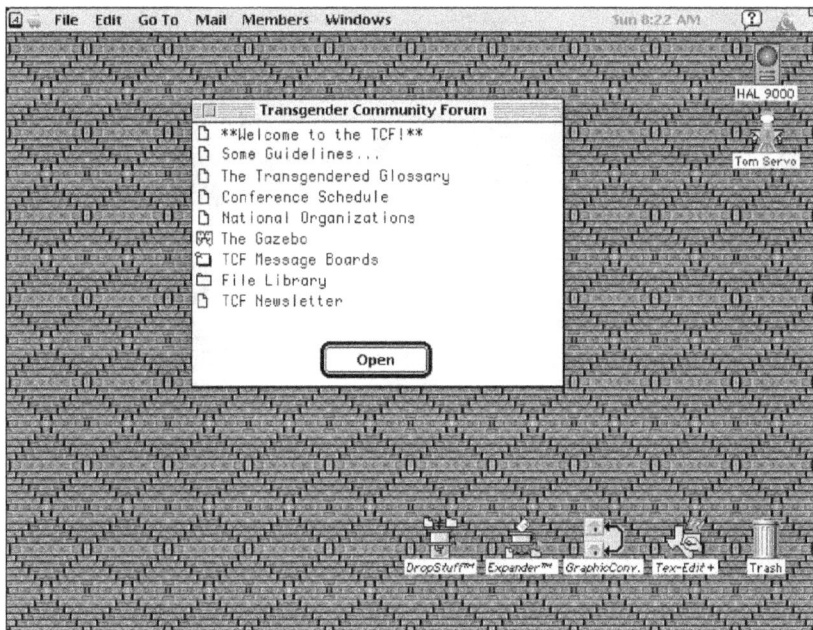

Figure 2.3. Screenshot of the Transgender Community Forum's main screen in January 1995, taken by TCF coordinator Gwendolyn Ann Smith. Image courtesy of Gwendolyn Ann Smith.

Figure 2.4. Screenshot of the Transgender Community Forum's main screen in October 1995, following America Online's move to a visual interface. The header image was designed by Smith, who was known as GLCF Wendy at the time. Image courtesy of Gwendolyn Ann Smith.

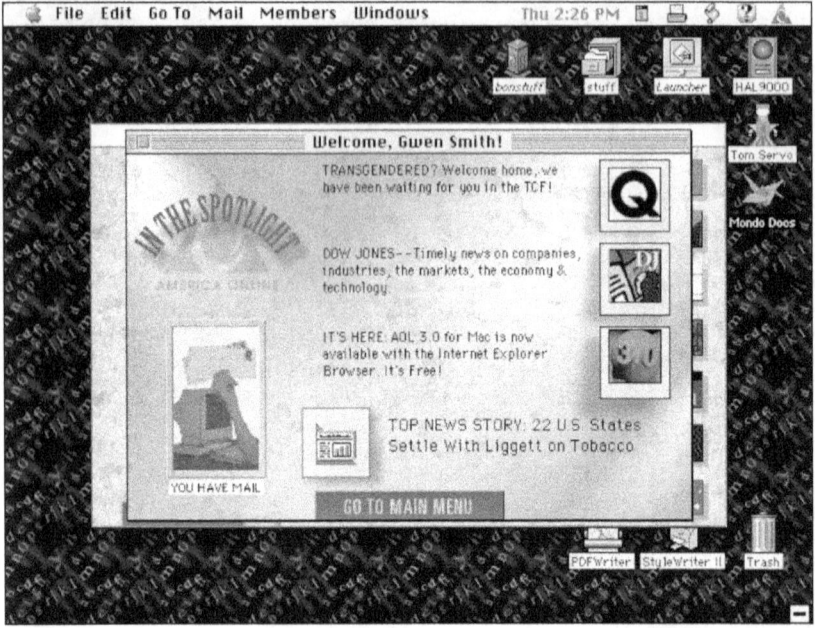

Figure 2.5. Different communities were regularly featured on AOL's main landing page, and the TCF finally had its turn on March 20, 1997. Image courtesy of Gwendolyn Ann Smith.

In the Gazebo, users felt comfortable coming out and seeking support; for some, being able to chat online gave them the courage to seek out in-person offline clubs and support groups. Trans users in particular continued to have some of the lowest churn rates, prompting AOL executives to at one point request a meeting with TCF manager Smith to discuss how she'd managed to so successfully retain users, thinking it was due to particular content or methods that could be replicated elsewhere. She knew, of course, what it really was: the TCF offered support and acceptance to a population that sorely needed it.[69]

However, the creation of the TCF wasn't the only change in AOL's relationship to its gay and lesbian user base. Though gay and lesbian individuals had always been a notable portion of AOL's base—the GLCF was one of the most popular areas on AOL, logging "close to 1.8 million hits a month"—the GLCF and its parent company QView had a fraught relationship with AOL. While AOL certainly valued gay and lesbian users' subscriptions, it rarely promoted the forum, according to QView's head of marketing.[70] Instead, marketing and promotion was left to QView, who organized volunteers to hand out free AOL trial discs at Pride.[71] Part of this reluctance stemmed from lingering associations between gay content and pornography. In 1995, QView proposed a community-specific AOL Free Trial disc, to be included with issues of the *Advocate* and *Out*. However, QView's proposed tagline "Now Your Playground Just Got Bigger" was initially rejected by AOL for potentially sexualized interpretations of "Playground." Instead, discs in the *Advocate* used the more generic tagline "Join Our Exciting Online Community," while QView eventually convinced AOL to release discs to *Out* with the "Playground" tagline.[72] Print ads that ran in these magazines a year later were equally circumspect, featuring the forum's keyword "GLCF" in white block text on a black background, accompanied by the (possibly unintentionally) ironic tagline at the bottom: "America Online's Best Kept Secret."[73] Though these ads still focused on gay and lesbian users, QView recognized that both the GLCF's own changing demographics and wider political shifts toward the GLBT initialism meant that the

Figure 2.6. Screenshot of the onQ frontpage from October 11, 1997. This screenshot was collected as evidence of a malicious hacking attempt targeting onQ. Image courtesy of AOLSucks.org.

forum was due for a rebranding. In August 1996, it would relaunch as the more-inclusive onQ, though the TCF would retain its name.

Just as onQ was beginning to market itself as the LGBT destination on AOL, commercial services were increasingly targeting LGBT consumers as a desirable market instead of an uncomfortable, if inevitable, presence on their services. When Microsoft Network (MSN) launched in mid-1995, having a gay and lesbian area was, according to group project manager Larry Cohen, a "no-brainer." MSN was the first host of PlanetOut, founded by Digital Queers founder Tom O'Reilly.[74] One month after onQ's relaunch, AOL added PlanetOut, which had recently received funding from AOL's content incubator Project Greenhouse. Though AOL president Ted Leonsis pitched the addition of PlanetOut as allowing AOL to offer "the widest choice for our lesbian and gay audience,"

Figure 2.7. Pride Media's home page for Pride! Universe. Unlike text-only services, users created customizable avatars that they navigated through a series of 2D graphical locales, including outdoor gardens, shopping malls, and an AIDS Memorial Hall. Users also had their own personal "CyberPad" they could furnish and decorate. Archived November 8, 1997. Archived copy courtesy of the Internet Archive.

QView was frustrated by the move and interpreted it as a direct threat to their revenue, since onQ would no longer by users' primary destination for LGBT content.[75] AOL wasn't the only major commercial service reconsidering its relationship to its LGBT customers. CompuServe, which had struggled to remain competitive with AOL, contracted with Pride Media to entirely reconceive their LGBT forums. This move replaced the medicalized connotations of CompuServe's previous classifications for LGBT content, "Alternative Lifestyles" or "Human Sexuality," with "Pride"-branded forums: Pride Central, Pride Men, Pride Women, Pride Bi, and Pride Trans*. They also oversaw a LGBT-specific, outer-space-themed version of "virtual world" program WorldsAway (already licensed by CompuServe) named "Pride! Universe." Following the rebranding, Pride Media claimed that the new forums were "already logging over 1,000,000 hits per month, demonstrating that the need for such services is strong."[76]

Nevertheless, the presence of PlanetOut was a sign of the larger existential threat to commercial services' business model: the World Wide Web. For much of their existence, commercial services had focused on developing curated content for their users, but those users were increasingly interested in reaching beyond their walls to the World Wide Web, and they were leaving AOL for ISPs, who charged not by the hour, but a monthly flat fee. In December 1996, AOL converted to a flat $19.95 monthly fee, launching the "America On Hold" debacle, as AOL members were forced to wait long hours to log in to AOL, if they could log in at all. For content developers, the switch to flat-fee pricing meant that they were no longer paid by use time but by advertising views. Though onQ hosted "over 300,000 unique screen names in its community spaces" monthly and "logged over $10 million in usage hours for AOL" in 1996 before the flat-fee switch in December, those numbers no longer had the same meaning in an advertising-based model.[77] Whereas the low-churn model rewarded content developers who kept users online, an advertising-based model rewarded content developers who emphasized rapid user turnover in order to squeeze out more ad views.[78] In this environment, the transgender community's deep engagement in the TCF's services transformed them from a valuable asset into a possible loss leader. Ultimately, onQ would leave AOL in 2000 for Gay.com—whose parent company, Online Partners, Ltd. had acquired QView in

2000—over an advertising-related contract dispute.[79] onQ and the TCF (now known as the Transgender Gazebo) would remain active on Gay .com until 2003, but they would never again have the same stature and level of attention as they had during the mid-1990s. onQ's content developer model, primarily designed to hold user attention within a walled garden, was not always well suited to the wide-open World Wide Web, where users had any number of possible options for socializing and consuming content. Moreover, user interest and attention was beginning to shift away from the "channel" model—which assumed users would, as they had historically for television, primarily want all of their topic-specific content in one "area"—toward a social network model, where users would have customizable individual profiles that could also be used for socializing in shared group spaces. Yet the TCF remains an important part of contemporary trans history as an example of the way trans users and their allies were able to organize around their shared identification to demand space and recognition on what was America's number-one online service.

3

Politics and "Petty Useless Bickering"

Transgender Usenet and the Emergence of "Cisgender"

Few social media platforms are so often simultaneously lauded and derided as Twitter. On one hand, Twitter is the facilitator of conversation, a place where users can connect and organize around key political issues. On the other, it's the mimetically dubbed "hellsite," where honest conversation goes to die in a fire of furious trolling. However, Twitter wasn't the first platform to play this dual role. That honor would go to Usenet, one of the earliest noncommercial communication networks to span the globe. Initially developed in 1979 as the "poor man's" version of the more "professional" Department of Defense–funded ARPANET, which would later become the backbone for the Internet folks use today, Usenet grew over the years to become one of the most popular and widely used international platforms available online. Yet Usenet would also be the first place where email spam, as we'd recognize it in the modern sense, would become widespread.[1] Most importantly, the platform was infamous for its lack of moderation, with ongoing, often vicious, flame wars that ran on for years. Ultimately, Usenet might be best summed up by Gene Spafford—early Usenet sysadmin, maintainer of the "official" newsgroup list, and member of the "Backbone Cabal" that partially oversaw Usenet's maintenance—when he compared it to "a herd of performing elephants with diarrhea—massive, difficult to redirect, awe-inspiring, entertaining, and a source of mind-boggling amounts of excrement when you least expect it."[2]

This quote could also aptly describe the transgender-themed newsgroups on Usenet. In their names, organization, governing charters, and FAQS, transgender Usenet newsgroups mirror the fractured political environment of the 1990s and early 2000s, with each group reflecting conflicting strains of thought. Compared to other transgender discussion fora, both print and digital, trans newsgroups were considered highly visible niche spaces dominated by posters whose arguments were otherwise excluded from the in-group discursive mainstream. As a result, these newsgroups eventually came to form their own discursive sphere, powered by cross-posting between groups. Usenet discussion was driven by a core set of regular posters, some of whom maintained acrimonious relationships for much of their time posting there. Yet these feuds, and the flame wars that fueled them, also popularized one of the most important additions to the transgender lexicon in the last thirty years: cisgender.

This chapter examines the place of Usenet in trans life online from the mid-1990s until the mid-2000s, when posting began to drop off significantly, by studying the shifting use and adoption of "cisgender" and associated terms. Notably, this investigation doesn't aim to recover a definitive point of origin or exact timeline of transmission. Instead, I consider how the social infrastructure and affordances of Usenet, specifically around the posting and circulation of content, allowed specific understandings of the term "cisgender" to gain visibility. Though the current ubiquity of "cisgender" would suggest a trajectory of increasing adoption of the term, for many years only a small subset of Usenet posters actively used it. However, these posters possessed a particular set of qualities, such as frequent posting and a propensity for confrontation, that made their posts more likely to draw not only an audience but also a variety of responses.

While many definitions now position "cisgender" as a value-neutral adjective, I argue that the term's contemporary adoption can be attributed to the political and ideological meaning early Usenet posters imbued it with. Significantly, these users applied a specific interpretation of "cisgender" that prioritized gender performance over embodiment as the primary site of difference between trans and non-trans individuals. This move circumvented existing hierarchies within trans spaces that prioritized gender normative presentation and one's ability to "pass," focusing instead on the oppressive nature of wider social norms. These posters used "cisgender" to construct an "us/them" dynamic that emphasized members' shared oppression, giving them a basis for collective organizing.

Usenet: "A herd of performing elephants with diarrhea"

Unlike most modern social media platforms, Usenet lacks both dedicated central servers and a dedicated administrative team overseeing its maintenance. Instead, its core architecture is distributed across a large, constantly shifting collection of servers ferrying user messages to subscribers across the network, making it nearly impossible for governments to successfully regulate it. In format, Usenet messages themselves largely mirror email, with designated headers containing preset information, including a unique Message-ID, and message content below. Posts made in response to another post included that post's Message-ID under its "References" header, which a Usenet newsreader—software specifically designed for reading and posting to Usenet—would use to create a message "thread" to follow.

All messages were required to designate at least one newsgroup to receive them. Though their name implies a static structure, newsgroups are little more than loose collections of topic-specific messages users would subscribe to, receiving a new load of posts each time they logged in. Following the "Great Renaming" of newsgroups in 1987 by the Backbone Cabal, a group of news administrators who oversaw some of the network's key servers, Usenet was organized into first seven, then eight "official" hierarchies, known as the Big 8: comp.*, misc.*, news.*, rec.*, sci.*, soc.*, humanities.* and talk.*.[3] Newsgroup names are organized in order of increasing specificity of topic; for example, humanities.music.composers.wagner focuses on academic discussion of the music of a specific composer, Wagner. The alt.* hierarchy was created after the Great Renaming as an alternative hierarchy, with fewer rules and restrictions around newsgroup creation. As early news admin Eric Ziegast humorously put it, "ALT stands for 'Anarchists, Lunatics, and Terrorists.'"[4] Posts were not limited to a specific newsgroup, however. Much like the long lists of hashtags used with posts on contemporary platforms like Instagram or Tumblr, messages could be simultaneously sent, or cross-posted, to a variety of (possibly unrelated) newsgroups, allowing them to enter into a variety of different discussion spaces. While cross-posting increased the level of interactivity in Usenet, often bringing in new perspectives, it also went against the rules of Usenet "netiquette" and led to some of the first instances of spam.[5]

For prospective spammers, it would be easy to avoid accountability: as a decentralized network, newsgroups did not have membership or signup requirements. Instead, one's Usenet "identity" was tied to one's email address, which could easily be anonymized or spoofed. Usenet's reliance on email addresses also made it platform agnostic: any single platform, from a BBS to a commercial provider like Delphi, CompuServe, or even AOL, could (and did) allow users to send and receive Usenet messages. Usenet was one of the first unregulated cross-platform discussion platforms available to a variety of audiences—much to early Usenet regulars' chagrin. Though Usenet's userbase initially tended toward the technically savvy, it ballooned with perceived "clueless newbies" as commercial providers added access, beginning with AOL in September 1993.[6] These changes marked the beginning of the "Eternal September," referencing the annual influx of clueless college freshman who, flush with their first taste of Internet access, flooded Usenet at that time every year.[7]

However, it's possible these Septemberites understood Usenet as simply another feature within the garden ecosystem, if they understood it as separate at all: many GUIs and browsers, as well as the numerous platform- or software-specific Internet "explainer" texts that filled bookstore shelves in the mid to late 1990s, referred to Usenet as "Internet News," "Newsgroups," or simply "News."[8] This connection was, in some cases, visually reinforced: Mosaic, for example, used a newspaper icon for its "newsgroups" button. Moreover, these interfaces could, in some cases, break the flow of discussion on Usenet. Many veteran users used specialized newsreader software that included a variety of now familiar affordances, like message threading, marking messages as read, and message quoting. These newsreaders presented Usenet in its least altered form; any filtering was specified by the user, not the service provider. However, users who accessed Usenet via readers built-in to their browsers or commercial platform might not have had many of these affordances. For example, being able to quote previous messages was particularly important in the fast and furious flow of Usenet. Keeping track of ongoing discussions across multiple messages and newsgroups could still prove difficult, and posters relied heavily on quoting prior messages to track the conversation. Quoting allowed readers who hadn't been in the conversation to more easily jump in midstream, without having to read all of the earlier messages, which they might not have yet received. Yet many nonnewsreader interfaces had poorly implemented—or entirely lacked—versions of such essential affordances. While Netscape Navigator was packaged with a fully fledged newsreader built-in, early versions of Internet Explorer didn't include threading.[9] AOL users relying on early versions of their built-in Usenet GUI could neither quote previous messages nor search message content, and AOL's message threading was poor at best.[10] As such, early AOL users would be at a distinct disadvantage, as they would have to manually quote another poster—a possibly time-consuming process. Those accessing Usenet via Mosaic were the most limited by far: they could only read newsgroups at the moment they were accessed, since Mosaic didn't allow subscribing, replying, or posting to Usenet.[11] Lastly, there's no evidence any of these platforms or browsers (beyond Netscape) allowed users to killfile, or block, specific email addresses of other posters they did not wish to read. Some of these services also engaged in benign censorship: some newsgroup names and descriptions on AOL did not match those distributed elsewhere, while CompuServe's default list of newsgroups did not include possibly objectionable groups, such as those under the alt.sex designation; instead, users had to subscribe to these groups manually.[12] The lack of advanced features, as compared to other parts of their chosen digital platform, might have oriented these users toward only reading Usenet instead of posting.

As the network grew, Usenet's membership was dominated by a vast "invisible crowd" of readers who consumed content produced by a small but highly active core membership.[13] According to one study, 27 percent of newsgroup messages came from "singleton posters," or posters who contributed only once to a given newsgroup, while an average 25 percent of all newsgroup posts were made by a "tiny percentage" (2.9 percent) of the larger newsgroup poster population.[14] Highly active posters often became familiar presences within a newsgroup, and their familiarity made their posts more likely to draw a response.[15] Usenet's social and political culture, in many ways, mirrored its architecture: a loose confederation of principles centered around keeping the anarchic platform afloat. Collected institutional knowledge was shared and passed down through metadiscourse on the purpose and direction of Usenet.[16] Debates about platform structure and organization emphasized solutions based in pseudodemocratic processes focused on "punish[ing] only those actions that threaten the network's ability to function as a forum for deliberative debate."[17] At the newsgroup level, users' activity was loosely governed by a variety of informal rules and documentation like newsgroup charters and FAQs, which lay down the rules of group "netiquette" and helped foster a collective group identity.[18] In some communities, mentor-mentee structures solidified institutional knowledge, as mentors enculturated newbies in both the technical skills and social norms needed to successfully navigate Usenet.[19] While group flame wars around unofficial group rules did occur, these debates sometimes had the side effect of reemphasizing and preserving established social norms.[20]

However, violators were equally as likely to find their inbox flooded with furious flames from other posters. Usenet posters' propensity for vituperative debate, including flaming, reflects the platform's wider reputation of anarchism, insularity, and prodigious production of content. In his study of flaming on Usenet, media scholar Joseph Kayany defines "flames" as messages that contain both hostility and lack of restraint, often marked by "swearing, calling names, ridiculing, and hurling insults towards another person, his/her character, religion, race, intelligence, and physical or mental ability."[21] Posters' response to being flamed varied, including denunciation, avoidant strategies like withdrawal or apology, to tension-defusion through jokes.[22] Over time, flaming could become an accepted social norm in a given newsgroup, and flame wars ended "only when both parties become bored with them."[23] Long-running and recurrent flame wars, particularly around technical issues, could take on the status of "holy wars," defined in Eric Raymond's *Jargon File* as ongoing arguments where "most of the participants spend their time trying to pass off personal value choices and cultural attachments as objective technical evaluations."[24] Though newsgroup moderation was possible, only 12 percent of all newsgroups were moderated.[25] Moderating a newsgroup could be a significant time investment, as it required a dedicated individual or set of individuals to approve all items posted to the group. Moderators could stem the tide of posts, but their presence had no effect on the overall level of interactivity in a newsgroup. Instead, interactivity and social restrictions existed in an inverse relationship: the fewer social or technical restrictions there were to posting, the more interactive a newsgroup would be.[26]

Transgender Newsgroups on Usenet

Transgender-themed newsgroups first emerged on Usenet in 1992, beginning with alt.transgendered. According to the alt.transgendered FAQ, the newsgroup was founded in late 1992 in reaction to the creation of an "unapproved" newsgroup, alt.sex.trans. Concerned the group's alt.sex designation, which was commonly associated with erotica and fetish groups, meant it would not be widely distributed, Usenet poster Kristine created alt.transgendered in October 1992. However, from the outset, posters remained concerned that being in the unofficial alt.* hierarchy would still limit how many servers carried the newsgroup. For them, the ultimate goal was to have a trans-specific newsgroup under soc.*, where it would be seen as a respectable newsgroup worth carrying. However, any groups nominated for the official hierarchies required a formal proposal, including a charter, and were held to a vote. In 1994, poster Amy would propose the creation of "soc.support.transgendered." Discussion of the proposal was widely in favor of the group, and many posters pointed to the wider potential for propagation as an important consideration. In her post supporting soc.support.transgendered's creation, Joan described the importance of the newsgroup's creation in stark terms: "If only one life is saved by the creation of this group, wouldn't it be worth it? It's only a communications medium, and people are needlessly losing their lives and wasting their potential in self-destructive, maladaptive, denial-bases coping strategies. The loss to our society is great, and needless. . . . If [soc.support.transgendered] gets us talking, it can't be bad." Opposition to the newsgroup proposal primarily focused on the soc.support.* designation, which opponents felt too closely tied cross-gender interests to medicalization, as compared to a top-level group, soc.transgendered. In July 1994, the proposal would pass, with 298 yes votes to 72 no votes, a roughly 80 percent approval rate. alt.tg and SST (as they were commonly referred to) would continue to be the two most visible and active trans-specific newsgroups, though several more would be founded in the alt.* hierarchy over the next ten years, including the three others studied in this chapter: alt.support.crossdressing, alt.fashion.crossdressing, and alt.support.srs.

Except for alt.support.srs, all of these groups were founded around 1994 and 1995, just as transgender publications were helping users get wired. Though very little data was collected on Usenet usage, some general hints as to user demographics and newsgroup propagation across the wider Usenet network are available. Early Usenet administrator Brian Reed's semimonthly Usenet readership survey, which tracked a variety of metrics for highly active newsgroups, included alt.transgendered from January 1993 to July 1995. From month to month, alt.transgendered averaged an estimated 21,130 readers worldwide and was received by a little less than half of all Usenet servers. As more transgender-related newsgroups were founded, the percentage of messages cross-posted between alt.transgendered and other newsgroups grew substantially, reaching 51 percent by July 1995. Poster activity in trans newsgroups mirrored Usenet at large: in existing Usenet Archives, unique email addresses with over one hundred posts make up a small percentage of the total posters; in contrast, over 50 percent of all unique email addresses make only 1 post to each group (table 3.1).

Posts covered a wide range of topics, including support or advice about coming out; tips on makeup, dress, and passing; and the philosophy and theology of cross-gender desires. The most active threads often delved into hotly contested political issues within the community and could run on for weeks. At times, discussion threads focused on users' other passions, such as golf or science fiction. Very little recorded information exists regarding poster demographics in transgender newsgroups. One poster did conduct an informal voluntary survey of alt.

TABLE 3.1. Upper and lower post counts per unique email (all percentages rounded up to the nearest whole number). Email addresses are not aggregated in instances when poster changed their primary Usenet address.

Newsgroup	Upper and Lower Poster Rankings
soc.support.transgendered	Upper (over 100 posts): 211/11750 (2%) Lower (1 post): 6306/11750 (54%)
alt.transgendered	Upper (over 100 posts): 41/19775 (0.2%) Lower (1 post): 12577/19775 (63%)
alt.fashion.crossdressing	Upper (over 100 posts): 86/12428 (0.7%) Lower (1 post): 7117/12428 (57%)
alt.support.crossdressing	Upper (over 100 posts): 91/8473 (1%) Lower (1 post): 4738/8473 (56%)
alt.support.srs	Upper (over 100 posts): 216/6586 (3%) Lower (1 post): 3367/6586 (51%)

transgendered posters in 1993, and the results were later republished in online e-zine *The Subversive* prior to 1997.[27] According to their results, the average survey respondent was 32.7 years old, likely from the United States (78.9 percent of respondents), and lived in an "urban environment" (80.3 percent). Self-identifications were roughly even split between transsexual (42.1 percent) and transvestite (47.3 percent), with 5.3 percent identifying as "interested third party." However, respondents had few other connections to transgender media outside of alt.transgendered: a little over half (59.2 percent) of the survey respondents were not members of a support group other than alt.transgendered, and only 22.4 percent subscribed to any gender community publications.[28] Part of respondents' disconnect from established community groups could be attributed to the survey's date: distributed a month after AOL, the first of the big three commercial platforms, added Usenet access, but before the wave of explainer articles in transgender publications. Thus, the survey respondent pool would likely be biased toward those who were already technically savvy but lacked connections to the existing gender community.

Yet newsgroup populations no doubt grew once users began to log on in earnest in 1994. Within transgender publications, authors did not always present Usenet as a stand-alone network, often referencing simply the "news" or "newsgroups" online. Few of these authors discussed using Usenet newsreaders, the implication being that the user already had or would get access via their existing service. In example, an article on newsgroups in the October 1996 issue of the newsletter of Delta Chi Educational Association, *The Pinnacle*, author Diane Kaye told readers that "your service provider should have a 'newsgroup' icon to get into them to start." She discussed her own Usenet access as coming two different ways: via Netscape 2.0 at home, and MOSAIC at work.[29] Not only did Kaye not differentiate Usenet as an independent network with its own technical infrastructure or social norms; she never even used the term "Usenet." Authors' attitudes toward Usenet also influenced its image within the wider discursive sphere. By the late 1990s, few authors had anything good to say about Usenet. Though Usenet newsgroups were occasionally suggested as a possible resource, most discussion focused on the sheer volume of user flaming and vitriol. JoAnn Roberts noted in 1997 that she'd stopped mentioning Usenet in her monthly columns because it was "mostly hot air that fills the cyberscape. If someone isn't flaming someone else, then it's sleazy porn spam scrolling through my newsreader. I've pretty much tuned out that part of the net as useless."[30] Usenet's notoriety was most evocatively described in an episode of the serialized pulp-style detective series *Dawn Benedict, TV Detective*, published in 1996 on TGForum.com. Author Rachel Robbins offers an appropriately pulpy description of Usenet via transvestite detective Benedict:

> I was staring at the screen of my personal computer, tuned into the transgender news groups, when I heard about Merilee Parker's encounter with the ice pick. Yet another on-line battle had erupted between the transsexual thought police and avatars of the great, unwashed masses of heterosexual crossdressers. The arguments were as old as the first time ancient man had put on falsies and sashayed across a runway. Transvestites were not really women, just men playing at it, and not much better than perverts or nasty old drag queens. Transsexuals were elitist snobs who thought they had a lock on womanhood. TVs were chicks with dicks, TSs had $20,000 vaginas. And on and on, ad nauseam. I toyed with the idea of finding a more peaceful newsgroup, such as "soc.skinheads" or "alt.aryan.nation", but continued to read the transgendered groups with kind of a sick fascination—caught like a bug in the headlights of an oncoming truck. I'd just read the heartfelt farewell from one of the old-timers in the group ("this is no longer a safe space for newcomers") and the sensitive reply ("don't let the door hit your ass on the way out") when I heard the phone ringing in the outer office.[31]

As Robbins's description suggests, the arguments between Usenet posters were by no means unique to the platform. The history of gender (and later transgender) community spaces has long been shaped by ambivalence regarding their shared, collective identity, effectively becoming a community-specific equivalent of a holy war. Transsexual individuals at times felt that the presence of cross-dressers would seem to undercut the validity of their gender identities. Alternately, cross-dressers and nonbinary individuals, whose presence at community events increased significantly in the 2000s, disliked the fact that their experiences were often obscured by events and publications that focused their attention on medical transition.³² As discussed in later sections, these tensions underlaid most flame wars between Usenet regulars, sharing many qualities with contemporary flame wars on Twitter or Tumblr, where users who adhere to strict medicalized definitions of transness duke it out with individuals who embrace a more expansive definition centered around challenging binary gender norms. And, as with any good flame war, each side has their own derisive term for their opponent: those who argue for a limited medical definition are labeled with the portmanteau "truscum" and their opponents are derided in turn as "transtrenders" or "tucutes."³³

Usenet's level of vitriol made some worry that it would keep vulnerable individuals from attending in-person support groups. In the July 1996 issue of the newsletter for the Tennessee Vals, a long-running support group, author Marisa Richmond described being "both shocked and appalled by the general tone present on the *alt.transgendered* and *soc.support.transgendered* Usenet groups. While there is no rule saying we must all agree, the personal attacks leveled at visible, active members of the community by others is totally uncalled for." As a result, she worried that posters' hostility toward each other would "[scare] away a lot of potentially active new members who feel that local support groups are probably just as nasty." She reassured Web-based readers that "nothing could be farther from the truth."³⁴

Nominally, user behavior in trans newsgroups was loosely governed by their founding charters and FAQs, often the work of one or two individuals who then asked for (or were given unasked-for) feedback from users at large. Charters functioned as the "founding document" of a newsgroup, outlining its purpose, on-topic and off-topic posts, and any other appropriate or inappropriate behaviors. Trans newsgroups' FAQs were often more detailed expansions of these categories, focused on a set of key elements: a definition and historical context of the group, basic community definitions and information, and community-specific appropriate and inappropriate behaviors. The group definition and history in particular presented users with a shared context, a sense of the group's larger purpose. For example, the authors of the soc.support.transgendered FAQ emphasized that soc.support.transgendered was primarily for posters seeking social support, while alt.transgendered was the appropriate venue for "discussions about the philosophy of crossdressing and transsexualism.[35] The alt.fashion.crossdressing charter, in contrast, specified that "articles posted to this newsgroup should be about fashion, cross-dressing, or about the newsgroup itself."[36]

However, the lack of central authority in trans newsgroups meant that enforcing these rules and structures in any way outside of social condemnation, like flaming, proved challenging. Though several of these newsgroups actively discouraged flaming in their FAQs and charters, such social norms were nearly impossible to enforce without an active moderation team. Instead, aggressive debate and flaming were frequent occurrences, leading to attempts to moderate or replace existing newsgroups.[37] As one poster put it in her unsuccessful proposal in alt.config to establish a new trans newsgroup, alt.support.transpeople, in 2000:

> Of the TG newsgroups that exist, (not including Trans-porn groups), only one has not been overrun with petty bickering and feuds, and that one group is slowly becoming a porn group. on alt.support.srs and soc.support.transgendered especially, honest advice and support has become difficult to find, because a group of about 5 people spam the groups with constant disparaging remarks and flames, and will not cease doing so. alt.support.transpeople would hopefully be an escape from such petty useless bickering, and be the supportive environment the others used to be.[38]

Despite this poster's concerns, the limited amount of trans-related venues, rapid production of content, and nonexistent self-moderation were, retrospectively, one of Usenet's greatest strengths in circulating discourse online. Although "honest advice and support" might have come only rarely, discussions of intracommunity ideology were constant. In this environment, debaters honed their rhetorical flourishes and arguments to a razor-fine point. On Usenet, the limited number of appropriate venues meant active posters were repeatedly engaging their ideological opponents, without any moderators to slow or stop the flow of discussion. Yet, despite their negative image in the eyes of the movement mainstream, newsgroups' unmoderated nature made them an essential outlet for those individuals whose viewpoints fell outside the mainstream, particularly regarding transgender's increasing prominence as an organizing umbrella identity. While major movement figures like Dallas Denny, JoAnn Roberts, and Kymberleigh Richards were active on Usenet, discussion in trans newsgroups was dominated by Usenet "regulars" and their primary areas of interest. On Usenet, these users were not subject to the kind of editorial oversight that limited them to occasional appearances in major periodicals' letter columns. When they felt that mainstream venues, or even existing newsgroups, failed to offer adequate space for discussing their concerns, these users could make new topic-specific newsgroups—a driving force behind the creation of both alt.support.crossdressing and alt.fashion.crossdressing.[39] Out of all this "petty useless bickering," then, would emerge one of the core underlying concepts of modern transgender activism: the category of "cisgender."

Defining Who We Are Not

As a term, "cisgender" combines the Latin prefix "cis-," meaning "on this side," with "gender," in contrast to transgender, where the prefix "trans-" signals that something is "across" or "on the other side." Generally, the term is used to signify an individual who identifies with the gender they were assigned at birth and likely doesn't identify as trans. Prior to the mid-2000s, "cisgender" was a relatively uncommon term until trans author and activist Julia Serano's 2007 book *Whipping Girl: A Transsexual Woman on Sexism and the Scapegoating of Femininity*, which is largely credited with the wide adoption and popularization of the term. In 2015, the *Oxford English Dictionary* added an entry for "cisgender," a move that then-head of US dictionaries Katherine Connor Martin presented as reflecting the English language's wider expansion of its vocabulary "to reflect changes in the way that people discuss gender, race, and other aspects of personal identity and social classifications."[40]

The increasing omnipresence of "cisgender" hasn't come without critique. Most critics argue that the term's usage represents an unnecessary imposition, though they differ on why. More conservative critics contend that it functions as a way for trans individuals to claim naming power over non-trans individuals, effectively "minoritizing" them.[41] Radical feminists, in contrast, assert that the term acts to detrimentally reinforce the gender binary or undermines the non-transgender individual's gender identity.[42] Notably, cisgender's nonspecificity can obscure the ways in which gender intersects with other aspects of individuals' experiences, like race and class.⁴³ Beyond these critiques and limitations, some commentators have expressed skepticism of the term's staying power. Writing in the *Atlantic* in 2014, linguist Paula Blank expressed concern that cisgender, as a neologism, lacked "user-friendliness," and that its amorphous definition might undermine its long-term survival.⁴⁴ In response, well-known advice columnist Dan Savage pointed to his anecdotal experience with "monosexual," a neologism coined by bisexual activists in the 1990s. Though both terms seemed to Savage "like the kind of queer jargon that straight people would never embrace," use of "cisgender" by straight-identified letter writers increased from the mid-2000s onward, while "monosexual" use remains confined to specific bisexual circles. In Savage's opinion, "I think 'cisgender' is here to stay."⁴⁵

"Cisgender" certainly wasn't the first term in the community lexicon to differentiate gender community members from those outside the community. For many years, most individuals used either "Genetic Girl," "Genuine Girl," "Genetic Guy," "genny"—all of which were often shortened to "GG"—or the term "natal" (i.e., natal female and natal male) to differentiate between trans and non-trans men and women. Some cross-dressers also used the abbreviation "RG" for "Real Girl," though this was less common. In comparison, "cisgender" seemingly places less focus on biology and "realness" and more on differing senses of self-identity. Yet an in-depth examination of the term's etymology suggests that its exact meaning was relatively nebulous for many years.⁴⁶ The term's most frequently cited origins are two different posts, a year apart, in the Usenet newsgroup alt.transgendered: a 1994 post by Dana Leland Defosse, then a biologist at the University of Minnesota, and a 1995 post by Carl Buijs, a Dutch transman, who claims to have coined the term. In both cases, "cisgender" is used in a way that suggests its contrast with "transgender"/"transgendered" would be contextually self-evident; in Defosse's case, the term is part of one of the items ("attitudes of the queer community and cisgendered people") in a list of "issues of interest" related to a larger question about campus climate. In a 1996 post on the topic in soc.support.transgendered, Buijs said he "just made [cisgender] up. I just kept running into the problem of what to call non-T*people in various discussions, and one day it just hit me: non-trans = cis. Therefore, cisgendered."

Outside of Usenet, however, the term is absent from print archives (retrieved from the Digital Transgender Archive) of transgender publications, few transgender-specific websites from the time period adopted it, and anecdotal reports mostly identify its use as being confined to Usenet. Andrea James's Transgender Roadmap (previously TS-Roadmap), one of the longest-standing transgender resources online, initially defined "cisgendered" in 2001 as "a rarely-used term," while a glossary James recommended noted that "cisgendered" "has become trendy in the late 1990's."[47] The most consistent etymological record comes from the "cisgender" Wikipedia page, which is in turn referenced by the most commonly cited piece about the term, historian Finn Enke's 2012 essay "The Education of Little Cis: Cisgender and the Discipline of Opposing Bodies."[48] The first "official" definition, a single line defining "cisgender" as "a neologism meaning 'not transgender,'" appeared on Wikipedia in August 2002. The first significant additions came almost a year later, in May 2003, when user Next Paige added information about the term's use and origins, specifically citing Carl Buijs's 1996 post. A reference to Defosse would be added three years later, in 2006, followed by a comment on the talk page from a user claiming to be Defosse, elaborating on her intention: "Cis and trans are not just where something is, however; they extend to the realms of their respective effects. . . . I think the use of cisgender also captures a subtle and nondualistic aspect of the issue at hand; cisgender reinforces and reflects itself, while transgender originates where cisgender begins but extends into a greater dimension by 'crossing over.'"[49] Following Next Paige's initial expansion in 2003, most substantial edits to the entry, as well as associated talk page discussion, center either on the term's validity and related arguments as to what constituted "real" gender, or, ironically, the lack of "reliable sources" offering secondary documentation regarding its use and etymology beyond academic sources. In 2014, all references to Usenet were scrubbed from the article for failing to qualify as reliable sources.[50] Nevertheless, when the *Oxford English Dictionary* added "cisgender" and associated terms in 2015, its earliest cited use case comes from a post to soc.support.transgendered.[51]

Yet, given its absence in other gender community platforms and periodicals of the 1990s and early 2000s, it remains unclear, etymologically, how the term spread to users beyond Usenet. One of the references removed from Wikipedia in 2014, however, offers the clearest connection: a glossary of trans-related terms maintained by active Usenet poster Donna Lynn Matthews, which included a definition of "cisgender" and identified Buijs as its creator.[52] For those who supported using the term, Matthews's glossary was an authoritative source. Trans activist and author Emi Koyama linked to it in a 2002 post to the Women's Studies Listserv (WMST-L), archived on her website, explaining the term's meaning and origins.[53] It was this post, according to Serano, that would inspire her to adopt the term and use it and the related term "cissexual" in *Whipping Girl*.[54] Matthews's glossary, however, is dated as being written in May 1999, leaving five unexplained years between its creation and Defosse's first post in 1994. These five years would play a formative role beyond developing the term's usage and definition—in ways that directly challenged the dominant direction of mainstream trans organizing.

Spreading the Word

At least initially, the Usenet archive would seem to validate narratives that position Defosse as the "creator" of cisgender. The very next post to use "cisgender," however, casts doubt on Defosse's role in creating it. Exactly five months to the day, on October 25, 1994, poster Jennileigh replied to a message from another poster who was worried about attending a local cross-dressing support group. She reassured them that they needn't worry, and, after all, "we shouldn't judge each other on appearances. That's what the cis-gendered, narrow-minded people do." Like Defosse, Jennileigh offers no contextual explanation of what "cis-gendered" means. The next archived post to use "cisgender" came two years later, in 1996—well after the Buijs creation date. Some of these inconsistencies can be attributed to the limitations and gaps in many early Usenet archives, which were erratically collected for many years. Yet the existence of Jennileigh's post, her unexplained hyphenation of "cis-gendered," and the term's specific, contextual use suggests another trajectory entirely.

Although Defosse may be cited as a possible creator, Jennileigh's use embodies the particular contextual and ideological meanings underlying most Usenet posters' use of "cisgender."[55] Like its modern form, "cisgender" most often differentiated between transgender and non-transgender individuals, but who exactly was identified as "cisgender" and "transgender" differed significantly. As noted in the introduction, in the mid-1990s major movement periodicals like *Tapestry* urged readers to adopt "transgender" as a uniform umbrella identity category. However, most Usenet posters continued to position "transgender" and "transsexual" as distinct categories, which reflected posters' differing self-identifications: transsexual users, who had received or sought SRS, and transgender users, who either did not desire SRS or were ideologically opposed to it. Posters were also split on the question of what the core goal of emergent trans activism should be. Some adopted a civil rights framework, focusing on legal and civil recognition, while others emphasized resistance to the societal focus on linking sexed embodiment to gender identity. Usenet posters' location within these two differing binaries served as a reliable predictor of the likelihood that they would use "cisgender." Transsexual and transgender users who were in favor of a civil rights approach rarely used "cisgender" and preferred terms like "GG" or "natal." Transgender users who prioritized challenging the sex-gender link preferred "cisgender," using it to identify *anyone* whose gender presentation and sex were aligned—even transsexuals who'd had or desired SRS. So, when Jennileigh spoke dismissively of those "cis-gendered, narrow-minded people," it's possible she was identifying a wide swath of individuals who shared one commonality: they presented their gender in ways that matched their sexed embodiment.

Looking at the archive of trans Usenet groups as a whole, though, it becomes clear that the population of users who actively used the term "cisgender" was relatively small. However, these individuals were among the most active posters in this corner of Usenet, engaging in extended debates that often devolved into out-and-out flame wars. This high level of activity meant that unless a reader had specifically blocked a given poster, they were guaranteed to repeatedly encounter these threads. Moreover, posters extensively relied on quoting previous messages, designated by a ">" at the beginning of each quoted line, in highly active threads (see figure 3.1).[56] In this way, quotes embedded the flow of discussion within the message itself, reproducing much of the content that came before it within the post. As a result, a term like "cisgender" could continue to appear and reappear in quotes from earlier posters, even if it wasn't adopted by other posters.

> From: ANONYMIZED
> Subject: Re: Hello again
> Date: 1997/05/10
> Message-ID: ANONYMIZED
> X-Deja-AN: 240585557
> References: ANONYMIZED
> X-XS4ALL-Date: Sat, 10 May 1997 16:51:30 CEST
> Organization: The mirror of her dreams
> Newsgroups: soc.support.transgendered
> NAME REDACTED wrote:
> > Tomorrow I check on a higher paying job that i applied for. Tomorrow i
> > sell my stocks to help pay the bills. Tomorrow I agonise over going out
> > en femme for the first time ever. Tomorrow may be the first day that
> > NAME truly gets to live. I have a lot of tomorrows and I have just now
> > realised it.
> Well NAME, today it's tomorrow and please tell us how things did go by the time tomorrow is yesterday.
> ANONYMIZED

Figure 3.1. Sample Usenet post, including quotation, from Usenet Historical Collection. Names and other identifying information redacted.

This drastically increases the term's overall visibility within the newsgroup. In the two network graphs (figures 3.2–3.3), each node represents a post in the archive where "cisgender," "cisgendered," and variants either appeared or were used in response to one of these posts, making it a part of the overall thread.[57] Posts are colored to differentiate between those that only use "cisgender" and variants (dark gray), posts that only quote these terms (medium gray), posts that both use and quote the terms (light gray), posts that neither use nor quote the terms (white), and posts that are referenced but not included in the archive (black). Node size in figure 3.2 is determined by number of posts that are responding to this specific post (as determined by the References header), while node size in figure 3.3 is determined by the number of posts earlier in the thread that this specific post included in its References header; more of these meant that it came later in a discussion.

As these networks show, archived posts that included "cisgender" and variants are was roughly split between posts that exclusively use the term and posts that exclusively quote the term. However, posts that only used the term were more likely to be referenced, or replied to, by other posters (fig. 3.1). Thus, these posts sparked a high level of response from other posters. In contrast, posts that came further downthread in a

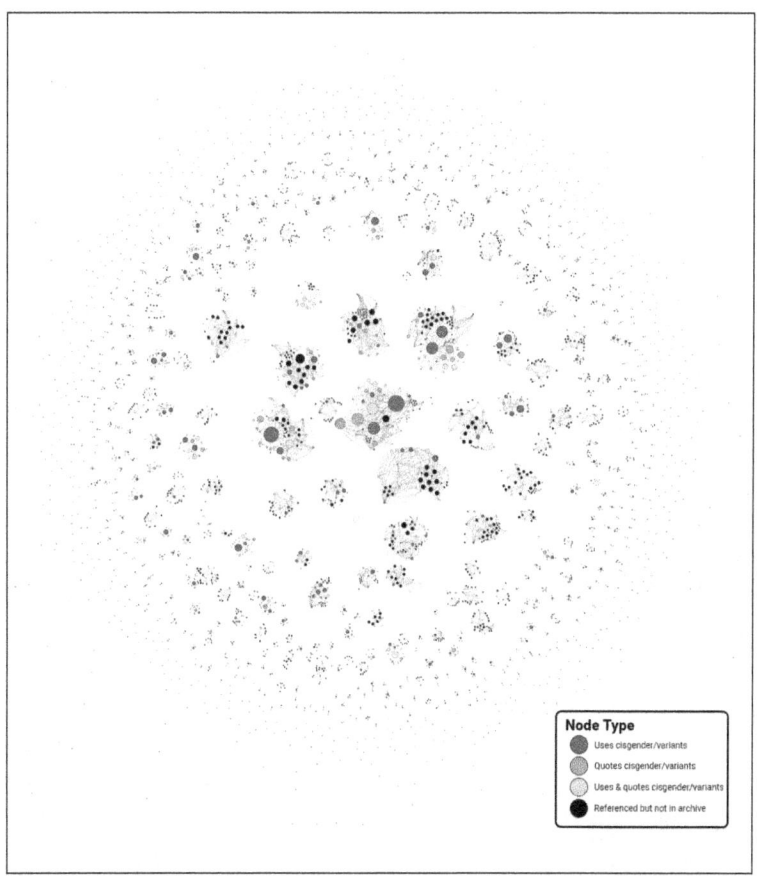

Figure 3.2. Network of posts using "cisgender" and variants. Nodes sized by in-degree of connections, or number of responses to that post. "Null" nodes are posts not included in the archive.

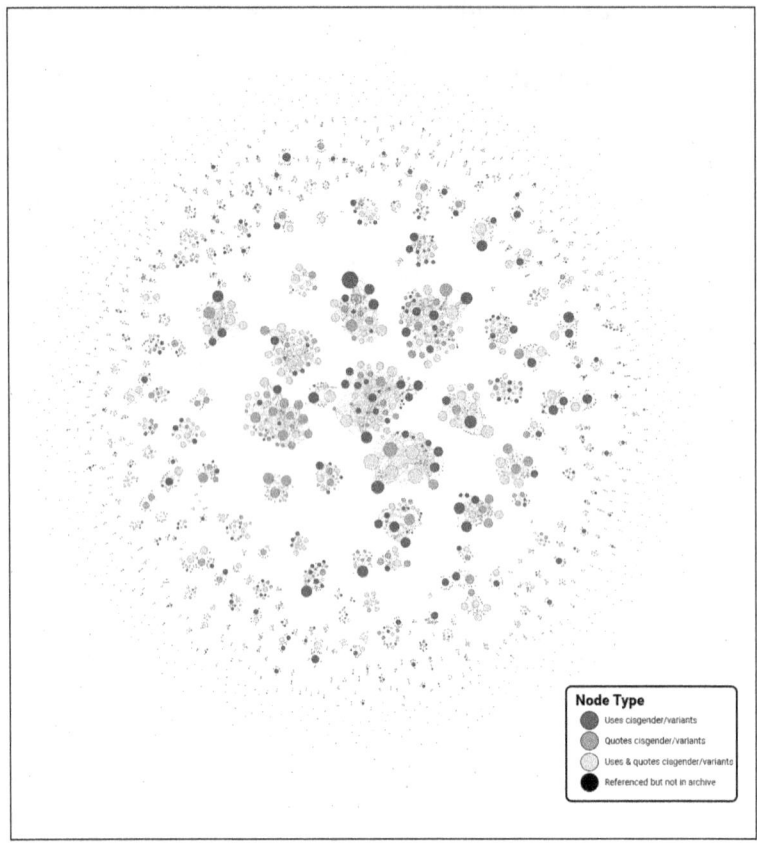

Figure 3.3. Network of posts using "cisgender" and variants. Nodes are sized by out-degree of connections, or the number of prior posts that single node is responding to. "Null" nodes are posts not included in the archive.

discussion, which often had more Message IDs listed in their reference headers, were more likely to only quote other posters using "cisgender" and variants, though some did mix use and quotation (fig. 3.2). Thus, prior posters' use of the term was frequently quoted in replies, even as these posters did not adopt the term themselves. Of the overall dataset, only a small portion of regular Usenet posters made the vast majority of all uses of the term. Not only that, only sixteen of these posters used it in ten or more posts in the archive (fig. 3.3). These users were either highly active posters who specifically identified as "transgender," or, in several cases, these users' most ardent opponents. One user stands out among them all, with 354 posts: Laura Blake.

Who Was Laura Blake?

Of all the regular posters to the transgender corner of Usenet, Blake was no doubt one of the most infamous and prolific. While Blake's presence was felt across the major trans newsgroups, she was active throughout the early to late 1990s, shifting most of her posting activity post-2000 to alt.support.crossdressing, of which she claimed to be a founding member. alt.support.crossdressing was distinct from alt.transgendered and soc.support.transgendered in that poster discussions focused not on what were perceived as "transsexual" concerns, such as sex reassignment surgery, but questions around gender identity and performance. Most of Blake's long-form writing was posted to alt.support.crossdressing and occasionally its sister group, alt.fashion.crossdressing. Though Blake rarely labeled herself, she would most likely define herself as a "transgenderist," an individual who engages in "crossliving," which she vaguely defines as "the complete immersion into one of the many transgendered

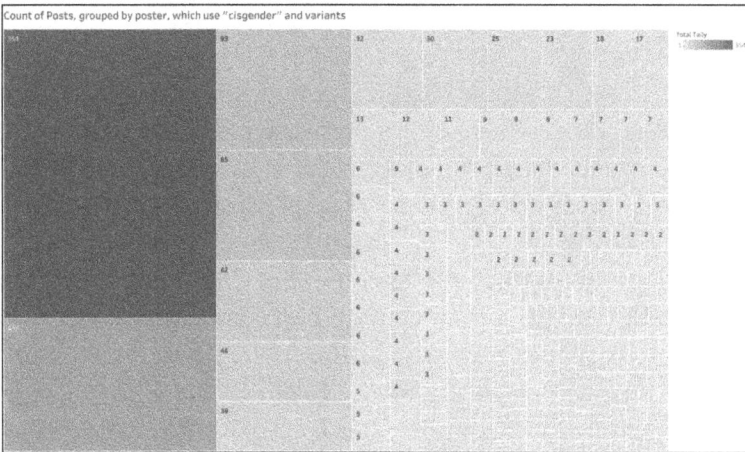

Figure 3.4. This treemap tracks the number of posts made by individual posters in the archive using "cisgender" and variants. Because posters sometimes changed their email addresses over time, these have aggregated under the name the poster most commonly used on Usenet.

lifestyles" and "the complete abandonment of the cisgender lifestyle." As a poster, Blake was more than willing to repeatedly engage opponents in lengthy and sometimes vitriolic debate. As she once said to an opponent, "If people would stop attacking, I'd be more than happy to stop retaliating." Moreover, Blake had a propensity for targeted and aggressive insults. When challenged by an opponent to offer evidence of her trans activism compared to the Transexual Menace, she retorted: "Well, in my personal instance, I was probably at the bargaining table trying to establish workable legal recourse against most of the stuff you have suffered. Where were the rest of them? Ramming bits of cold plastic up their brand new cunts!" Blake's tendency to rapidly resort to flaming opponents into submission had long been a hallmark of her online presence. According to anecdotal reports from other Usenet posters, Blake's history in digital transgender spaces began on TGNet and the Fidonet GENDER Echo; she would eventually be banned from accessing both platforms for flaming.

Through her posts, Blake serves as the missing link between Usenet and the popularization of "cisgender": Donna Lynn Matthews, herself an adopter of the term who credited Blake with her own self-awakening into transgender identity, hosted an archive of Blake's essays on her site.[58] The *OED* indirectly recognizes Blake's importance, as the Usenet use case cited in the *OED* definition of "cisgender" is a direct, if uncredited, quote from one of Blake's posts. Furthermore, Blake, more than any other poster, established the "Carl Buijs as creator" narrative on Usenet. She would repeat the Buijs origin narrative every time another user asked her to define the term; however, she consistently put the creation year as 1995, which would later vacillate between 1995 and 1996 upon retelling by other users.

Beyond participating in discussion online, Blake presented herself as the founder and head of an Ontario-based paralegal service turned Canadian transgender advocacy organization, TransEqual, on whose behalf she claimed to regularly advocate with Ontario's provincial government.[59] While it's unclear how much contact she actually had with governmental entities, two of her publications are cited as sources in the Ontario Human Rights Commission's 1999 discussion paper "Toward a Commission Policy on Gender Identity," and she claimed in 1993 to have worked with the Canadian Human Rights Commission to develop new trans-specific polices for filing human rights complaints.⁶⁰ Blake also made a point to increase TransEqual's reach beyond Usenet, having copies of her writing included in the TCF library on AOL.⁶¹ As head of TransEqual, she used the pseudonym Laura Masters in all of the organizations' publications, correspondence, and press interviews.⁶² From 1993 to 1995, she submitted short articles and letters to both *Tapestry* and *Cross-Talk* on her experiences lobbying the Canadian government. These articles offer a window into Blake's specific political positions within the changing movement landscape. With their legalistic tone, they present a stark contrast to the vitriol of her posts on Usenet.⁶³ Unlike mainstream figures such as Phyllis Frye, Blake felt that the best path forward was separatism of various stripes, which she described in detail in a 1993 essay in *Tapestry* titled "Achieving Equality." Going against prevailing movement trends, she argued that activists had to acknowledge that while "transsexuals, transgenderists, and transvestites" did need to organize together, they were "indeed three separate groups with different agendas." She also strongly resisted allying with gay and lesbian individuals and was concerned it would compound the prejudice transsexual and transgender individuals faced. In her view, any move to work with gay and lesbian individuals would merely reinforce public perception that those with cross-gender desires were "motivated by extensions of homosexuality." And she vehemently rejected any attempt to medicalize transgender or transsexual identities, as well as any activist who advocated working with medical authorities. Activists' efforts, according to her, would be better directed at working outside of established systems for broader societal change around gender nonconformity. "Our problems," she argued, "are imposed upon us by an unaccepting society. We do not need to change, they do."⁶⁴

Living Up to the "Cisgender Ideal"

These same ideological threads would appear in Blake's Usenet posts, and by 1996, she began using a new term to identify and define the "unaccepting society"—"cisgender." For her, "cisgender" was a "conversational strategy . . . that parallels het-homo, bringing many of our issues into a more conventionally understood 'us-them' semantic."⁶⁵ In her view, Buijs's invention was revolutionary, as she explained in a post in 2000: "Carl Buijs once made a simple comment 'How come there's no name for people who are not transgendered?' and offered us the word 'Cisgendered' . . . this profoundly clarified our relationship to the rest of the world and resulted in a change in my thinking that has allowed me to tackle many previously unfathomable problems."

In her "Coming Out FAQ," Blake most clearly defines how she understands "cisgender" and "cisgendered." She first composed the FAQ in 2001 and revised it in 2004 to add an entry on the "Cisgender Ideal." The FAQ represents the culmination of her ideological positions, which she imbues in her use of "cisgender," as well as its political applications. Blake's choice to use an FAQ lends her writing not only a specific structure, question and answer, but also contextual meaning. As noted earlier, FAQs on Usenet were primarily introductory documents, laying out the social and discursive norms for a newsgroup. Blake's FAQ was intended to provide the recently out individual with necessary frameworks for understanding their experience and the road ahead. The audience targeted by Blake is crucial to the document's rhetorical impact: by offering definitions not for the existing community but for those just coming out, Blake meets these individuals at the moment when they're just beginning to adopt a "transgender" worldview and build their subcultural vocabulary. By getting in on the ground floor, Blake constructs the cisgender/transgender binary as a foundational aspect of their developing identity. In fact, the order of questions places "cisgender" right after the first three concepts defined, sex, gender, and sexual orientation, but before "transgender" or related concepts, such as "coming out" or "passing."

Placement, then, is reflective of relative importance: before the reader can understand what transgender is, they must be able to recognize and understand what it *is not*. In the FAQ, Blake's definition of "cisgender" is grounded in gender performance: "Cisgendered people are males who live exclusively masculine lives and females who live exclusively in the feminine lifestyles. It's about the combination of sex and gender; man-male or woman-female. This is the gender polarized and stereotypical norm of society." Blake's choice to use "polarized" instead of "binary" and emphasize the connections of "cisgender" to "stereotypical norms" forefronts gender's socially constructed and normative nature. Though it doesn't say so outright, this definition implies that the cisgendered individual adopts a simplistic view of gender that uncritically reproduces received knowledge. The transgendered individual, in contrast, takes a much more complex view, as reflected in Blake's definition of "transgender": "When a male prefers a feminine lifestyle or a female prefers the masculine they are said to be 'Transgendered.' This is about combinations of sex and gender; man-female and woman-male. It is estimated that about 1% of the world's population are transgendered. Within society, 'Transgender' most often means 'Not Cisgendered' in that it is a broadly based term applied to anyone who's gender and sex do not fit the 'Cisgender Ideal.'"

Here Blake offers readers a third path beyond one's birth-assigned gender and transsexuality: "transgenderism," which prioritizes gender performance over embodiment. Gender identity and performance are flexible, individualized categories that vary from person to person and determine one's position in the cisgender/transgender binary. However, unlike contemporary understandings of "transgender," Blake considers sex—"what you got between your legs"—as an unchangeable fact of biology that signals membership in one of three categories: Male, Female, or Intersex. For Blake, anyone whose genital makeup matched their gender identity, including transsexuals who'd had SRS, was cisgender; everyone outside of this category was transgender. Other transgenderist posters also used the term in this sense, though often with far less vitriol. This distinction is also central to Matthews's "authoritative" definition, cited for many years both on the Wikipedia page and by Koyama in 2002: that "one's identity and presentation *matches* their physical morphology."[66] The choice of "morphology," which refers to one's bodily form (alterable by SRS) instead of their birth-assigned sex is a core distinction in transgenderists' use of the term.

Far from being a value-neutral binary, "cisgender" was, to Blake, an essential tool for dismantling societal gender norms. It was the centerpiece of one of her most commonly cited, quoted, and adopted rhetorical flourishes: the "cisgender ideal." Mention of the "cisgender ideal" was so common, in fact, it inspired a rule in the "Laura Blake Drinking Game," developed by a regular alt.transgendered poster: "Every time Laura says 'cisgender' the first person to call out 'Ideal!' gets her drink paid for by the person to her left." Though Blake used the phrase frequently, often with minimal context, she specifically defines it in the FAQ:

> This is the widely held notion that everyone is Cisgendered and those who are not should be. It is [the] mistaken belief that Transgender is an invalid state—one created by failure or disorder—that needs to be fixed. The Cisgender Ideal can most easily be summarized by 4 simple rules.
>
> The Cisgender Rules:
>
> Everyone is Cisgendered by default.
> It is wrong to be anything but Cisgendered.
> Those who are not Cisgendered must appear Cisgendered.
> Those who do not appear Cisgendered are beneath consideration.
>
> You don't have to be a rocket scientist to figure out how much trouble the Cisgender Ideal has caused transgendered people, over the last couple of centuries. These rules actually describe transphobia.

In this definition, Blake draws a clear us/them distinction between trans and cisgender individuals, with the cisgender ideal serving as a weaponized version of stereotypical gender norms. Cisgender individuals, in their presumed adoption of the cisgender ideal, actively or passively undermine transgender individuals' right to exist as they are. Moreover, Blake's choice to name her concept an "ideal" over the more seemingly transparent "rules" emphasizes the impossibility of normative standards of gender. Under the cisgender ideal, trying to pass or hide your transgender status is a sign of false consciousness, identifying with the power of the oppressor even as they actively discriminate against you. Blake's solution, then, is to establish and respect transgender and cisgender as two equally valid self-identifications. Cisgender and transgender individuals would each occupy different spots on the spectrum of sex, gender, and sexuality, and each person's lifestyle would be treated as a value-neutral aspect of their personality. This understanding most closely reflects "cisgender" in its modern usage: as a (presumably) value-neutral descriptor of different states of being. Similarly, the cisgender ideal and its rules embody a variety of practices which are still used to deny trans individuals' right to exist. Though it's difficult to know just how many users were exposed to Blake's frameworks, at least one thread offers a window into the view of a self-identified "newbie." In 2000, long-time lurker Toni posted her first message to alt.support. crossdressing, where she admits to her "fascination" with Blake:

> I am fascinated by Laura Blake. She is the most inspirational person I've ever read in any newsgroup. I've done a lot of thinking about the things she says. Her four rules of the cisgendered ideal make me slap my forehead and say, "darn, why didn't I think of that?"
>
> Laura, you've made me feel so much better about myself, and you've given me courage to try to be myself. I would hate to see you leave, although it does seem like you often take quite a beating—I think I can understand how you might feel. I don't for a minute, however, believe that I am the only lurker or newbie that owes you sincere thanks.

For Toni, the underlying ideas of the ideal—that she had a right to express her gender identity without fearing recrimination or violence—helped her come to terms with her desire to cross-dress. Blake's own prodigious posting habits (measured in fig. 3.3) would help "cisgender," the "cisgender ideal," and its associated "rules" achieve a far greater reach than they might have otherwise. She would often compose lengthy, detailed responses to other posters, quoting users quoting her at length and prominently featuring the "cisgender ideal" and "cisgender rules." This process, as I noted earlier, meant that the term would appear and reappear with regularity. Often, these posts would become flammable flash points of activity driving discussion and spawning a variety of new, spin-off discussions, sometimes retaining only a tenuous connection to the original flashpoint via a stray backwards Reference. In practice, discussion flow might only be discernible after close reading, where the reader could identify posters' interlocutors through in-message quotes.

The two social networks below offer a visual representation of how these terms would appear in a thread. Each node represents a post in the collection that either includes the terms "cisgender ideal," "cisgendered ideal," or "cisgender rules" or was part of the larger thread. As with the earlier graphs, posts are colored to differentiate between those that

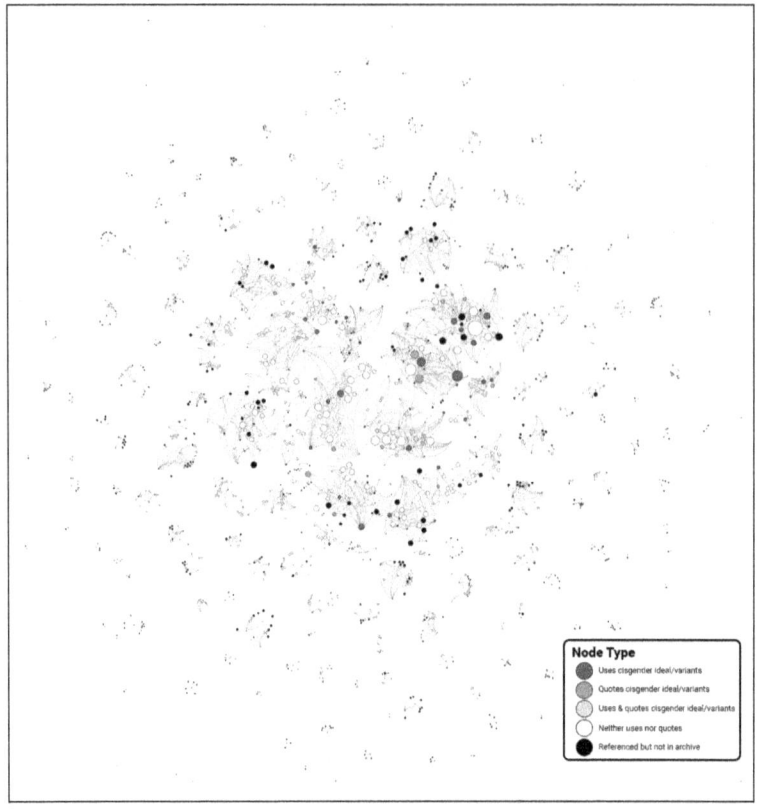

Figure 3.5. Network of posts using "cisgender ideal," "cisgendered ideal," and "cisgender rules." Nodes sized by in-degree of connections, or posts responding to this post. "Null" nodes are posts not included in the archive.

only use "cisgender ideal" and associated terms (dark gray), posts that only quote these terms (medium gray), posts that both use and quote them (light gray), posts that neither use nor quote them (white), and posts that are referenced but not included in the archive (black). Nodes in figure 3.5 are sized based on the number of posts that are responding to this post, while nodes in figure 3.6 are sized by the number of previous posts listed in its Reference header, meaning it came later in a thread.

As figure 3.5 illustrates, posts early on in discussions (which are more frequently referenced in responses) rarely use "cisgender ideal" or similar terms. As a discussion progresses, however, the likelihood that the "cisgender ideal" or its associated "rules" will appear increases significantly. This is evident in the vast disparity in nodes between figures 3.5 and 3.6: in 3.5, posts that use or quote these terms are rarely referenced compared to posts that don't use these terms (white nodes). In figure 3.6, the white nonuse nodes, despite making up over half the network, virtually disappear. Instead, posts with many connections outward to other posts—which would have had to come later in a discussion thread—either use or quote these terms. As these two networks illustrate, once

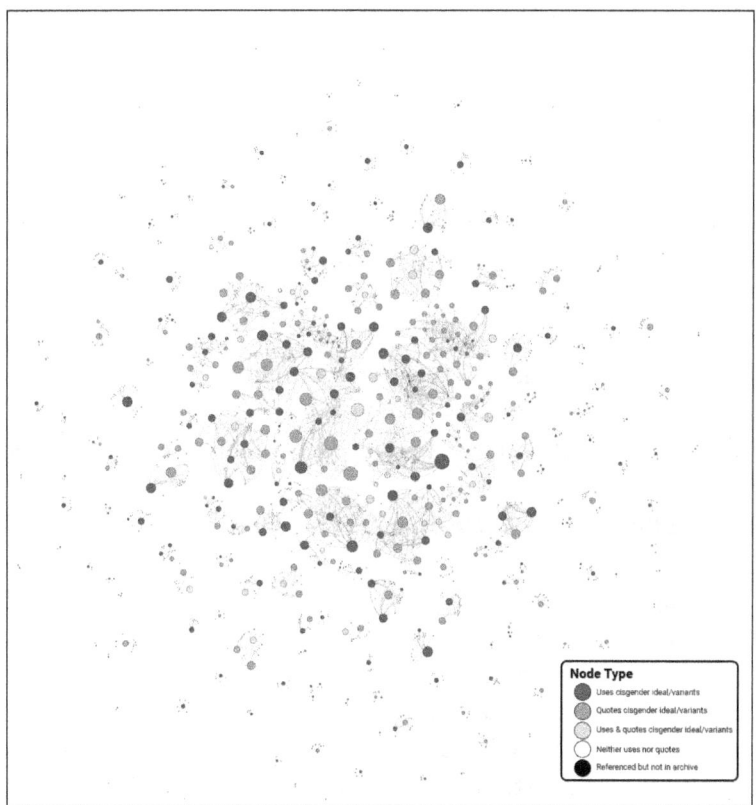

Figure 3.6. Network of posts using "cisgender ideal," "cisgendered ideal," and "cisgender rules." Nodes sized by out-degree of connections, or number of prior posts a single post is responding to. "Null" nodes are posts not included in the archive.

the "cisgendered ideal" had been introduced into a thread, it replaced the original post as the primary topic of discussion.

The impact of these flash points is evident in threads like "What Joann Has Been Up To" at final count, the total thread (in the archive, at least) takes up 176 posts spread out over seventeen days. The thread begins with an update from Usenet regular Joann on her most recent activities with several social cross-dressing organizations, as well as a mention of her increasing interest in transgender activism. She closes her post directing readers to visit her new home page, where she discusses this advocacy work in detail. Following this post, Usenet's aforementioned affordances (lack of content moderation, imbalanced poster to reader ratio, extensive use of quoting, and widespread readership) come into play. The first few responses offer generally positive feedback and advice, but the tone of the discussion changes drastically once Blake enters the conversation. To her, the site is "quite boring . . . just more of the usual plap and smargle I've come to expect from crossdressers. . . . Same old same old." She presents Joann, representative of cross-dressers as a whole, as buying into the false consciousness of cisgendered norms (styling retained from original message):

> **We *insist* that crossdressing be seen as a playful diversion because again we recognize that it offers to undo the cisgender construct in which we so ambitiously seek membership. We are so wrapped up in status-quo and inclusion that we seem to be forgetting one very central fact of our lives:**
> **WE ARE NOT CISGENDERED and we can never be cisgendered!**

By complying to existing gender and medical norms, such as the Standards of Care, Blake argues that these individuals reinforce the "the mechanism of self-oppression." In doing so, they "believe the cisgendered ideal, [they] endorse it, and [they] *demand* that our peers play along with it." Instead of "seeking freedom for our peers . . . they are merely a form of substitute oppression, imposed upon us, this time, by our own kind. These things are the very sickness of transgendered life. . . . Internalized transphobia." Blake closes her post telling Joann, "You are part of the problem not part of the solution. Your page should be taken down . . . post haste!" Though several posters attempt to refocus discussion on Joann's original post, the thread quickly devolves into an extended argument on the value of Blake's arguments regarding transgender identity and activism. The first response to Blake suggests that she could find a more civil format to express her ideas, while the second poster comes out in support of her, calling her post "one of your better explanations of our problem. . . . I hope people see she isn't what the problem is, the whole cisgendered ideal is the problem." Several posters continue the earlier social thread, but once another poster redirects attention to Blake's post, the thread turns into an extended argument about whether or not Joann (and, by extension, all those who hold a similar position) are dupes of the larger cisgendered world. By engaging Blake, Joann gives her ideas, including the "cisgender ideal," far greater visibility than they might have had otherwise, as Blake's core arguments are reiterated and quoted many times over the course of the thread.

As Toni's quote earlier alludes to and the above example illustrates, Blake was a divisive—and in some cases despised—figure on Usenet. She regularly used "cisgender" to emphasize the unbridgeable gap, in her view, between transsexuals and transgenderists, in the process furthering her larger separatist agenda. For Blake, one's transgender status was directly connected to one's gender practices, as reflected in how she defines the "transcommunity" in her FAQ: "The congregation of transgendered people and lifestyles . . . In many ways the transcommunity is defined by what it is not, i.e. 'Not Cisgendered', a catch basin for all those who do not easily fit the Cisgender ideal." Blake's lifestyle approach and transcommunity, however, did not allow for transsexuals, which she defines under "What Is 'Transsexualism'?": "Transsexualism is about obtaining sex-change surgery. No matter how it is justified, this amounts to rejection of one's own transgendered state and a desire to end membership in the transcommunity. The 'treatment' for transsexualism does offer symptomatic relief for Internalized Transphobia but the end goal—to become Cisgendered—is Unachievable." Transsexuals, as Blake presents them, are misled by their false consciousness to believe that they can become cisgendered, or have their sex and gender align. Nothing, in Blake's worldview, can change one's sex, and transsexuals who try are simply in denial.[67] For Blake, living a transgender lifestyle is an all-or-nothing endeavor, and any attempts to pass amount to little more than deception: "In general 'Passing' means trying to get people to believe you are someone you are not. (e.g. Gays who pass as straight.) For a transgendered individual this means pretending to be cisgendered; hiding that one is transgendered. Most commonly this is a reference to males who try to deceive people into thinking they are female or females who ask people to believe they are male but Passing also applies to anyone who hides their transgender identity through denial or omission."

In all of these cases, Blake's position is entirely black and white: one is out or in, one is transgender or cisgender, and no in-between is allowed. Passing is not about one's gender presentation being validated by others, as in its most common contemporary form, but about acting out of denial. In Blake's view, mainstream transgender activists limited trans freedom to those that fit within the "cisgender ideal." Blake encapsulates this viewpoint in response to another poster: "If I want to shave my head, grow a ZZ-Top beard, wear pink tights and a burgandy mini-skirt with a yellow sport coat and orange tie. . . . Acceptance means that's just fine. Anything short of that, anything that prevents it, or causes me to hesitate about doing it, is not freedom . . . it's a state of oppression." Mainstream activists "don't understand what it means to be free as a transie . . . they just want permission to be one."

Blake's strident tone, combativeness, and insistence on ideological purity are hallmarks of her posts. An excellent example of these qualities in combination came following the 2001 release of regular poster Lacey Leigh's self-published book, *Out & About—The Emancipated Crossdresser*. While it's difficult to know just how many people read or purchased *Out & About*, it was one of the texts cross-dressing organization Tri-Ess regularly donated to public libraries.[68] Included in the book was a version or copy, depending on the poster's interpretation, of Blake's "Cisgender Rules," attributed to an unnamed "transgender advocate" described in the acknowledgments as "one of the 'regulars' who held court in that cyber community": a "curmudgeonly Canadian activist whose mission seemed to be one of rubbing us raw with the revolutionary idea of self acceptance and then picking at the scabs of those wounds so they wouldn't scar; sort of 'tough love' approach." According to Leigh, Blake's approach "worked," as "she, and countless supportive others, led, pushed, cajoled, bullied, and harassed me into thinking clearly about all this for the first time."

Whatever goodwill prompted Leigh's acknowledgment was not evident in posters' ensuing debate over whether or not Blake had been properly attributed. The debate-cum-flame war raged in alt.support.crossdressing for much of 2001 and 2002; at its height, posts to alt.support.crossdressing including the word "book" would make up 6 percent of all posts archived in the Usenet Historical Collection—a sizable percentage for the eternally spam-prone Usenet. Leigh claimed that Blake had explicitly asked not to be named as the rules' author; Blake claimed Leigh had stolen her intellectual property outright and threatened to sue. Reflecting the depths to which arguments on Usenet could plunge, Blake would accuse Leigh of being a "sociopath" who was in it for the money, leading Leigh to retort that Blake was herself a "screaming, agenda driven, mouth foaming, bi-polar, schitzo/paranoid zealot." Following Blake's accusations, Leigh posted that the next edition of *Out & About* would be a "'LB free zone'. No mention, no implication, no hint, no name, no acknowledgement, no credit-by-description, nada." Ironically, Leigh would then go on to say that "cisgender" was "not a very important concept in the long run (and in fact sounds rather angry)," leading to her decision to replace the rules with a short paragraph.

Spreading the Good Word

Though Leigh might not have seen "cisgender" as being very important in the long run, the concept has persisted. Since it first began appearing on Usenet, "cisgender" has been adopted and used in a variety of wider publics, and many now employ it to signal their status as a transgender ally.[69] In many ways, at the national level, contemporary transgender activism relies on the "'us-them' semantic" Blake found so useful in her arguments: both the National Center for Transgender Equality and the Transgender Law Center, two of the most visible national trans advocacy organizations, have adopted the term on their websites and in their surveys, reports, and other public documents. However, Blake's own preferred use of "transgender" has largely faded, and concepts like "genderqueer" have taken its place. This shift is reflected in a 2006 addendum that Matthews, a Blake admirer, makes to her 1997 essay "Crossdressing and Society": "It's been a long time since I wrote this essay and much has happened in my life since then. I no longer identify as a 'crossdresser'. I identify as solidly Transgender, borderline Transsexual—but most specifically as Genderqueer."[70] In effect, transgender and cisgender have reversed their scope: while "transgender" now covers a broad swath of identities, united by their nonidentification with their birth-assigned gender, "cisgender" has narrowed significantly from a category for all whose gender identity aligns to those who identify only with their birth-assigned sex. In modern definitions, morphology has given way to biology. The adoption of "cisgender" by allies no doubt contributed to this narrowing: as allies became cisgender, they excluded those they might be allied with from the category—namely, anyone under the "transgender" umbrella. However, Blake and other transgenderists' legacy lives on through the way "cisgender" shifted attention from "wrong" and "right" bodies to gender identity and performance. This legacy wouldn't have been possible, however, without the free-wheeling, flame-throwing, and spam-prone world that was Usenet.

4

Always On

Information, Circulation, and the World Wide Web

December 1, 1996, marked a monumental change for AOL's millions of subscribers: the first day of flat-fee pricing. From that day on, instead of having to pay by the hour after using up your prepaid hours, all AOL customers received unlimited time online for $19.95 a month. Though the company had resisted changing its existing by-hour pricing model, increasing pressure from a new competitor, the Internet service provider, forced AOL's hand. From then on, eager AOL users could stay logged on as long as they liked without fear they'd be facing a huge bill come the end of the month. And stay logged on they did, by the millions. Less than three weeks after the switch, an AOL spokesperson estimated that "seven million AOL customers in the United States were conducting 30 percent more daily online sessions, lasting an average of 20 percent longer."[1] However, the high volume of users strained AOL's underprepared network, which had been fine-tuned to accommodate those who logged on in short bursts to avoid blowing through their prepaid time.[2] A study conducted by a technology firm in December 1996 found that, out of 3,136 attempts to dial in to AOL, 41 percent failed to connect, and that, during "peak hours" (6 p.m. to midnight local time) that number leapt to 61 percent.[3] By early January 1997, angry customers were demanding refunds, and growing interest in a class action lawsuit drew the attention of multiple states' attorney generals.[4] AOL would eventually relieve the strain through concentrated investments in infrastructure, while CEO Steve Case assured customers in a nationwide commercial that "at America Online we are focused on one thing: working to serve your needs."[5]

What was it, though, that kept customers logging on more often, and for longer stretches of time? The reason: access to the rapidly growing

World Wide Web, which had by now established itself as the primary appeal of the Internet. As Thomas Streeter discusses in *Net Effect*, the "dreamlike, compulsive quality" of surfing the Web in its earliest years led users to feel as though they were immersed in "an endless what's next?"[6] For walled garden subscribers accustomed to the closed corporate ecosystem, the open Web offered a very different vision of interaction online, where there was minimal corporate oversight and seemingly limitless possibilities. But it wasn't just the sense of freedom and exploratory anticipation that made websites so attractive; compared to a dial-up BBS, they were more practical places to post and store information and files for downloading. Lastly, Web-based discussions allowed users previously used to Usenet's restriction against posting media files—for fear they would unnecessarily eat up network bandwidth—the freedom to visually represent themselves in a new medium: the home page.

This chapter considers how the Web transformed trans information seeking and self-representation practices. By the mid to late 1990s, the Web radically changed how information within the trans community was disseminated. Not only did it make mass dissemination affordable for small organizations, but it also opened up the possibility of publishing to a far larger portion of the community. Trans organizations saw the website as a golden opportunity to provide information, raise awareness, and attract new members, while trans individuals embraced the personalized home page as a space for low-risk self-expression. On their home page, trans users could keep a public, semipermanent archive of anything they wanted, including resource pages, personal journals and memoirs, curated photo collections, and essays discussing major social or political issues within trans discourse. These home pages represent an early example of hypertext's possibilities to transform both how trans individuals represented themselves and how their representations were read. Increased visibility online, however, fueled already existing fears about minors' access to what some classified as "indecent" material. Absent a concerned response from major trans organizations, trans home page creators engaged in self-protective practices that, in the process, reinforced cultural assumptions about the "indecency" of trans topics.

Finding Out More

As discussed in chapter 1, access to an information library was one of the key benefits of joining a gender community group. Through the group library, information seekers could gain access to a variety of community-produced resources, largely developed by small independent presses and nonprofit information clearinghouses like the Erickson Education Fund (EEF). Funded by philanthropist and trans man Reed Erickson, the EEF offered pamphlets and brochures on a variety of topics, including *Guidelines for Transsexuals* and *Legal Aspects of Transsexualism*.[7] Though the EEF would close its doors in 1977, its materials continued to be updated and offered into the early 1990s through two offshoots: first the Janus Information Facility, and then J2CP Information Services. By the mid-1980s, several small community presses, such as JoAnn Roberts' Creative Design Services, offered texts and videos for both transsexual and cross-dressing individuals. CDS was one of the most prolific publishers, its offerings including a layman's guide to hormone replacement therapy, workbooks on feminine deportment, makeup application guides, and an essay collection on cross-dressing and Christianity. However, publishing for the gender community was not exactly financially lucrative. Only Roberts was able to make a living as head of CDS; most other groups were primarily funded through grants, subscriptions, and donations.

Without access to the shared group library, the cost of acquiring a personal library of these materials could add up quickly. One author estimated that a transsexual just coming out should budget at least $100 to acquire all the books and videos they'd need early in transition, since "reading will save you a lot of lost time, motion, and money."[8] These costs could also come on top of other trans-related expenditures, from therapy to an alternate wardrobe. However, group membership allowed individuals to defray some of these costs by borrowing items from the group library. These libraries, maintained by a group librarian, contained a variety of books, press clippings, photo albums, periodicals, and videos that members could either read at meetings or check out (sometimes after placing a small deposit). Groups would also host "video nights," where members could watch and discuss tapes. Recognizing the importance of information access, one of Renaissance

Education Association's first major projects was building up and cataloging its library, as well as developing an annotated bibliography of material discussing cross-dressing and transsexualism. An article on their efforts drew upon readers' shared experience of finding their first encounter with a text on "their unique interest" as less-than-supportive of cross-dressing, often conflating it with mental illness. REA's annotated bibliography would offer members a list of positive alternatives—which, ideally, would eventually be available in their library.[9] Computer databases, BBSes, and commercial services largely operated on the same model, hosting a variety of digital files on topics related to the gender community. Unlike the group library, indexing was handled by the hosting platform, and individual members could acquire and contribute materials of their own volition. However, technical limitations at times restricted the size and kinds of files that could be hosted, while libraries on corporate platforms like AOL were limited in what kinds of content they could host.

Yet, to activist Dallas Denny, these pre-Web technologies were "merely making the old model more efficient."[10] Based on her experience as director of the American Educational Gender Information Service (AEGIS), Denny felt that the information clearinghouse model would remain unsustainable due to the constant buildup of costs from staffing, printing, photocopying, postage, storage space, among other expenses. While digital systems relieved some of these, like postage, they added new tasks, all of which came at the cost of time. In a memorable passage, Denny recounts her responsibilities as director of AEGIS:

> As spokesperson—and, in fact, the major and usually the only volunteer—I answered the phone and handled the mail (and, after 1993, e-mail), conversing with and corresponding daily with transsexuals, journalists, researchers, clinicians, spouses and other family members, and appearing on radio and television on occasion. I also wrote almost all of AEGIS' material; edited and laid out the journal and newsletter; maintained the databases of helping professionals and subscribers to Chrysalis; kept the bibliography up to date; ran the Internet news feed, the publishing house, and the bookstore; programmed the automated telephone system and the computers; bought office supplies and maintained

the equipment; did all mailings and filled all orders for the bookstore; and folded, collated, hand-assembled, and stapled 1300 copies of Chrysalis when the flat pages arrived from the printer (we could not afford to have this done by the printer). I lugged the AEGIS bookstore to dozens of transgender conferences and spoke to hundreds of college classes and civic groups. I did all this day-in-and-day-out for nine years, without pay and usually without assistance, all the while holding down a full-time position as a civil servant.[11]

The advent of the World Wide Web, however, offered a far more sustainable alternative. Web-hosted content required a limited set of identifiable startup costs (e.g., design, hosting, site maintenance) and came with none of the traditional infrastructure of a clearinghouse, such as physical space, staffing, or printing/photocopying equipment. Moreover, with the industry-wide shift toward a monthly subscription model in the late 1990s, users' search time was increasingly not limited by per-hour access fees.

To Denny, "the advantages of this no-rent, no-electric-bill, no-typewriter-ribbons-or-printer-cartridges, no-postage-stamps, no-salaries, no-need-to-sell-things-or-solicit-money model were obvious as early as 1994; no nonprofit could afford to ignore them—although many did."[12] In a 1998 column on the future of the transgender community (part of a larger "Vision 2001" series) Denny and coauthor Jessica Xavier contrasted the traditional print-and-mail distribution model with using an Internet search engine, which can return over four thousand results for the term "transsexual." "With such a wealth available in seconds," they argue, "who in the future will be inclined to wait a couple of weeks for an information packet from a gender organization? And which organization will be able to afford packets sent by mail at a cost of a dollar or two apiece, when a Web site can disperse ten or a hundred or a thousand times as much information instantly and for free?"[13] This would be the attitude that guided Denny as head of AEGIS's successor organization, Gender Education and Advocacy (GEA), whose primary mission was providing accurate information for interested parties and educators, free of charge, on their website, gender.org (fig. 4.1).

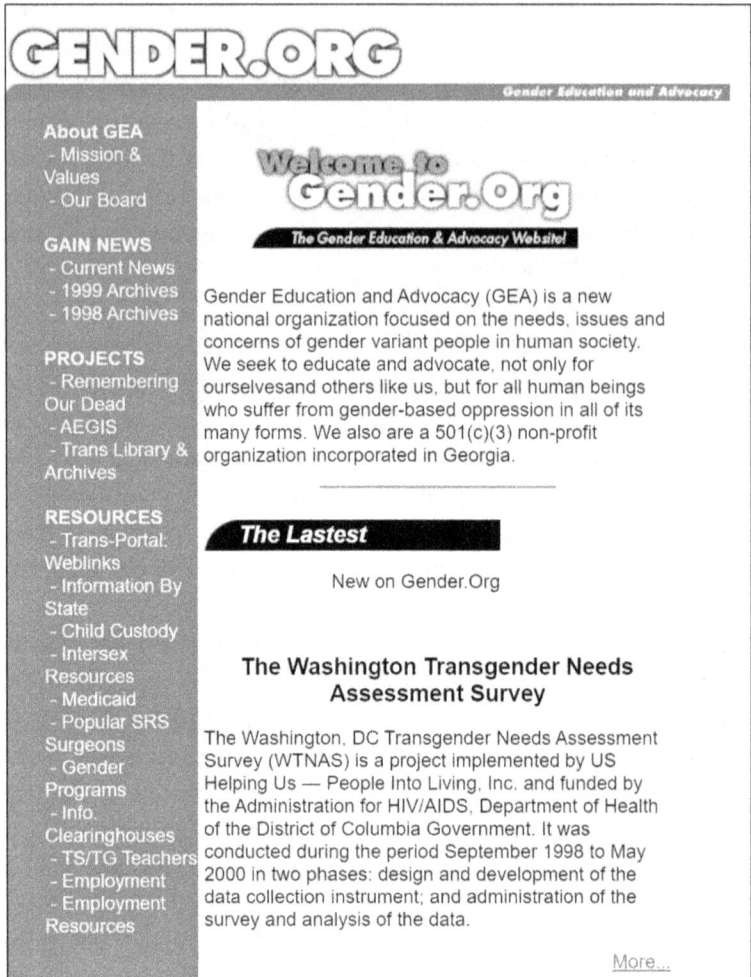

Figure 4.1. Screenshot of Gender.org, archived December 5, 2000. Retrieved from the Internet Archive's Wayback Machine.

Getting Online

At the same moment as Denny's first epiphany in 1994, wider cultural interest in the World Wide Web was growing. A major driver of this interest came with the 1993 release of Mosaic, the first graphical web browser. While websites had existed prior to the release of Mosaic, the advent of graphics added a whole other layer of interactivity and "wow" factor to the Web. One of the most notable websites launched during this period was Transgender Forum (TG Forum), founded by Cindy Martin and Jamie Faye Fenton in February 1995 (fig. 4.2). Though it began as an informational site, it quickly transitioned to a community-focused e-zine once site management shifted over to 3-D Communications, Inc., a company cofounded in January 1996 by Martin, Fenton, and JoAnn Roberts. As a digital publication, TG Forum had a number of advantages over similar print media: lower publication thresholds, as well as a wider potential audience and reach. Independent informational sites also began to emerge, like Gender Web (genderweb.org); Susan's Place (susans.org); and TS Roadmap (tsroadmap.com), now Transgender Roadmap (transgendermap.com) several years later. However, in most cases, these sites were developed or indirectly supported by computer-savvy individuals who owned servers for hosting.

The permanence of the Web also allowed room for brand new projects, such as Remembering Our Dead, founded by Gwendolyn Ann

Figure 4.2. Screenshot of one of the earliest versions of the TGForum.com landing page, archived October 2, 1996. Retrieved from the Internet Archive's Wayback Machine.

Figure 4.3. Screenshot of the Remembering Our Dead memorial page, listing transgender individuals who died as a result of transphobic violence. Archived October 13, 1999. Retrieved from the Internet Archive's Wayback Machine.

Smith, then-moderator of the Transgender Community Forum on AOL, in late 1998 and hosted on the GEA site (fig. 4.3). As Smith recounted in her 1999 column discussing the site, when she drew connections between the 1998 murder of Rita Hester, a trans woman of color from Boston, with the deaths of Debra Forte and Chanelle Pickett three years earlier, she was surprised to find that no one else remembered who they were. "Is our community's memory so short," she wondered, "that one of the more important benchmarks of recent trans-activism, from less than a handful of years before, is largely forgotten?" Remembering Our Dead, then, aimed to "provide a way to preserve the memories of those who have fallen along the way, as well as make a statement about these human beings who were treated as something much less than that."[14] Functionally, the site was designed to replicate existing memorials, with somber black-and-white graphics—a stark contrast to existing web design trends' emphasis on high-impact imagery.

A Room of One's Own

By 1996, TGForum had begun offering subscribers a new, highly desirable service: web hosting. Though TGForum's hosting was community-oriented (e-zine subscribers received a set amount of space, while organizations could receive space free of charge), a variety of other options also existed, from popular ad-supported services like Tripod, Angelfire, and GeoCities to service providers like AOL. Not only were folks getting online; they were also increasingly interested in making a home on the web. Corporate rhetoric reinforced this spatial orientation: AOL named their Web-hosting service "Hometown," while Geocities initially allowed users—dubbed "homesteaders," in distinctly colonialist company rhetoric—to organize in themed "neighborhoods" where they were assigned a specific "street address." Mirroring offline geography, LGBT-related pages were located in WestHollywood, named after a well-known LGBT neighborhood and tourist destination in Los Angeles County. Though it's difficult to calculate the number being made during the mid to late 1990s, both Geocities and Tripod estimated in 2000 that they each hosted approximately four million web pages, though some estimates put GeoCities' size at the substantially larger seven million.[15] However, compared to large-scale professional sites like TGForum or Remembering Our Dead, sites hosted on these services reflected their creators' more modest or personal ambitions; many local and regional groups created their first sites using them. These sites lacked the interactivity of a TGForum, having much more in common with what was derisively described in the industry as "brochureware": mere "collections of scanned documents slapped on a web page."[16] However, for such perpetually time- and cash-strapped organizations, the very ability to create and publish a digital "brochure" was a huge boon. The group website offered both current and prospective members an always-on, one-stop-shop for group information, communication, and outreach that required little planning or maintenance. In discussions around groups' websites, outreach was one of the most frequently cited needs. Given public attitudes toward gender community groups, most organizations had small-to-no budgets for public advertising, many times limited to a spot in the local classifieds.[17] A website, in comparison, could both cost far less to maintain and give questioning individuals access to far more information about the group without the risk of interception—a fear keeping many hotline callers from agreeing to receive brochures or information packets via postal mail. Moreover, unlike a hotline, a website didn't require regular staffing at specific times. For example,

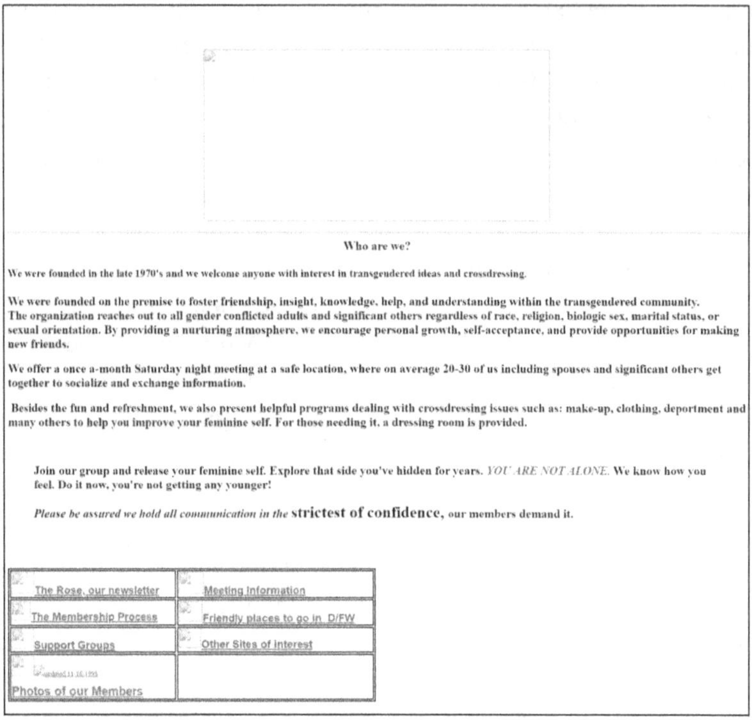

Figure 4.4. Earliest archived version of the Delta Omega Website, archived December 5, 1998. Retrieved from the Internet Archive's Wayback Machine.

while readers could use the website to email the Dallas/Fort Worth–based Metroplex Cross Dressers Club (also known as the Delta Omega chapter of Tri-Ess) at any hour of the day, their hotline was only "live" for two hours a week.[18]

In terms of design, many organizational sites had (at least initially) bare-bones designs, reflecting the often-growing skill of their creators, who sometimes relied heavily on services' built-in design tools and templates. For example, the first archived iteration of the Metroplex Site is primarily left-aligned text and tables, with limited use of color (fig. 4.4). The site's features grow with each passing year: increasing use of multiple alignments, color and images, a visitor meter, and even that most infamous of late 1990s website features, an embedded midi file (fig. 4.5). Though many organizations were committed to maintaining member privacy, a website allowed members greater control over their public presence. Online, members could self-select to share photos and other information, providing questioning, often anxious searchers with a welcoming face whose smile ran contrary to the popular image of the furtive, maladjusted cross-dresser hiding in their bedroom. In some cases, the launch of an organization's website was accompanied by a newsletter article explaining how to access and use the site.

Groups also used their websites and newsletters to publicize members' sites, either through "links" pages or regular columns in the style of "hotlinks" lists. For, at the same time as groups were building sites, many more trans individuals were creating home pages online. Though no complete index exists, one GeoCities-based directory indexed at least 2,500 trans-related home pages on that hosting service alone. This growth reflected wider cultural trends, with GeoCities registering 18,000 new users a day in the late 1990s.[19] Unlike the trans

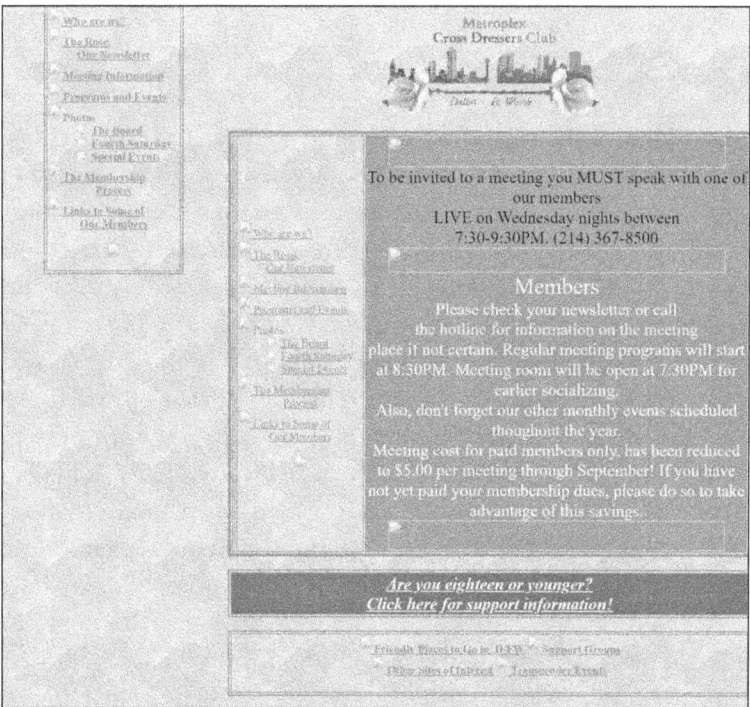

Figure 4.5. Later iteration of the Delta Omega Website, archived December 1, 2002. Retrieved from the Internet Archive's Wayback Machine.

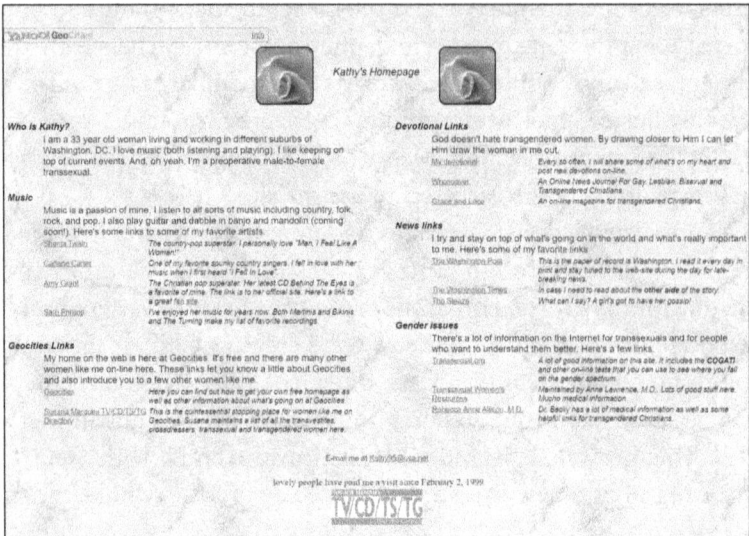

Figure 4.6. A single-page home page, archived October 23, 1999. Retrieved from the Internet Archive's Wayback Machine.

group's digital "brochure," trans creators often constructed their pages as an extension of their identity, either lived or *en femme*. Home page content varied widely: some were little more than a one-page profile, containing a short biography, a list of interests, and links to other sites (see fig. 4.6), while others sprawled across a variety of different pages, including photo galleries, poetry, or pages dedicated to hobbies (fig. 4.7). Though its hand-coded aesthetic bears visual similarities to zines—and many e-zines were in fact hosted on services like GeoCities—the home page is effectively an early ancestor of the social media profile. While some home page creators did discuss erotic interests or desires related to cross-dressing, most focused on more public-facing aspects of daily life, remixing elements of familiar formats including personal ads, scrapbooks, photo albums, and personal journals. Unlike these earlier documents, however, the home page could reach a sizable audience. Most importantly, it allowed the trans creator to represent themselves in ways that challenged existing mass representations.

How Do We Tell You Who We Are?

In American mass media during this period, representations of trans individuals were most commonly available in two formats: the transition memoir, and the tabloid talk show. The memoir offered trans individuals an accessible way to represent themselves and their experiences. Early trans memoirs offered a retrospective view of the individual's progress through a highly formalized set of stages, from suffering and the epiphany of self-discovery to the transformation of transition and the final comfort of reassignment.[20] Trans individuals, particularly

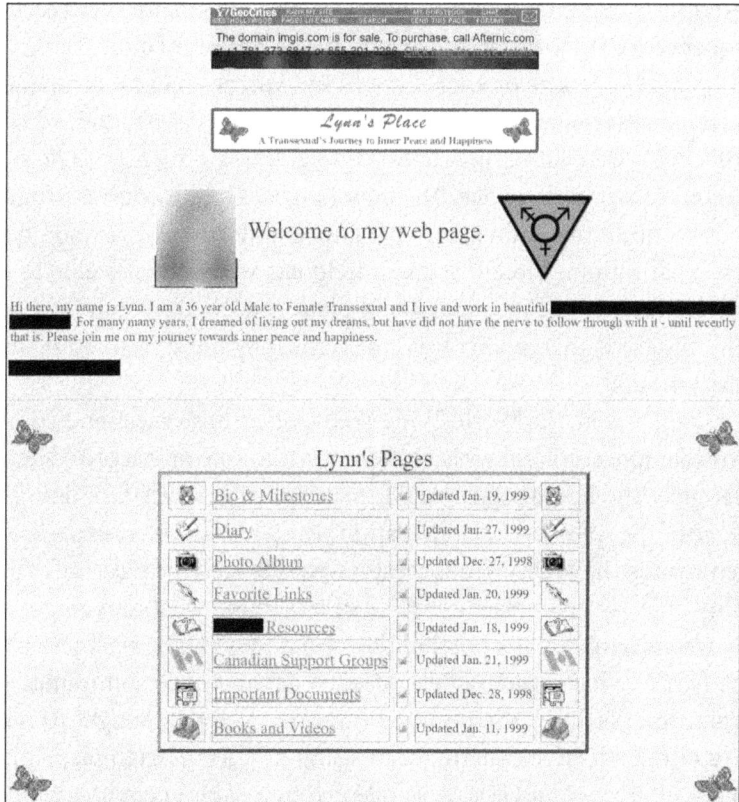

Figure 4.7. A home page with multiple branching pages, archived January 28, 1999. Retrieved from the Internet Archive's Wayback Machine.

prior to their exposure to trans print culture, voraciously consumed these texts. Though dismissed by medical experts as unreliable, the memoir genre offered trans readers narratives that centered around the trans individual's lived experience of gender transition, in contrast to the diagnostic focus of medical texts like Harry Benjamin's *The Transsexual Phenomenon*. These medical gatekeepers had outsize influence over individuals' progress through the transition process, as well as their gender performance, which could not deviate from wider heteronormative social scripts. Departure from the established narrative could and did leave individuals at risk of being denied care, since they appeared to not meet the specific diagnostic criteria of Gender Identity Disorder, despite their protests. These memoirs, then, implicitly or explicitly offered their audience "recipes" they could use to ensure they received adequate care.[21] However, those who didn't desire medical transition, such as cross-dressers or androgynous individuals, had no comparable model for processing one's life narrative; most texts aimed toward non-transsexuals were either instructional (e.g., explaining how to do one's makeup) or personal advice. The tabloid talk show, in contrast, framed topics around trans individuals' presumed abnormality, dishonesty, or oversexualization. Though trans individuals were at times able to use their appearances as an educational platform, in effect "talking back" to the audience, their ability was constrained by the structured realities of the format.[22]

In comparison, the World Wide Web made trans spaces and content accessible to a similarly wide audience, with none of the producer interference. The home page opened space for infinite self-fashioning, an inverse of the "pleasure of anticipation" early Mosaic users experienced when surfing the Web.[23] Trans creators experienced the pleasure of possibility on early home pages: instead of imagining what they might see, they were excited by the possibility of what they might *be*. These users were part of what media scholar Megan Sapnar Ankserson frames as a "structure of feeling" surrounding the early web that sought to make sense of the affective experience of using it.[24] As an example, Ankerson cites *Wired* writer Gary Wolf's description of his encounter with the home page of a CERN scientist's three-year-old son: "It was a type of voyeurism, yes, but it was less like peeking into a person's window and more like dropping in on a small seminar with a cloak of invisibility.

One thing it was not like: it was not like being in a library. The whole experience gave an intense illusion, not of information, but of *personality*" (emphasis added).[25] Trans users conveyed this personality through three key affordances of the home page and web browser: its basis in HTML, hypertext's nonlinear structure, and the ability to embed media. Compared to the apparently static print text, work created in HTML offered far more flexibility. If they wished, creators could write, erase, and rewrite their work as many times as they desired. Unlike the memoir, they were not required to present a coherent, unitary self, but could explore different chosen names and gender performances, including their discomfort with limiting themselves to one end of the gender binary. And, as creators grew more confident in their self-identity, their home page could change to reflect their growing confidence.

Creator Davita's home page is an excellent example of how one's identity can change over time, reflecting both her growing fluency with the language and her shifting sense of self as someone whose cross-gender desires lie outside the linear progress of transition. In 1999, when her home page was first archived, Davita self-identified as a "life-long cross-dresser" and framed much of her self-identity around her relationship with her wife, including a photo of herself *en drab* with her (fig. 4.8). By 2001, she'd removed all discussion of her wife, as well as photos of herself en drab. Whereas she'd previously thought the gown featured on her site was "too pretty to have my face ruin it," she updated her site to include a copy of the photo with her face clearly visible (fig. 4.9). A year later, her narrative had transformed further, along with a site redesign. Following in-community trends, Davita identified herself as "transgender" and described her recent visits to a psychologist, who diagnosed her as "transgendered but undetermined" (fig. 4.10). She, like many individuals who began identifying as "transgender" during this period, fell outside the strict categories (transsexual or transvestistic fetishism) of DSM IV-era diagnoses. By 2007, her site header emphasized her in-between status, featuring photos of her both en drab and *en femme* as Davita (fig. 4.11).

In a similar vein, hypertext's nonlinear structure changed how trans narratives could be both constructed and read. The trans memoir, much like the medical process it emulates, emphasizes linear forward motion. Stages of transition had to be completed in sequence with the approval of a medical gatekeeper; any attempt to avoid or skip a stage in the

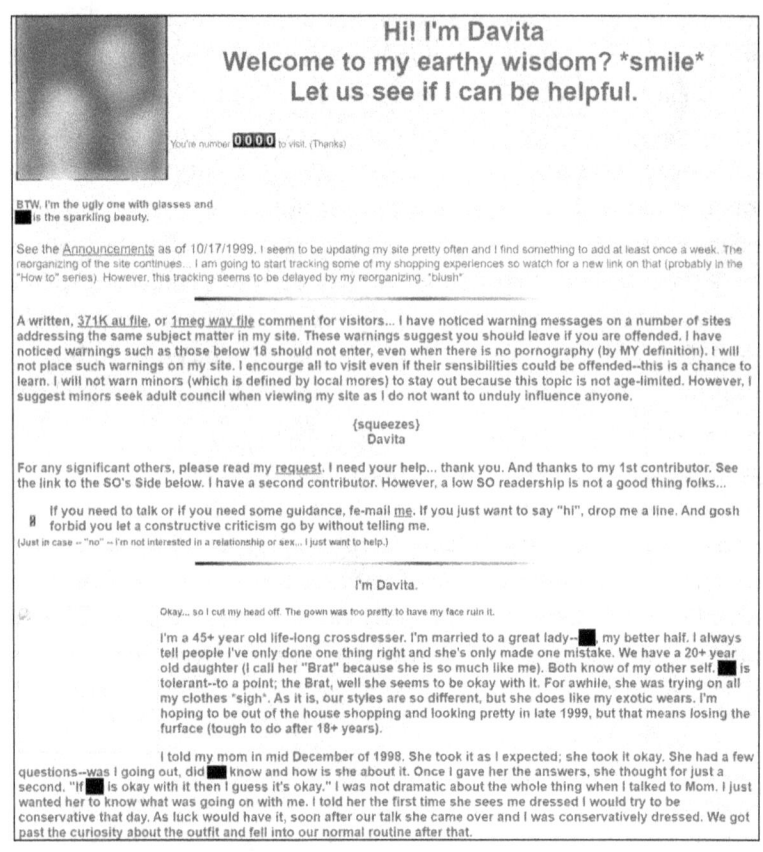

Figure 4.8. Davita's home page, archived October 18, 1999. Retrieved from the Internet Archive's Wayback Machine.

process could be taken as evidence that one wasn't a "real" transsexual. In a hypertext environment, however, content could be encountered in any number of different ways. Creators could apportion their lived experience into self-contained pages, which could easily be consumed "out of order," as readers skipped ahead according to their own interests and desires (see figs. 4.7 and 4.10). These readers were not confined to one site or narrative, either, as they followed hyperlinks from home page to home page. The numerous linked perspectives they could find online made room for readers to fully conceptualize the variety of different experiences collected under the "transgender" umbrella.

Similarly, creators were not required, as in the transsexual memoir, to organize their photographs within the expected "Before and After" framing.[26] On a home page, they were able to engage in a variety of curatorial practices, self-selecting the image they presented to others (fig. 4.12). Whereas the memoir centered transition as the most important (and interesting) aspect of the trans person's identity, on their home pages creators could make room for unrelated aspects of their identity, such as their professional accomplishments, hobbies, or fan interests. By design, the trans home page resembled not the memoir's single master narrative but an interconnected assemblage of different, sometimes contradictory, aspects of self. These could be further reinforced in creators' graphical and design choices, allowing creators to explore self-representation outside of bodily modification. Creators could "gender"

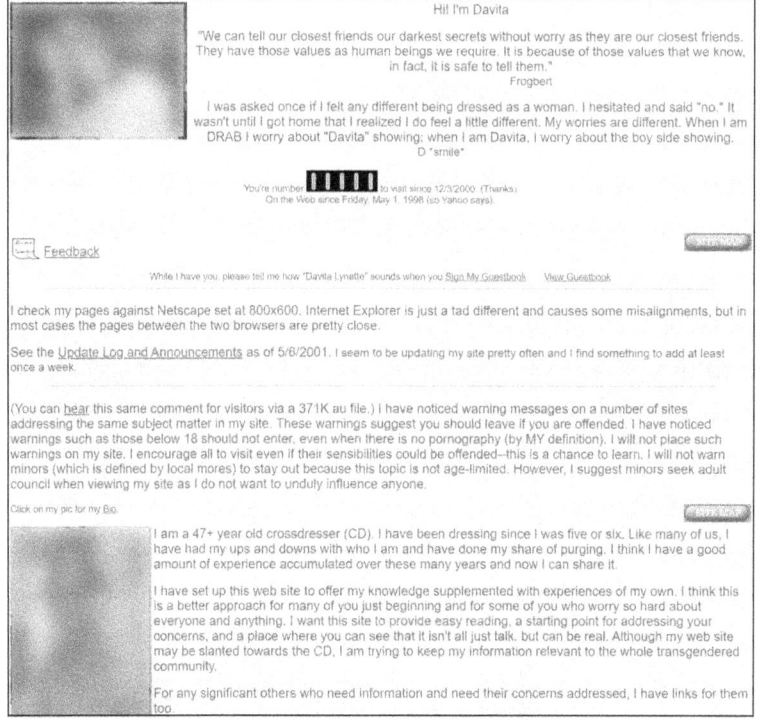

Figure 4.9. Davita's home page, archived May 7, 2001. Retrieved from the Internet Archive's Wayback Machine.

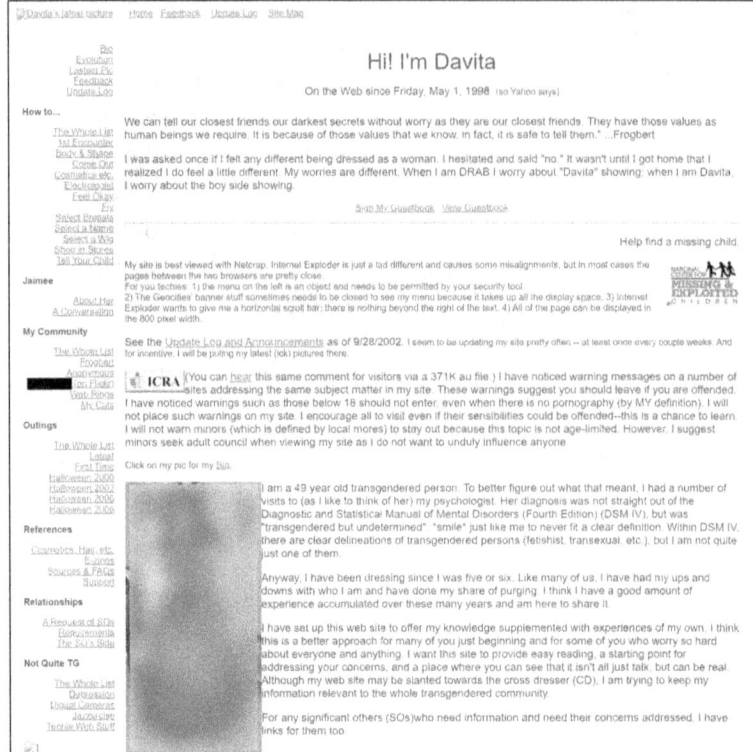

Figure 4.10. Davita's home page, archived October 3, 2002. Retrieved from the Internet Archive's Wayback Machine.

their pages to best represent their lived (or aspired) gender identity and change this presentation as many times as they liked. Alternately, users could present their gender in ways that fell outside gatekeepers' prescribed norms, without risking they would later be denied care. Users with no other semipublic outlet for their femininity, for example, could fill their home page with gendered visual markers—liberal use of pink, purple, and other gendered colors; looping script typefaces; iconography like flowers, butterflies, makeup items, and high heels—in whatever configuration they wished (see fig. 4.13). This is not to suggest all home page creators embraced such hypergendering, but simply that they *could*. The design of the home page was also understood as an extension of its creator; in a 1997 column on member home pages from the Gulf Coast Transgender Community Transmission Line, author Vanessa Edwards noted that member Jenifer's site was, like her personality, "very showy and flashy with all the bells and whistles. Make that all the graphics and Java-style animation!"[27]

Not only were home pages a space of self-representation; they were also inherently social documents. Creators made a point of encouraging readers to contact them via email or sign their guestbook. Many creators joined at least one webring, connecting with other creators who shared similar identities or interests. Functionally, webrings were collections of sites organized around specific topics or themes. Unlike contemporaneous search engines, whose overreliance on keywords could limit their usefulness, webrings offered a more "curated" perspective on a topic.[28] The depth of connection within any one ring varied: some represented existing friend groups who communicated regularly, while others had membership numbers in the thousands.[29] The most extensive directory

Figure 4.11. Davita's home page, archived November 13, 2007. Retrieved from the Internet Archive's Wayback Machine.

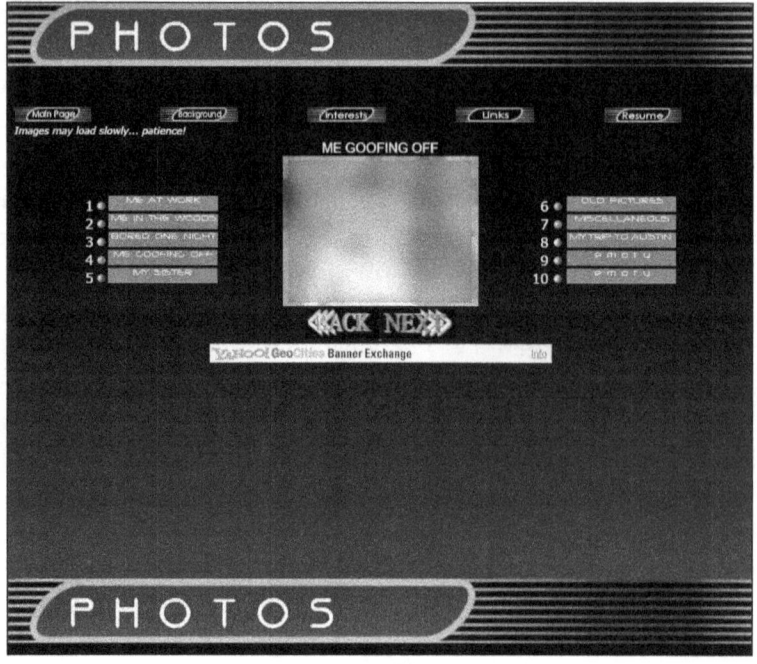

Figure 4.12. Photo gallery from a home page featuring a variety of subjects. archived February 29, 2000. Retrieved from the Internet Archive's Wayback Machine.

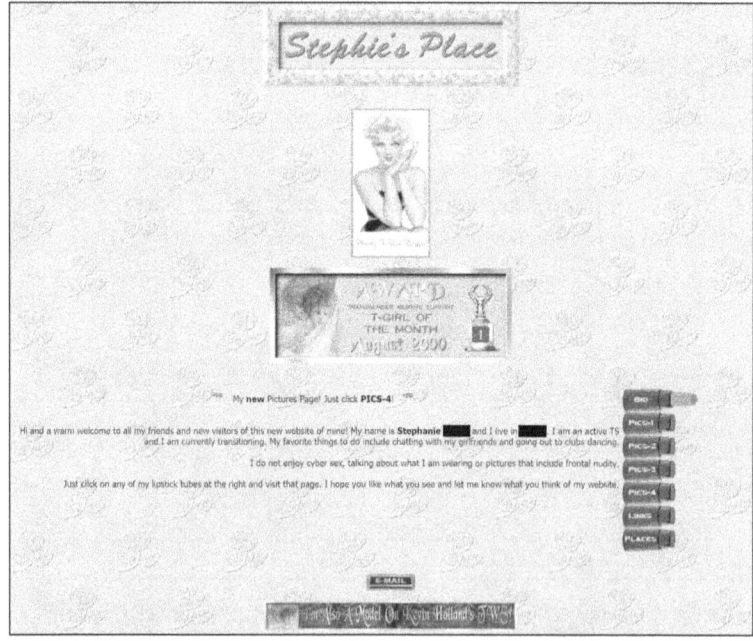

Figure 4.13. Example of gendering practices in home page design. Archived April 07, 2001. Retrieved from the Internet Archive's Wayback Machine.

of trans home pages was maintained by Susana Marques, a Portuguese cross-dresser (fig. 4.14). The site, which she regularly updated through 2007, included member sites from at least sixty-two countries, though most members were from North America and Europe. In 2001, the directory listed 2,771 trans-related home pages—including self-identified cross-dressers, transvestites, drag queens, trans women, and trans men—within the Geocities WestHollywood neighborhood alone, and nearly half of those were just cross-dressers. Yet its listings weren't limited to GeoCities, and it served as a key hub of connection with the wider trans Web.

In some cases, the webring was fused with existing offline models to create new, digital variants. The most notable of these groups was the Vanity Club, which billed itself as an online variant on Tri-Ess's sorority model. An adamantly nonpolitical group, membership centered around

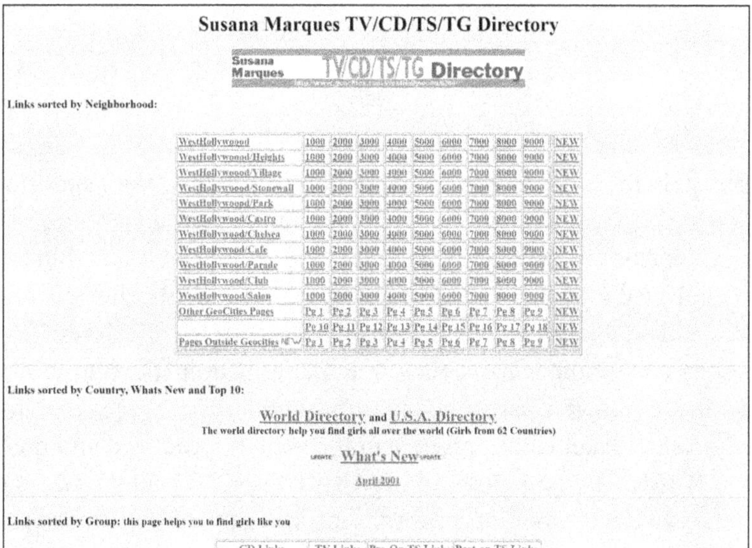

Figure 4.14. Screenshot of Susana Marques TV/CD/TS/TG Directory home page. Archived May 6, 2001. Retrieved from the Internet Archive's Wayback Machine.

the "Vanity Club Ideal, "the freedom of expression with our particular desire to emulate and/or attain womanhood," which required members to "ALWAYS maintain the highest possible standards of beauty, elegance, glamour, sophistication and style" in their daily life.[30] Prospective members, once nominated by an existing member, submitted a photo and questionnaire for review by members, who voted whether or not to grant membership. While a home page was not a requirement, having a web presence was seen as an "enhancing" factor, and members would help each other build home pages if they didn't currently have them.[31] Unsurprisingly, as a primarily digital organization, many club members' first introduction to the transgender community came via the Internet—though the Club made it a point to note that "an unspoken but important goal for each member is to meet her Sorority Sisters in *real time* in the *real world!*"[32]

On the part of corporate hosts, GeoCities in particular set itself apart through its neighborhood model, which aimed to foster community among its users by extending the spatial metaphor and mimicking core features of the offline neighborhood.[33] In LGBT-centric WestHollywood, where the vast majority of trans pages were located, numerical "blocks" were assigned their own "community leader," a volunteer responsible for welcoming new neighbors, answering their questions, reviewing page content, and contributing to the shared community resources, including the neighborhood "cyberzine." The leadership team also approved and forwarded applications for neighborhood sites to be recognized by GeoCities as "featured homesteaders." Nevertheless, the archives are unclear on how much connection trans individuals had with the larger WestHollywood community. There appears to have been no significant trans presence in the content produced and posted at the WestHollywood Community Center, nor did many trans pages join the WestHollywood-specific webring, as compared to trans-specific webrings.

Being Good Digital Citizens

Beyond content and webring links, a substantial number of home pages also included another feature: a disclaimer. Placed either near the top of the site's main page or on a separate page, often index.html (so it would automatically be designated the site landing page), this text warned potential readers of the site's transgender content. While some were fairly generic (figs. 4.15–4.16), others adopted more legalistic language (fig. 4.17). Disinterested, offended, or presumably underaged readers, the upper limit ranging from under eighteen to twenty-one years old, were urged to use their browser's back button and head elsewhere. Some disclaimers also offered alternative sites that might be more to these individuals' tastes, including both mundane options (Yahoo.com or Geocitites.com) and more tongue-in-cheek choices (Disney.com). The disclaimer emerged from the confluence of three ongoing cultural shifts in the mid-to-late 1990s: the rising dominance of the World Wide Web, corresponding fears about children's access to obscene content online, and trans individuals' increasing media visibility.

As discussed in chapter 2, the responsibility of managing content was handled by commercial services, who set their own rules and standards for what counted as appropriate, as well as imposing restrictions on access. On these platforms, authority lay with the platform's corporate management, and concerned individuals could identify with whom to express their concerns. As a theoretically open platform, though, the World Wide Web lacked the same clear hierarchy and oversight. This contrast is best captured in in the opening graph of Philip Elmer-DeWitt's infamous 1995 *Time* magazine cover story "On a Screen Near You": "Sex is everywhere these days—in books, magazines, films, television, music videos and bus-stop perfume ads. . . . Most Americans have become so inured to the open display of eroticism—and the arguments for why it enjoys special status under the First Amendment—that they hardly notice it's there. Something about the combination of sex and computers, however, seems to make otherwise worldly-wise adults a little crazy."[34] Elmer-DeWitt's story focused on a study published in the *Georgetown University Law Journal*, "Marketing Pornography on the Information Superhighway." Primarily authored by Carnegie Mellon undergrad Marty Rimm, the study, as described by Elmer-DeWitt, presented an image of a network dominated by pornographic imagery within easy reach of any casual user. Though Rimm's study was later widely debunked, the shocking statistics he quoted helped to fuel a cyberporn technopanic. In a technopanic, as defined by media scholar Alice Marwick, anxieties about new technologies and the theoretical

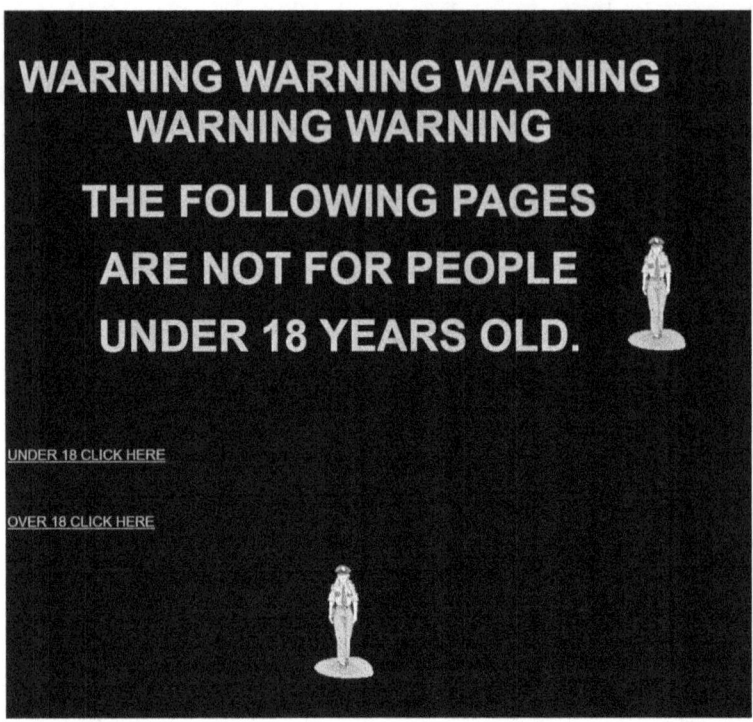

Figure 4.15 and Figure 4.16. Examples of general site disclaimers on a landing page. Archived October 3, 1999 (fig. 4.15) and October 9, 1999 (fig. 4.16). Retrieved from the Internet Archive's Wayback Machine.

threat posed to youth lead to public pathologization of youth media use, culminating in moves to regulate or control their behaviors either through platform self-regulation or legal means. In the cyberporn panic, adults' fears over youth use of the Internet, as well as anonymous email and chat—supposedly infected with all manner of pornographic talk and images—led to increased focus on regulating these spaces, culminating in the 1996 passage of the now-overturned Communications Decency Act (CDA).[35]

Drawing on existing zoning legislation, the CDA intended to "zone" the Internet in order to keep minors from accessing "obscene or indecent" material, requiring that this content be accessible only with age-restricted payment methods or access codes.[36] Unlike the "Miller test" for obscenity, however, the CDA did not include a "community standard" provision for determining obscenity, so who determined what counted as "obscene" material was unclear. This lack of clarity put trans groups and individuals in an uncomfortable position. To some, trans as a concept still invoked associations with indecency, underlined by the Rimm study's inclusion of "transsexual" and "transvestite" content within the "paraphilia" category (they are, in fact, the first paraphilias listed in the authors' description of the class). Yet they rarely appear in panic-related media coverage; the most notable mention is one offhand

Figure 4.17. Example of a legalistic site disclaimer. Archived October 2, 1999. Retrieved from the Internet Archive's Wayback Machine.

reference attributed to Ken Layne, then-editor of *ComputorEdge*, a weekly San Diego computer magazine, that negligent parents who fail to supervise their children's computer use "shouldn't complain when they find that little Jimmy has been talking to a transvestite."[37] Within community publications, discussion is equally absent, limited to a brief mention of the state of the case in one of JoAnn Roberts's HotBuzz columns (run in April and May 1996 in two separate publications), where she noted that, "if the CDA is upheld, many of the web sites with information about transgender behavior could shut down."[38] Roberts's brief warning notwithstanding, trans-specific concerns are absent from any of the legal documents filed as part of *ACLU et al. v. Reno*, the case that struck down the CDA. In fact, the only mention comes in the Queer Resource Directory's affidavit, where they describe the site as "one of the most comprehensive Internet archives pertaining to lesbian, gay, bisexual, transsexual, and transgender issues."[39] Following the failure of the CDA, filtering software emerged as the go-to method for content restriction. Many popular filtering software relied on some combination of word filtering dictionaries, prebuilt blacklists, and domain filtering. Users had some control over the severity of filtering, but they were often a blunt instrument: some by default blocked entire domains for popular home page hosts like Geocities and Tripod or only allowed "all or nothing" blocking options. They also consistently blocked LGBT sites on various topics, though only one, cybersITTER, explicitly listed "Homosexuality / Transgender Sites" as a specific target of filtering.[40] For their part, major home page hosts' terms of service did restrict members from posting content that, in their terms, didn't reflect the spirit of the community. GeoCities was the most explicit, stating in their FAQ: "By popular opinion, our guidelines have been carefully crafted to promote the free flowing exchange of ideas about your interests, activities and hobbies, and at the same time maintain standards consistent with the Internet community and the societies of the world at large." This included not allowing nudity or pornography, which they defined as "images and text which do not reflect the concept of community which we cherish and offer to our homesteaders, visitors and sponsors."[41]

Given the risk legislation like the CDA and filtering software posed to the trans Net, they would seem to have raised more concern within the community. However, when considered in its contemporaneous political context, the trans community's limited public advocacy makes sense. As discussed in the introduction and chapter 2, respectability politics had long been a central pillar of both transgender media advocacy and formal political lobbying. Under this politic approach, trans individuals focused primarily on advocating for changes that allowed them to fit into existing infrastructure without challenging its foundational assumptions.[42] Online, this meant framing the trans subject as a good digital citizen, who followed the terms of service and easily fit into corporate and social expectations. The focus on promoting "good citizen" status has a long history as an advocacy tactic, adopted by movements ranging from post–World War II Mexican American civil rights organizations to post-9/11 trans organizing around the Real ID.[43] For example, advocates targeting AOL didn't challenge that obscene trans-related material, such as chats of a sexual nature involving trans topics, was obscene. Instead, they made a point of differentiating AOLGG as a respectable space full of good citizens, where such content was not welcome.[44] However, this good-citizen narrative was at odds with the core focus of the CDA: first, defining what counted as "sexually explicit" material, and, second, explaining why allowing access to supposedly "indecent" material was important.[45] If any trans groups or individuals had become involved in cases opposing the CDA, they risked guilt by association; if they'd long argued what they did wasn't sexual or deviant, why were they involved in a case centered on what counted as "sexually explicit"?

Lawsuits opposing filtering software, in contrast, allowed trans groups to maintain their public position against indecency, as in the 1998 case of *Mainstream Loudoun v. Loudoun County Library*. In it, a coalition of residents of Loudoun, Virginia, represented by People for the American Way, alleged that the library system's "Policy on Internet Sexual Harassment" and the Internet filtering software used to enforce it, X-Stop, violated their First Amendment rights. In 1998, the ACLU intervened in the case to represent a group of plaintiffs whose sites were blocked by X-Stop as pornographic, including the Renaissance Transgender Association. Renaissance's involvement in the case, beyond being represented by the ACLU, was limited to a deposition given by Angela Gardner, then–executive director of Renaissance. Throughout the case, framings of Renaissance emphasize its legitimacy, including the social status of its board members and nonsexual content of its site and associated publications.[46] Prior to the final verdict, X-Stop would in fact admit that Renaissance's site contained no "prohibited material" and unblock the site.[47] Yet none of the plaintiffs in the case opposed the idea that *some* content on the Internet was inappropriate for minors, and that the library had a right to limit their access.

I draw this distinction not to take an absolutist First Amendment position but to highlight how public arguments for trans content's legitimacy centered on clearly differentiating between good (not indecent) content produced by proper digital citizens and bad (indecent) trans-related online content that could safely be excluded. While previous cases involved trans groups, home page creators held sole responsibility for their content. The home page disclaimer, then, could serve two purposes, depending on the creator's intent: protect them from perceived legal liability while signaling that they were producing "good" trans content. Certainly, some home pages bore more than a passing resemblance to personal ads in trans-themed contact magazines, listing vital statistics, orientation, and interests, accompanied by an email address and photographs; in fact, by the late 1990s, many ads in such magazines were little more than a home page address.[48] While they didn't technically violate GeoCities' policy against pornography or erotica, creators' presentation was at times highly sexualized. However, as a *self*-presentation, creators wielded agency over all aspects of how said presentation was sexualized.

Alternately, other creators used the disclaimer to deter any connotations of sexualization and reinforce a more respectable image (as in fig. 4.16). The disclaimer was, in a way, a double-edged sword: while it actively refuted sexualization, its existence implicitly reminded readers that trans individuals were sexualized within wider culture. This fact was most often reinforced by unprompted contact from chasers: individuals, primarily straight-identified cisgender men, whose interest in cross-dressers and trans women was almost entirely sexual. As Angela Gardner noted in her column on the increased visibility of chasers online, "Men who have admired transgender pulchritude from afar are now able to log on and get the finest TG porno downloaded to their laptop."⁴⁹ Some creators bemoaned the number of emails they received from chasers. Underneath the disclaimer at the top of her site, creator Michelle left a warning: "I have been getting alot of people under the age of 18 trying to talk dirty with me and I dont like it, Not at all, if thats all you want to do is talk dirty then go to a pay site and talk dirty to them, and stay away from mine thank you!!!! Some days I wonder why we are put on this blessed earth do you? if you know why send me some e-mail to the address's below." While the way she determined her correspondents' ages was unclear, her frustration was not. For her, the chasers' presence was diametrically opposed to the more gentle, feminine persona of her site, communicated through liberal use of "cute" GIFs, rose imagery, and soft pinks.

In some cases, the lack of a disclaimer may have itself been a deliberate choice as well. In the earliest archived iteration of her site (as seen in fig. 4.8), Davita noted that she had "noticed warning messages on a number of sites addressing the same subject matter in my site. These warnings suggest you should leave if you are offended. I have noticed warnings such as those below 18 should not enter, even when there is no pornography (by MY definition)." In contrast, she chose not to "place such warnings on my site" and encouraged "all to visit even if their sensibilities could be offended—this is a chance to learn." As to the risk to minors, she chose to not warn them, both because the status was "defined by local mores," and "this topic is not age-limited." Nevertheless, she did "suggest minors seek adult council when viewing my site as I do not want to unduly influence anyone." Even absent legally concerning material, some creators clearly remained concerned about the presence of minors within their readership.

Presumably, parental perspectives on minors' Internet use would be enforced through their use of filtering software, with the disclaimer acting as a final deterrent. Creators had the option to participate in these filtering regimes, and some authorities encouraged them to rate their sites as a method of self-protection. On the "Rating Your Website" page, first archived in 1997 as part of the WestHollywood Community Center, community leader Toantom noted that while "we are all extremely blessed to have a home on the Web like WestHollywood . . . there are still people out there who would like to get rid of all our home pages, merely because they related to alternative sexual lifestyles." Voluntary participation in site rating programs like RSACi (the Recreational Software Advisory Council on the Internet) and SafeSurf allowed creators to protect themselves from false claims or filtering. Both systems used the W3C's (now unsupported) Platform for Internet Content Selection (PICS) specification to create metadata tags used by browsers or filtering software to control access to websites. A variety of popular browsers and filtering services supported RSACi, SafeSurf, and the PICS standard during the late 1990s, including Internet Explorer, Netscape, CompuServe's native browser, and popular filtering software CyberPatrol. However, the two standards varied in how strictly they rated content. The RSACi, an Internet-focused variant of the now-defunct Recreational Software Advisory Council's proprietary video game rating system, allowed users to self-rate their sites on a scale of 0 to 4 as to its level of nudity, sex, language, and violence. SafeSurf, in contrast, was a far more detailed system that included ratings not only for sex and language but also "Homosexual" or "Heterosexual Themes," as well as the ability to designate a site's target age group. Given the implication of censorship in this scheme, Toantom emphasized that SafeSurf's inclusion of these categories was meant to empower parents to "determine whether or not their children can see sites with these ratings." He went on to estimate that "the majority of sites in WestHollywood should be rated for Ages 15 & Up, with an appropriate rating for the Heterosexual or Homesexual [sic] Content (or both if applicable)." At the end of the page, Toantom reminds readers that "these ratings systems are **entirely voluntary**, and **you** rate your own pages. Nobody will force these ratings on you, and the acceptance of the rating you give your pages is entirely at the discretion of the Ratings providers" (emphasis in original). Yet participation, even when voluntary, failed to challenge the social norms that made such ratings necessary. As with disclaimers, self-rating ensured that WestHollywood pages could be deemed respectable to parents and other authorities using filtering systems. In effect, either through their participating in filtering regimes or use of age-restrictive disclaimers, creators were clearly establishing that queer content was for adults only. Yet all of these efforts to shield minors from indecent materials are also indicative of just how many youth were getting online. But, unlike the print periodicals and newsletters that dominated the 1980s, youth could produce their own supposedly panic-inducing content. On a platform like GeoCitites, trans youth home pages lived right next door to content made by adults. These two factors—the Web's growing ubiquity and the increasingly visible presence of trans youth—would help usher in a transformative generational shift within the trans community.

5

Becoming "Obsolete in Your Own Lifetime"

Membership Declines and Generation Gaps

In her keynote address to the 1990 Texas T-Party, an annual cross-dressers' convention in San Antonio, activist Bette Lee Johnson describes taking H. G. Wells's time machine to the "far away" future of 2010. In the "metropolis" of San Antonio, she said, "people look at us, and no doubt read us, but just don't seem to care. There seems to be an attitude with the public that we are doing what we want, and expressing ourselves as must we do, and that seems to be fine. Restaurants and clubs, well of course. Welcome ladies. Table for six? Please follow me. Is this suitable? Enjoy your dinner. Stigma and discrimination seem to be gone."[1]

In Johnson's imagined 2010, "the cross-dresser seems to have been assimilated into the mainstream of society, as we have seen happen so often with ethnic classes in this country over the centuries." Gender community groups now primarily fill social, not supportive, roles. According to a "lady of 2010," national support organizations like Tri-Ess and IFGE (International Foundation for Gender Education) still exist, but "Tri-Ess had major difficulties in 1991 and 1992, because it had problems trying to adapt to changing times. IFGE is still with us, but its thrust had changed significantly since the '90s."[2] Returning to 1990, Johnson presents 1990 as a moment of supreme opportunity, building on her repeated refrain "we are an idea whose time has come":

> There is a time for everything. We are an idea whose time has come. Our time is now. We have emerged from the dark ages of the '70s. Clubs are being organized . . . more each day . . . Statistics tell us that there are six million cross-dressers just like us out there, who think they are all alone and unique and different, and don't know that our clubs exist. Well they are not alone, they are not unique—different, yes, and vive la différence! Our clubs do exist, and we desperately need to reach out to those who

desperately need us. It is a desperate situation to be alone like this, and lives can be at stake. I know of two lives that I believe we have saved through our club in Dallas, just by 'being there.' But . . . we won't reach these people, or achieve the euphoria of 2010 unless we collectively work at it to make it happen.[3]

Johnson closes her speech urging her audience to get involved with their local clubs, pay their dues, and participate in outreach; all of these tiny actions, when combined, can spark true social change. Giving this speech on the cusp of the digital explosion of the 1990s, Johnson could not have known how prophetic it would be, or just how different the landscape would look once she and her audience entered 2010. This chapter considers how the Web fundamentally changed not only the infrastructure of transgender organizing but also transgender life. For many questioning individuals, being able to communicate online was an essential lifeline that allowed them to find self-acceptance. However, not all of those coming out online were getting involved in the smaller regional and local organizations that had long served as the backbone of the "gender community." The leaders of some organizations, who relied on member participation and dues to thrive, worried that the Internet's ease of access presented an existential threat to their groups. Furthermore, although youth who'd grown up with Internet access were claiming transgender identities in increasing numbers, they weren't seeking out seeking traditional organizations, who could be unprepared to or uninterested in addressing their specific concerns. While in-person space and support remained essential to trans life, youth were finding and creating these spaces well outside the existing community infrastructure.

Coming Out Online

By the late 1990s, a new coming out narrative was emerging in letter columns and "cover girl" interviews for community magazines. Unlike their predecessors, these individuals first came out online, and many maintained strong connections to online fora even after getting involved in offline groups and events. While some were aware of and had consumed gender community-specific print publications, the anonymity and interactivity of chat rooms and forums offered them the comfort they needed to come out. In her interview for *LadyLike* in 1999, "cover girl" Sarah described how she was turned off by "sleazy contact magazines," but had been engaged by in-person meetings and the Internet. Given its impact, she wondered not just "where many of us would be without it," but "where many of us would be now if we had it 20 years ago," and "how many would have transitioned if the web was there for us during our early years?"[4] As editor Angela Gardner put it in an editorial from the same issue, early Internet use by trans individuals was "an adjunct to their magazine and TV paperback lives," where they communicated mostly via P.O. box. Now the trans person "in the middle of nowhere can live in her PC" and meet others "in any guise they care to assume."[5] *LadyLike* cover girl Amanda described how getting a household Internet connection in 1997 transformed her identity: "The vast amount of resources I discovered there simply astounded me. For nearly a year I spent every spare moment surfing the Net." For Amanda, "to be able to reach out to girls all around the globe in an instant was absolutely incredible!" She became so engaged online, her wife became like an "Internet widow," and Amanda warned readers they should do "everything in moderation," because "it is very easy to be pulled deep into cyberspace."[6] Community practices were changing as well, as photo sharing became an increasingly important part of one's Internet presence—so much so that JoAnn Roberts ran a column in a 1999 issue of *LadyLike* on digital image formats, hoping to stem the deluge of emails she received with unprintable GIFs and JPGs attached.[7] Trans men and trans masculine individuals also made up a sizable portion of those coming out into visibility. Though trans women remained the most notable population within shared forums, trans men were developing their own spaces online. Home pages were particularly popular, connected via FTM-specific webrings like the FTM Pride Ring.

That same year Amanda got her first household Internet connection, activist Melanie Yarborough declared in a report in the annual IFGE conference, "The communications revolution of e-mail and the Internet, which is reshaping America, has also helped to bring us [transgender individuals] together as a community. Thanks to the net, we know there are a lot more of us out there than we thought, that we're a very, very diverse crowd, and that we need to unite."[8] However, while this "diverse crowd" brought together by the Internet may have had a variety of gender identities, in other areas they were relatively homogenous. For small and regional groups, membership demographics did in some ways reflect their geographic region. Nevertheless, the wider community and national organizations had a long history of prioritizing white perspectives and individuals, often of some economic means, who also had the free time to acquire a variety of clothing and travel to events.[9] Of the 934 respondents to a nonclinical survey of the gender community, conducted over three years and published in 1994, approximately 90 percent of respondents self-identified as white, and over 50 percent had an annual household income above $30,000 (approximately $56,300 adjusted for inflation), roughly the US median income at the time.[10]

Community leaders recognized this inequity, and some did encourage groups to identify ways they could diversify their membership in terms of race, ethnicity, and class.[11] In her keynote speech to the 1994 IFGE conference (republished in *Tapestry*, *Cross-Talk*, and several other publications), Phyllis Frye urged her audience to reject and challenge racism: in her words, going "through the awkwardness of telling that person that their 'white sheet' is showing and you do not approve." She also encouraged them to conduct outreach in community-specific media outlets, such as on Spanish-language radio stations, to reach their "sisters and brothers." Not only could the move increase group membership; it would also "enrich your own life through learning" and "reinforce the argument that we are indeed everywhere and we are in every culture."[12] However, Frye's framing of why trans individuals should reject racism—that transgender individuals are "one of today's" n-words—highlights the whiteness of the gender community. Though meant to facilitate empathetic identification in her presumably largely white audience, Frye's usage decontextualized the term from its historic roots and placed it in a new, racially ambiguous context—a move only possible if made from a location of white privilege.[13] Even when leaders offered more direct criticism, they were still careful to frame their critique as a suggestion for improvement, not highlighting others' active failures. In a 1998 column, Riki Anne Wilchins, then–executive director of GenderPAC, the largest transgender-specific political action committee, reflected on comments by several different activists that she should "be careful that things like race and class don't make GenderPAC 'lose its focus.'" Wilchins noted that such remarks could only come from white individuals, who "have the luxury of choosing [their] focus," which is itself helped "when one has the luxury of a one-dimensional oppression"—a luxury unavailable to people of color. However, Wilchins stopped short of committing GenderPAC to taking a fully intersectional focus, noting that, while issues of race and class did "overlap in important ways with gender," other groups "are already doing that work." Instead, she said, GenderPAC would "continue to stress that overlap, because I believe it represents the reality for so many of us whose lives are not simple, straightforward, or one-dimensional."[14]

Yet rather than increase the possibilities for representation and participation, interest in the Internet among both organizations and community members merely reinforced then-existing inequalities within the community. Writing in 1998, trans activist and academic Stephen Whittle declared that "the communion of the transgender community has been realized within the space outside of space." In his view, "what happens on the street—happens on the Net—happens on the street . . . the Net could have been said to become the street on which the transgender community lives."[15] On this street, users' virtual online selves could more easily transform into their actual, correctly gendered selves without having to pass for others. Lost within this communion, though, was the nuances of participants' lived experiences as classed and raced individuals. Online, as in the offline transgender mainstream, gender was placed at the forefront, while other aspects of trans users' experience were understood as at least partially tied to their "escaped" physical bodies. Key to this escape was the mode via which one's actual self was signified online: according to Whittle, "the pure signifier of the self—the name."[16] Within trans spaces, one's first name is often the first aspect enacted of one's chosen gender identity; even if one isn't read by others as their identified gender, they can still use the name to signal and lay claim to it. Choosing a female or femme name was a very personal process, but columns on naming noted several common themes: acronyms or the feminizing of given, traditionally male names, such as Robert to Roberta or Bobbi; names of female celebrities, such as Marilyn, Sophia, or Lauren; or choices that followed contemporary baby naming trends.[17] However, readers were discouraged from choosing androgynous names that could lead others to question an individual's gender, or selecting "unique" or "unusual" names that would require repeated explanation or spelling correction.[18] Moreover, none of these authors discussed names with non-white cultural connotations, or naming practices specific to languages without established feminization practices, like the addition of *-ita* in Spanish. Community naming practices, then, emphasized Anglo and European names as the most appropriate. In contrast, wider naming practices in text-only fora online encouraged experimentation and exploration, at times up to digital blackface. As Lisa Nakamura notes in her work on self-representation in LambdaMOO, names were used by some as racialized signifiers, allowing them to reenact racist tropes that discouraged users of color from participating.[19]

In online trans fora, though, the emphasis on one's gendered first name (either as a handle or a name used by others) relegated all other aspects of the self to the background, reinforcing the community's preexisting whiteness. For example, a seventeen-year-old Chinese-Canadian began posting to the CDForum mailing in 1991 under her given name. In her introductory post, she talks about immigrating to Canada at 11, the place of her family and local community in her life, and her complicated relationship with her mother. At the end of her introduction, she notes that her given Chinese name "isn't a feminine name, but I choose that when I was five years old, and I haven't found a female name I like yet." By her next post, she's chosen a feminine name to use on CDForum: Susie. Susie includes no further explanation for why she's chosen this name, but her choice follows the common naming conventions of other posters, who use Anglo names such as Valerie, Steph, Amy, Debbie, and Heather. Whatever the reasoning for her choice, Susie's name clearly foregrounds her gender identity as the most important aspect of herself on CDForum.

Increased emphasis on the Internet as the primary mode of communication also reinforced English's place as the lingua franca for the transgender community—including outside of English-dominant regions. In a Fall 2001 article in *Tapestry*, Isabel Tamara, a member of Mexico-based transgender support group *Crisálida*, described the Internet's key role in her own self-discovery: within ten minutes of first getting online in 1997, she "started to get acquainted with my true self: a male-to-female transsexual."[20] The Internet, from her perspective, had been a huge boon.

For those who can "use a computer and have Internet access and some knowledge of English, a whole new world is arising right before our eyes. I can say for sure my life changed the very first day I became connected to the Internet. I was no longer a sick person and no longer alone."[21] However, Tamara's mention of "some knowledge of English" suggests the Internet's clear limitations: discussion on the most popular (and thus accessible) transgender fora was conducted in English for a primarily US-based audience. Beyond the limits of language and representation, few community organizations or leaders discussed the sometimes significant economic challenges to getting consistent Internet access. The only time any discussion appeared in *Tapestry* was a 1998 column by regular contributor and well-known trans psychologist Gianna E. Israel. In her column, she noted that, according to an informal survey of her nationwide clientele, Internet use directly correlated with education level. "Only 35% [of her clients] used or had access to the Internet," and of this population "approximately 15% have less than a high school education . . . a large percentage of persons in our community." She admonished readers—no doubt many of them Internet users—that they should remember that, "while on-line transgender men and women are busily debating" gender theory and medical standards of care, "there are others in the transgender community still struggling with their ABCs."[22] Though avenues of Internet access would increase through the late 1990s in the 2000s, these early norms continued to shape trans spaces online.

Unplanned Obsolesce

The rise of the Internet as the transgender "street" directly contributed to the declining prominence of some long-standing community institutions. The first ones to go would be gender community BBSes, whose affordances and offerings had been rapidly outpaced by the World Wide Web. While some sysops tried to course-correct by adding Telnet access or transitioning their business model toward providing web hosting or acting as a local ISP, most simply went offline. This was the case for Houston-based BBS Carolyn's Place, whose sysop noted in aletter announcing its closure in 1995 that "if a BBS does not have internet access, then it's really not worth logging onto."[23] Community-specific appeals also failed to stop the exodus of users. Recognizing

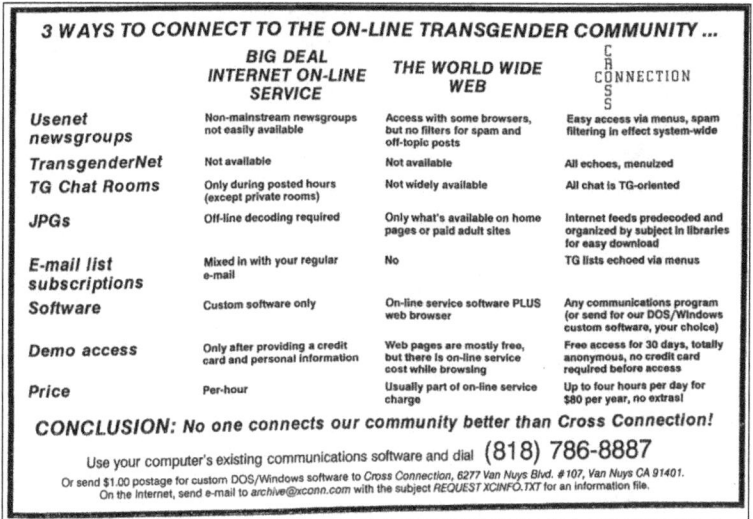

Figure 5.1. As the Internet overtook BBSes in popularity, prominent BBSes sought different ways to adapt, such as emphasizing their specificity and user-friendliness, as in this advertisement for the Cross Connection BBS service from the August 1996 issue of *Cross-Talk*. From *Cross-Talk: The Gender Community's News & Information Monthly* #82, courtesy of the Digital Transgender Archive.

that Cross Connections couldn't compete with the scope of the World Wide Web, sysop Kymberleigh Richards (who had inherited the board from the previous sysop) began in 1996 to market the board it as a gender community-specific "alternative" to big ISPs. These ads (fig. 5.1) emphasized the BBS's niche-specific qualities, all as evidence of the ad's final conclusion: "No one connects our community better than Cross Connection!" Richards' choice to break out the World Wide Web and "Internet On-Line Service" into comparative columns, though, obscured the BBS's limitations as a format. The BBS just couldn't offer the same interactive visual and aesthetic experience as a web page coded in HTML. Moreover, many BBSes were ill suited to offer always-on Internet access, which required a significant infrastructure investment.

However, such efforts came too little, too late for Cross Connections—particularly once popular services like AOL had switched to flat-fee pricing. By July 1997, both *Cross-Talk* and Cross Connections would shutter.

In her open letter to the community, posted to various transgender-specific Usenet groups (republished in the September 1997 issue of *Renaissance News & Views*), Richards questioned if transgender individuals could even be called a "community." In her view, "an attitude of selfishness" was destroying the "mutual support infrastructure" she and others had "worked very hard to create for you." She imagined a nightmare scenario where, due to lack of financial support and political will, transgender individuals "find ourselves thrust 40 years into our past," with no one to advocate for them. Richards ended her missive: "At least for me, the battle is over. For the rest of you, it is likely just beginning. Good luck to you all. You'll need it."[24] Like Richards, small and regional group leaders worried that their organizations, which already struggled with membership, would face even more difficulty recruiting and retaining members as a direct result of the Internet.[25] Given social disapproval of cross-gender interests and activities, meeting attendance could fluctuate widely, since members could not always safely set aside time to attend meetings. Group duties, therefore, tended to fall disproportionately on those who could regularly participate, which could in turn contribute to member turnover and burnout. Moreover, recruiting new members via postal mail and hotline inquiries required persuading individuals that the reward of group participation was greater than the perceived risk of meeting attendance. Meeting online, in contrast, significantly reduced the level of risk, while still offering some of the same rewards. In a 2001 editorial, JoAnn Roberts blamed the Internet for the decline in national organization membership, since "many t-people no longer feel they need to attend real meetings because they have virtual meetings online." But this emphasis on digital spaces meant that "in the year 2001, on the edge of a new year, a new century, and a new millennium, the transgender community is without focus and without leadership."[26] In response, organizations emphasized their importance as sources of safe, in-person meeting spaces. In their newsletter, leaders within the Central Illinois Gender Association blamed the group's declining membership on the "magic meeting place of chat rooms and e-mail," where prospective members did not face the "risk" of meeting face-to-face.[27] In a similar vein, a 1997 letter (republished in the newsletter for the Alpha Rho chapter of Tri-Ess) by Jayne Cresap, vice president of the Los Angeles–based Alpha chapter, described how the chapter's primary offerings for newly out cross-dresses, such as resources, shopping information, and social support, had largely been supplanted by the Internet. Yet, for those individuals who dismissed support groups as unnecessary, Cresap warned that their current sense of acceptance could vanish should "the cyberpolice deem us unfit for the internet," leaving organizations like the Alpha chapter as their only outlet. Instead of letting the group languish, Cresap argued that readers should focus their energy on modernizing organizations, for "the Net can't replace the support group."[28]

Linda Phillips, a longtime leader (alongside her wife, Cynthia) of Boulton & Park, the oldest cross-dressers' organization in San Antonio, Texas, was the most prominent figure to adopt this stance. The Phillipses had a long history within the community, regularly appeared on the television talk show circuit, served terms on the boards of IFGE and Tri-Ess, maintained an extensive newsletter exchange network, and were heavily involved in several major community events, including the Texas T-Party and SPICE (Spouses/Partners International Conference of Education). Phillips herself identified as the "new breed" of cross-dresser, a transgendered woman who lived full time as the opposite gender but did not desire any form of bodily modification beyond hormone treatment. In Boulton & Park's newsletter, *Gender Euphoria*, she frequently expressed her opinion of how digital communications were changing the community. An initial 1989 column spoke positively of their possibilities, comparing Phillips' conversations with cross-dressers online to the face-to-face encounters she had at the T-Party.[29] More often than not, however, Boulton & Park's digital communications, such as the BBS they maintained throughout 1993, were primarily created and run by other members.

By the mid-1990s, Phillips had grown more skeptical that computer communications could help individuals come out and become active community members. Part of her critique focused on how computer communication inclined users to remain in a "fantasy" world online, instead of using as a stepping-stone to living as a "real woman."[30] Whereas, prior to the Internet, individuals could only imagine their fantasies via fiction or calling the Boulton & Park helpline, now they could live them out online.[31] Yet, to Phillips, claiming a transgendered identity required that one live out this identity in physical spaces with other people, if only part time. This dichotomy is clear in Phillips's response to a letter writer who reached out after reading an interview with her. In her letter, the writer identified Phillips as a role model for her own cross-gender desires and then described her "mind blowing" experiences presenting as a bisexual woman on an adult BBS. In her response, Phillips emphasized that she, unlike the writer, did not live in "fantasy" but was a "real" woman in her day-to-day life. As she saw it, "actually 'real' women, which is what I consider myself, have no time for fantasy play on a machine. Why not get out into the real world and experience the things you only dream about?"[32] She regularly expressed this view in her columns for *Gender Euphoria* and used her position as a newsletter editor to reprint columns from other publications questioning the Internet's value for the gender community.[33]

Like Cresap, Phillips foresaw computer communication rapidly replacing the core functions of support groups, the newsletter in particular. A dedicated reader, she worried that newsletters would be "eaten" by the "bane of the sub-group, the Internet."[34] Moreover, Phillips believed the anonymity of the Internet allowed individuals to spread misinformation. Compared to the newsletter, she considered the Internet full of false facts about medical topics, from the reality of hormone treatments to the necessity of SRS. Writing in 1997 under the pseudonym Ms. High Heels, she argued that a "happy well adjusted" transgendered person did not "[spend] her time typing out advice to the transgendered every night."[35] Though Boulton & Park's web mistress would become a regular contributor to *Gender Euphoria* in 1997, she emphasized the Internet as a supplement, not a replacement, for group participation and newsletter subscription. As she wrote in 1998, the Internet had been "both a blessing and a curse for the transgendered community," simultaneously spreading both legitimate information and sensationalism, with little recourse to counter the latter's attention-grabbing "freak show atmosphere."[36] In 1999, Linda and Cynthia Phillips cited Boulton & Park's declining active membership as a key factor in their initial decision not to host their annual Texas T Party. In a column discussing this choice, Linda noted that Bouton & Park appeared to be "going to go the way of the dodo bird" and noted that "the outlook for Genderland and its many support groups is somewhat bleak, we hope things will improve, but we predict a long slow slide into the murky depths for this strangest of America's help groups."[37]

The next issue of the newsletter was ultimately to be their last. In it, Phillips blamed the Internet for the demise of *Gender Euphoria* newsletter and identified it as part of a larger pattern of extinction: "We have fallen victim to the bane of Genderworld, *the Internet*. We never thought it would end the way it has, but when over a year goes by without a new subscription, it is time to leave gracefully. . . . Every time we get another group's newsletter, we read the distressing news of not enough members at meetings, not enough input for the newsletter, etc."[38] Even as she mourned *Gender Euphoria*'s dissolution, Phillips recognized that the Genderworld she so often wrote about was changing around her, most of which she used her final newsletter to directly oppose. In her front-page editorial, she discussed her own discomfort with emergence of the LGBT initialism, which, she argued, disenfranchised heterosexual-identified cross-dressers, and the increasing emphasis within the community on coming out and refusing to pass.[39] Inside, she devoted an entire column to defending Virginia Prince's role in the creation of the term "transgendered" against those individuals who had, in her words, "decided to steal 'transgendered' as an umbrella term for the 'T community.'" Even despite Prince's importance, Phillips noted that those asking online about the term's origin didn't truly care about Prince's role; not only were they part of "the only special interest group in America which has a living founder," but they also belonged to "the only group who doesn't care." For Phillips, all of these changes had been a "sobering experience," as she watched herself "become obsolete in [her] own lifetime."[40]

Yet what Phillips interpreted as an endemic incuriosity and dismissal of her generation's perspective, others understood as an important evolution for the community. In a 2000 column, Gwendolyn Ann Smith argued that the community must embrace digital technology's possibilities or risk being left behind, for "the community that stands still is actually moving backwards." As an example, she compared her own experience seeking information after she came out with the contemporary moment: "When I initially started looking for information on transgenderism, there was precious little to find. It took a great amount of searching to go from having not the slightest inkling there was information out there to attending my first transgender support group. Today anyone can, with a few keystrokes, find information on any number of trans-related topics and hook up with others who travel similar paths. Thanks to this technology, a new generation of transpeople are finding information faster and are able to act on it at a younger age."[41] However, this new generation faced their own challenges in finding their place, if any, within the growing transgender community.

Youth Issues

Though rarely visible, gender nonconforming youth have long sought a place within gay and lesbian spaces, as well as the gender community. As historian Jules Gill-Peterson has chronicled in *Histories of the Transgender Child*, many youth reached out to Harry Benjamin to inquire about the possibilities for treatment, though Benjamin and other colleagues at his practice were largely dismissive of their efforts. Some of these youth were able to connect as pen pals, finding a sympathetic ear from peers in similar situations.[42] At the same time as they were writing to Benjamin, queer and trans street youth in San Francisco's Tenderloin district were mobilizing to form Vanguard, the first queer and trans youth organization in the United States, as well as publishing a magazine of the same name.[43] While Benjamin's relationship with trans youth was marked by medical paternalism, gender community organizations were caught between knowledge of their own histories and the perceived legal risks of youth outreach. For many transsexual individuals and cross-dressers, "inappropriate" cross-gender interests while young held a prominent place in their self-narratives. However, in their discussions of trans childhood, both medical professionals and some gender community members focused on considering how trans children and youths' cross-gender desires might be used to find an "explanation" for transness. A happy trans childhood, where one's cross-gender desires could be freely explored, appeared unthinkable.[44] By the mid-1990s, gender community groups theoretically had the ability to offer youth support, but many groups feared legal challenges from parents should they admit minors to their meetings, leading some to set strict restrictions on their attendance. For example, the Mu Sigma chapter of Tri-Ess, based in Jonesboro, Arkansas, required any minor who wished to join the group to get written and notarized permission from a custodial parent, who would be required to attend meetings with their child.[45] In a 1994 editorial "What about Teenaged Transgendered?," Kymberleigh Richards mused on what community groups primarily oriented toward middle-class adults could possibly offer teens. Though she considered the possibility of having professionals refer teens to her or to other community leaders for informal phone counseling, something she'd done independently, she worried that this method wouldn't be feasible without active professional oversight, lest the call become a "potentially dangerous situation" for the community member if the teen's parents felt the informal counselor was "contributing to the delinquency of a minor." In the end, Richards concluded that she "honestly [didn't] know" if there was anything organizations could do for youth and admitted she "[wouldn't] sleep well with that admission."[46]

In 1989, Sheila Kirk, long-time board member, board-certified OB-GYN, and medical consultant for IFGE, launched a longitudinal study of teenage cross-dressing, primarily through corresponding with teenagers ages twelve through nineteen and their parents, and placed an announcement in *Tapestry* asking readers to refer possible participants to her. Given the social shame surrounding cross-dressing, Kirk hoped study participation would "pacify and instruct both young crossdressers and their parents" and allow her to "work cooperatively with their counselors" to recommend more inclusive therapeutic approaches. Kirk was also careful to emphasize that all possible participants must have parental consent for the study to be valid, as well as in light of "the legal concerns that could arise."[47] But permission was not a guarantee that participants would remain in contact. In a 1996 article, Kirk reported that, while she had made some progress remaining in contact with participants, she had faced not insignificant challenges ranging from disapproving counselors, legal issues, and concerns about participant privacy, leading to "some 30 instances where parents have halted the informational exchange because they perceived a threat and/or insecurity."[48] Despite these issues, Kirk had found that her "real problem" was simply finding participants. Despite regular requests placed in both *Tapestry* and the IFGE newsletter, they had "yielded only an occasional referral." Kirk, like Richards, surmised that this lack resulted from the concern around parental approval: "Regrettably, we receive calls here at IFGE from teenagers who do not have parental consent and they cannot continue contact with us for that reason. There is no doubt that this happens more than occasionally with support groups nationwide, and understandably they are very reluctant to talk with and inform their teenage callers because of the potential legal consequences. The callers are frustrated and lost, and the individuals receiving the calls are equally troubled."[49]

The only positive, in Kirk's estimation, was for teens who early on adamantly claimed a transsexual identity, as they had a clear set of procedures and resources they could access.[50] Even when groups were open to hosting youth, they were aware that the age gap might present issues. In a 1996 column, Tennessee Vals president Marisa Richmond assured all theoretical "computer literate" teens reading their newsletter online that, while they may "prefer to interact with people their own age rather than with a bunch of gray hairs," the Vals "do understand the loneliness of being a transgendered teen." She assured her readers that "not only are you welcome to join us, but if you would prefer to be around others your own age," she could provide additional information on youth support groups who were open to trans youth.[51]

In their writing, both Richards and Richmond identify one possible bright spot for trans youth: the Internet. Examples of trans youth using digital platforms to learn more and find support existed as early as 1989, and they were an irregular presence within established trans spaces online.[52] By the mid-1990s, more and more LGBTQ youth in general were gaining Internet access, either at home or through their schools. Some of them could be quite circuitous: one queer youth described "borrow[ing] the principal's modem to jack into a beekeepers BBS and gopher his way to the Queer Resources Directory."[53] Many more used whatever popular commercial service their parents subscribed to, most often AOL. Like their adult counterparts, this change opened a variety of new avenues for information access and collective organizing. In a 1994 *Wired* article on queer youth online, journalist Steve Silberman compared the contemporary information landscape to the prior decade, when "the only queer info available to most teens was in a few dour psychology texts under the nose of the school librarian." Now, however, "libraries of files await them in the AOL forum and elsewhere—the Queer Resources Directory alone contains hundreds—and teens can join mailing lists like Queercampus and GayNet, or tap resources like the Bridges Project, a referral service that tells teens not only how to get in touch with queer youth groups, but how to jump-start one themselves."⁵⁴

The peer-to-peer contact and support these spaces offered became an essential resource for many LGBTQ youth, particularly those who didn't live in a metropolitan area with an established youth organization. As part of their case opposing the Communications Decency Act, the ACLU included affidavits from three queer youth—sixteen-year-old Rheana Parrenas, seventeen-year-old Hunter Allen, and eighteen-year-old Christine Soto—who were involved in YouthArts, an Internet-based arts workshop for LGBTQ youth. In her affidavit, Parrenas noted that access to the teen and people of color conferences in AOL's Gay and Lesbian Community Forum "reinforced the idea that I was not alone." Though there was only a small group of regular users, these spaces allowed them to build queer community, especially if they, like Parrenas, lived far from metropolitan areas.⁵⁵ According to her, Internet access "diminish[ed] the distance between users and organizations, capable of bringing the institution to one's home."⁵⁶ Allen said that the "only connection [he'd] ever made" with other gay youth "was through America Online." When he encountered gay spaces on AOL, "it was like discovering a whole new world. Every night for a week I would disappear into my room at night and listen on to the gay and lesbian chat lines, just watching other people's interactions, too nervous and scared to say anything myself." Eventually, he became pen pals over email with another teen, which allowed him to reach out beyond his "isolated world in Mountain View [California]" and "share my true self with a peer who could understand what I was going through."⁵⁷ Soto also framed the importance of youth spaces online in terms of peer role modeling, as online spaces gave users "the opportunity to look at other teens doing something positive." For her friends who struggled with "frustration, depression, and unhappiness," being able to access programs like YouthArts online could help them "use their own creativity to let out their emotions."⁵⁸

Some of the youth who might benefit from Internet access, however, faced stiff resistance from parents concerned about just what kinds of information they might find. The cyberporn technopanic of the mid-1990s, discussed in chapter 4, colored parental attitudes to youth Internet use. Media coverage largely centered on the threat pedophiles posed to presumably naive and vulnerable teens, particularly for LGBTQ youth. For many years, AOL infamously did not allow members to create chat rooms that included any combination of the words "gay," "teen," and "youth," and drew clear distinctions between "male" and "man."[59] In response to an inquiry by author David Batterson, published in a 1994 issue of *Computer Underground Digest*, an AOL Terms of Service adviser noted that it was company policy to convert any room whose title "could possibly be construed as sexual" from public to private. Thus, the chatroom title "Yng M 4 Yng M" would be made private, because, according to the adviser, the "ambiguous" M in the title "could mean 'male', hence underage male." Yng Men 4 Yng Men, in contrast, would remain public, since it "specifically states that the occupants seek to meet adults."[60] Some concerned users even protested allowing any discussion of gay or lesbian topics in existing approved teen chat rooms, arguing that allowing these discussions made them a "hunting ground for pedophiles," prompting GLAAD to organize users in counterprotest.[61]

Youth often pushed back at these characterizations by asserting their own agency. In Silberman's article, users described a variety of self-protection methods, including blocking predatory users and logging off IM to deter attention. As one anonymous user put it in a petition for AOL-approved gay teen chat rooms: "We are not defenseless, nor innocent."[62] Moreover, this user also wasn't convinced an approved "Youth onQ" section—which onQ had internally discussed but never followed up on—would be particularly effective.[63] In his view, such an "adult-centered approach" didn't "recognize the fact that most teenagers, sexually explorative or not, are uncomfortable by any adult presence." In his experience, "if teens know that an adult is present, we will IM (Instant Message) each other, and go to a private room." At times, trans adults expressed skepticism about the viability of youth-created fora. Though Richards applauded the idea of trans youth seeking out support online, she characterized a sixteen-year old Chicago-based crossdresser's efforts to create a youth-specific mailing list as "the equivalent of the old saying 'the blind leading the blind'"—a characterization that reinforced existing cultural narratives around youth inexperience and self-determination.[64]

Richards's dismissal notwithstanding, youth-run spaces thrived online. Youth users could access resources and fora supported by youth-led nonprofits like the Youth Assistance Organization (YAO, later Youth

Action Online) or Youth Guardian Services (YGS), or build and share information on their own sites; youth-oriented webrings were among the largest LGBT-specific rings at the height of the format's popularity. The relative ease of publishing online also fueled a small boom in queer youth publications, including *YouthArts, Blair!, elight, insideout,* and *Oasis*.[65] One of longest-running youth-founded spaces was soc.support.youth.gay-lesbian-bi (ssyglb), a moderated Usenet newsgroup founded in 1994. The group's charter emphasized its focus on providing a space where "young people [could] express their feelings and comfort others, and for adults to offer advice and friendship to youths." In fact, ssyglb's initial moderators met through their work at San Francisco's queer youth center, LYRIC, and, throughout its lifetime, it continued to be consistently moderated by individuals under thirty.[66] Trans youth were also welcome on ssyglb, but technical constraints related to newsgroup name length kept "trans" out of its name. In a similar vein, while trans youth were not restricted from the teen conference on GLCF, they didn't seem to have a significant presence.[67] While nonyouth did participate in discussion on ssyglb, youth primarily conversed with and about each other, "[gaining] strength, confidence, and a greater sense of well-being" from these interactions.[68]

Many of these sites and organizations included special sections specifically for trans youth, maintained by youth staff or volunteers. Alternately, youth created their own resources, in some cases specifically citing the lack of "mainstream" youth-focused trans resources as inspiration.[69] Unlike mainstream publications, these sites centered the voices and experiences of trans youth, from discussions of coming out in high school to navigating transition while a minor. The home page was a particularly important platform for trans youth, who used it to come out, claim a transgender identity, and make connections with other trans youth. Given the relatively rapid change in preferred platforms online, they also form one of the few still-accessible archives of youth communication online. Thus, while not all youth had home pages, those that were archived provide a rich source of insight into their perspectives during this period. The Transgendered Teens Web Directory, created in 1998 and last archived in 2002, included links, home pages, and email addresses for youth from thirty-two different states. They contained a variety of information, including advice on coming out, navigating being out in high school, and pursuing medical transition as a teen.

In some cases, pages included creator photographs, allowing readers to visualize what had seemed, to Richards, an impossible category. Many youth kept diaries online, describing their personal and social struggles and triumphs, and discussing their own relationships with gender identity, presentation, and what it meant to be "transgender." On his site, Dylan Jared self-identified against the dominant mode of FTM, instead stating that he did not identify as a "transsexual" but as an "intersex" individual because he viewed his experience as not "a psychological situation of one thing switching to another; instead, it is a medical mismatch of genitals and brain: something I consider unresearched as an intersexual condition." He also identified against dominant hegemonic masculine norms as "the epitome of boiwife," who loves "to cook, clean and keep things organized for daddy-types who falsely think they can take care of themselves." Through their home pages, youth could connect and build support networks otherwise inaccessible. For example, transgender teen Sarah's diary, which ran from 1997 to 2001, included repeated references to her ongoing email communication with a variety of other trans teens online, who helped her navigate her self-identity, come out to her parents, and build connections within the community. Some youth also used their home pages to share their coming-out letters to their parents, or even as the primary venue for their coming out. Sarah not only posted her coming out letters to her home page; she also changed her home computer's landing page to her letter pages, ensuring that her letters were the first thing her parents would read when they went online. In other cases, some were outed by their home pages. Fourteen-year-old Jennifer described how, after her mom walked in on her and read her home page as she slept, was now under "martial law." At the bottom of her page, she added an addendum: "MOM, IF YOU'RE READING THIS, LET ME BE WHO I WANT TO BE!" Several teens outed by their pages reported having their computer and Internet access severely restricted—a reminder of their limited autonomy in the era of the shared family computer, which, for many, was their primary mode of getting online.

Trans youth also recognized their sites' impact on readers, and many made a point to note that their sites were by teens for teens. For Dylan

Jared, one of the key inspirations in making his home page, he said, was his belief that "it's important for other trans/intersexed kids to be able to run across people like themselves. I always find myself wanting to look at pictures and read journals written by fellow gender-variant teens, so I am going to try to produce the same sort of thing I fancy stumbling upon. I'm also keeping up these pages because I think it helps a person to share some of himself with the world, even if it's only via internet." In their writings, youth showed that they were not "the blind leading the blind," as Richards had asserted, but seeing the world from a new perspective, exploring their identities and building their own support networks outside of existing infrastructure.

Making Institutional Connections

Over time, youth-led LGBT groups developed relationships with older, well-established nonprofits like the National Gay and Lesbian Task Force. For many years, YAO hosted the home page for the NGLTF's Youth Institute, which was begun as a way for the organization to "recognize young organizers and activists as leaders in their own right and to offer young people the opportunity to learn the skills necessary to create change."[70] In a similar vein, YGS for many years hosted the home page for T-NET, the trans-specific mailing list and network within PFLAG. Established transgender organizations, however, initially emphasized approaches that maintained the organizations' existing distance from youth themselves. In the fall of 1996, IFGE created a formal youth outreach committee, chaired by Kirk, which focused on pairing with and providing resources to existing youth-serving organizations.[71] Outside of such coordinated outreach, many other transgender organizations simply referred inquiring youth to PFLAG, who'd fully incorporated gender identity into its mission by 1998 and offered a pamphlet, *Our Trans Children*, coauthored by Jessica Xavier, then-director of AEGIS.[72]

At the same time, LGBT youth organizations were increasingly offering support groups and services specifically for trans youth, with limited to no input from transgender-focused organizations. Trans-Youth Services (TYS), a Philadelphia-based peer support group specifically for Black trans youth founded in 1996, was associated not with a major transgender organization, but with Unity, Inc., which focused on the needs of Black gay men.[73] While TYS did reach out to both IFGE and Renaissance, it's unclear what either group offered beyond, in IFGE's case, a pledge of support.[74] In her final column as outgoing director of AEGIS, published in April 1998, Jessica Xavier noted that, whereas transgender organizations lacked the funds to support comprehensive transgender community services, LGBT groups could quickly step into the gap. She cited the experience of Atlanta Gender Explorations—"a stable organization nearly ten years old"—who approached the local gay and lesbian youth organization OutPride, with the idea of creating a trans youth group. While AGE engaged in the slow process of deliberations about founding a group, OutPride "just did it," without any support from or affiliation with Atlanta's wider transgender community. To Xavier, this move was one more sign that the transgender community risked "dilution" by allying with LGB groups. She asked her readers, "Where do you [suppose] the members' allegiance will lie?"[75]

Yet I would argue that such allegiance, in retrospect, might not be entirely surprising, given some prevalent community attitudes toward trans youth. In 2000, a group of transgender individuals founded the Transgender Fund, a national charitable foundation focused on supporting the interests of the broader community. Later that year, fund chair Diane Dale announced their first initiative in a full-page advertisement in *LadyLike*: the Trans-Youth Select Initiative. Following an "informal assessment of our Community's attention" to youth, the trustees came to the conclusion that the community was "only in the very early stages of establishing practical resources specifically geared for these children."[76] LGBT agencies did offer support, but trustees characterized it as supplementary to their core focus. Trustees also found that the mentors available to facilitate trans youth support groups often had "so many overwhelming, unresolved personal issues that they are not well-suited for the task," citing as an example a group facilitated by "two active street workers," who, it is implied, cannot by the very nature of their lives offer a vision of a positive future for "highly vulnerable" trans youth.[77] Dale makes a point to note that issues of substance abuse and familial rejection are not limited to "urban trans-youth" but cut across "socio-economic layers"—though just who counted as "urban" was left unspoken. Based on this assessment, they conclude that "if there ever was a forgotten generation, it is today's transgender youth." The Fund, then, aimed to make 2001 "the Year of Our Transgender Children" by both offering direct support to "stabilize" youths' lives and "help them develop into viable human beings" and pursuing community outreach to reduce discrimination.[78] However, based on the archival record, such increased organizational attention and support for youth did not frequently appear to translate into empowerment within these organizations themselves. The fund's focus on developing trans youth into "viable human beings" offers a marked contrast from the NGLTF's Youth Initiative's conception of LGB youth as "leaders in their own right." Although offering youth support was key to their success, the fund and other organizations' characterization of youth emphasized their vulnerability and risk, not their potential to serve as leaders within the community.

A 2001 letter to *Tapestry* brought this contrast into stark relief. In it, twenty-two-year-old Krista asked if *Tapestry* has "any content that the young, information-hungry transexual boys and girls would find palatable," as her initial research revealed the magazine to be "geared towards the older crowd." While she'd previously used a trans-specific youth forum online, its closure had left her with "no place to go, and really nothing to look at for information."[79] In her response, editor Dallas Denny recognized that local support group membership was often predominated by "middle-aged non-transitioned MTFs," what a trans youth she'd met termed "Old Trans-Dudes." While these members were happy to help youth, younger attendees "often feel little in common with them" and preferred "youth-only groups." Denny suggested that Krista instead use her "Internet skills" to connect with organizations like PFLAG; Gay, Lesbian, and Straight Education Network (GLSEN); and the National Gay and Lesbian Task Force (NGLTF). Yet, in her response, Denny not only failed to include already established trans youth resources, but she also assumed Krista's priority to be finding an offline support group: the predigital model. Moreover, Denny's choice to recommend large, well-known LGBT groups carried an unstated implication: existing national-level transgender organizations couldn't provide what Krista sought because they were unprepared to serve or support youth not classified as at-risk.[80]

Tapestry would not feature content by trans youth until 2002, when it ran two short narratives by two Seattle-based trans youth activists discussing their experiences as transbois, and in the case of one author, a transboi of color.[81] Youth authors and concepts would be increasingly visible in *Tapestry* in the following years, but they were often marked as specific to youth and distinct from the trans mainstream. GEA's educational pamphlet *Gender Variance: A Primer* (republished in a 2003 special issue of *Tapestry* entitled, "Gender Education 101"), noted in their section on identities that "many transgendered youth prefer the term Gender Queer to describe themselves."[82] In practice, this characterization also recentered gender binaries as the dominant understanding for gender within the community, leading some youth to wonder if identifying as genderqueer meant they "weren't trans enough."[83]

These worries reflected wider changes within American trans institutional politics. At the same time as youth were founding their own platforms in the mid-1990s, a new style of transgender politics was emerging that emphasized more radical, direct-action activism, embodied in the organizations the Transexual (later Transgender) Menace and Transgender Nation. Founded by Riki Anne Wilchins and Denise Norris, TS Menace initially organized protests following Brandon Teena's 1993 murder and continued to mobilize to protest transphobic violence throughout the United States. Transgender Nation, begun as a caucus within Queer Nation, positioned "transgender" as an "explicitly" queer concept that had a place within radical politics. Though Transgender Nation would only be active from 1992 to 1994, during their existence they engaged in a variety of highly visible activism, including a 1993 protest of the annual meeting of the American Psychiatric Association.[84] The contrast between established transgender organizations' approach and newer activists' increased focus on queer politics came to a head in 2000 with the rebranding of the Gender Public Advocacy Coalition, otherwise known as GenderPAC. When founded in 1995, the organization was directed by Riki Wilchins, supported by a board drawn from a variety of major existing trans organizations, including AEGIS, IFGE, Renaissance Education Association, Tri-Ess, ICTLEP, and the Congress of Transgender Organizations. Much of GenderPAC's early energy was focused around lobbying the federal government on issues such as hate crimes legislation and the Employment Nondiscrimination Act (ENDA). Over time, GenderPAC became the "the de facto voice for transgender politics."[85] When the organization rebranded in 2000 to a broader "gender rights" focus, as opposed to being transgender-specific, the move sparked protest and multiple board resignations from long-time trans activists. While the change reflected Wilchins's own interest in breaking down gender binaries, activists argued that, in practice, it decentered the trans individuals most affected by gender-based discrimination in favor of gender-related "issues."[86]

However, the rebranding had a secondary effect: it created room for youth within the movement. As part of the change, GenderPAC launched a robust youth outreach program, GenderYOUTH, including scholarships to attend their national gender conference, offering Wilchins as a featured campus speaker, and a youth-specific college branch, GenderROOTS.[87] The first annual conference was, according to two attendees, "'full of college students expressing their gender in ways you can't even imagine' but not necessarily identifying with the term *transgender* or any identity labels," and "maybe less than 10% of the people there are what would be called 'traditionally transgender people.'" According to them, the presence of youth brought a new energy to the event, as compared to other trans conferences.[88] For these attendees, this new GenderPAC presumably offered them a place at the table that "transgender" did not. Given the loss of support from established trans organizations, it seems likely GenderPAC saw youth activists as an untapped source of on-the-ground activism and support. This was born out in the first two GenderPAC conferences and lobby days, whose attendees were, according to ethnographer Megan Davidson, "young, overwhelmingly White, raised middle-class, and born female-bodied."[89] Yet, as with their non youth-specific materials, while GenderYOUTH's promotional materials emphasized the issue of gender-based discrimination, they offered no materials that directly spoke to how gender nonconforming youth—the assumed target audience—might be empowered to embrace their identities.

Although GenderPAC implicitly branded themselves as more youth-friendly, by the mid-2000s gender nonconforming and trans youth had become a visible presence both online and at trans conferences and events.[90] Issues facing trans youth and their families were a major theme of IFGE's annual conference in 2004, though attendees still worried about the "ethical issues involved with having children at our conferences and particularly with them giving presentations."[91] Youth-focused nonprofits, such as San Francisco's Youth Gender Project (later Youth Trans and Intersex Education Services, YouthTIES), hosted youth-specific conferences like Gender Blast.[92] What had once seemed to some an impossible category too dangerous to openly acknowledge was now an active community in its own right.

Changing Generations

By the year 2010, the gender community—now firmly the transgender community—had certainly changed, but not entirely in the ways Johnson had anticipated. Tri-Ess experienced major difficulties throughout the 1990s and 2000s adapting to the changing times, but chapters did remain active, even if their membership increasingly skewed older. IFGE, in contrast, was no longer nearly as active, not because of increased acceptance of transgender individuals but changing management and depleted funds.[93] Groups not yet in their infancy in 1990, like GenderPAC, had already opened and closed shop.[94] While the cross-dresser was not yet "assimilated into the mainstream of society," cultural attitudes around gender identity and performance had undergone notable changes. Gender nonconformity, while always present within trans spaces, now had its own distinct umbrella category: "genderqueer."

The most significant change, however, was one that Johnson could not have foreseen: the decline of the trans clubs she considered so vital to achieving "the euphoria of 2010" and the accompanying rise of the Internet. While clubs have continued to be active, some groups' membership has increasingly skewed older. In a 2018 profile of the Chicago Gender Society (CGS), author Rowan Lynam reported that most members were "in their 60s and 70s," which members chalked up to both generational change and the Internet. Many CGS members, according to past CGS president Nicole Richmond, had only recently come out after a very different life trajectory: "Our families are developed, our children are grown, and we're entering retirement. It's time to be yourself."[95] The gap Richmond described was reflected in interviews I conducted in 2014 with trans individuals, many of whom were under thirty. Few of them reported attending formal transgender-related support groups, and all of them that did attend them found them lacking to differing degrees. Several individuals described groups dominated by older trans women whose life and transition experiences didn't match their own. One participant, who had been using digital communications since the early 1990s, had tried and failed several times to actively participate in local support groups, which, according to her, were consistently facing issues with growth and sustainability. For her, attending in-person meetings "just doesn't seem to resonate," which she suspected was "a generational thing." At an in-person meeting, she remarked on these generational issues: "This woman probably in her fifties, I wanta say, said, 'Well, that's you young kids. You don't need groups, you don't need us. You have online.' And I kind of nodded my head, sort of agreeing. It's like, yeah! I don't need the basement of the Unitarian church here. I'm fine."

Her experiences illuminate another generational difference: not only did she see group members' concerns as irrelevant to her personal experience, but the very format of an in-person weekly support group wasn't among her usual methods for seeking peer support, which were primarily online. Yet, even online, a generational divide became increasingly apparent in *where* trans individuals were seeking out community in the mid-to-late 2000s. If you were reading *Tapestry*, *LadyLike*, and other publications, the trans Internet would seem to be largely confined to standalone websites like TGForum or Susan's Place (as discussed in chapter 4), mailing lists, or IRC Channels like #tgcafe. Certainly, the editors and publishers of both magazines were by no means Internet skeptics, unlike some older trans individuals—a reader letter in a 2007 issue of *LadyLike* damningly contrasts the safety of print publications with the unsafe wilds of the Internet—but, by the early 2000s, popular modes of socializing online were shifting away from independent websites toward social platforms that in their design and branding emphasized personalization, participation, and sharing.[96] As noted in chapter 2, this shift was a key factor in the demise of Gay.com and the Transgender Gazebo. In spite of social platforms' growing prominence, there are few references, either in articles or reader letters, to contemporaneous sites like LiveJournal, Yahoo Groups, MySpace, or Facebook. LiveJournal (hereafter LJ) in particular was one of the most popular and active spaces for trans youth in the 2000s, at times replacing their existing home pages. Several trans youth whose sites were indexed in the Transgendered Teens Web Directory would move most of their social activity there, including their diaries. On LJ, users could maintain their own journals as well as participate in topic-specific, member-created groups, combining the individualized focus of the home page with the shared community space of the message board or mailing list. Relationships were framed in terms of "friends," but "friending" did not guarantee access to all of a user's posts. LJ had highly granular privacy settings, which allowed users not only to control post visibility for public, private, and friends, but also to create a variety of different filters for content—a particularly appealing affordance for trans users, who might not be out to all individuals in their various social circles.[97]

Fusing these two formats—individualized home page with the shared community space—had a profound effect on many existing communities with a sizable online presence, the best documented being English-language media fandom. Within fandom, the move to LJ "served to take the focus off the source [of one's fandom]," often the core topic of the mailing list, "and put it on the fan, and in turn, on fandom."[98] In a similar vein, trans users were able to maintain separate, individualized journals, where their trans identity formed one part of their self-identity, while also belonging to dedicated groups for discussing queer and trans-specific topics. In her work on the LJ community birls (a portmanteau of "boy" and "girls"), self-described as "a community dedicated to boyish/androgynous girls" also open to adjacently trans-identified individuals, media scholar Susan Driver notes that the community "creates coherence through an ability to dialogue, interpret, and personalize meanings" in individual users' posts.[99] Photo sharing formed a key point of connection, an opportunity for members to support each other through praise and compliments, which could also take on an eroticized quality. Such recognition of shared erotic desire also formed "an ongoing dynamic of community involvement, acting in performative ways to create a shared sense of their desirability as birls."[100] In this way, while gender remained an important topic of discussion, the primary focus of most posts to birls was the poster themselves.[101] There was also no standardized definition of a birl, however, and Driver argues that "naming oneself a birl is a celebrated act that encourages others to join in and get involved in the inventive development of self-presentation and interaction between birls."[102] LJ's affordances further ensured the community remained a relatively enclosed and safe space for collective dialogue and exploration. A single user post could not be automatically cross-posted across LJ communities—cross-posting required manual duplication of a post in each target community—and members had a granular level of control over who could see their posts, including indexing by search engines. Thus, nonmembers who were not actively seeking out a community may have had few opportunities to be exposed to that community's content.

Yet, by 2007, the kinds of participatory media valued and emphasized in public discourse were changing. "Blogging," which is what LJ was most often associated with (particularly after being acquired by Six Apart in 2005, who owned early WordPress competitor TypePad, later Moveable Type), was losing ground to "social networking," exemplified at the time by MySpace and Facebook. In a 2007 Associated Press piece on Six Apart's sale of LJ to Russian media firm SUP, business reporter Michael Liedtke made it a point to note that while LJ was increasingly popular in Russia, it was "facing a stiffer challenge in the United States" in comparison to contemporaneous social networks sites: "3.9 million U.S. visitors" in October 2007, in comparison to "72 million for MySpace and 32.9 million for Facebook."[103] In some ways, what LJ offered its users was not all that different from sites branded as "social networks": the ability to connect with and share content with other users. But LJ (at the time, at least) offered users a far greater degree of control over their user data, privacy, and overall visibility than many of the popular platforms that would follow. According to former staff, however, these same commitments became LJ's downfall. LJ had always struggled to be economically sustainable, and early efforts at monetization were widely resisted. For example, staff attempts to add in-page ads were stymied by past commitments to its userbase to remain ad-free. Staff also mishandled several different efforts to police content that violated the platform's terms of service, which led to user protest and gradual migration to other platforms, like Tumblr. Most importantly, though, LJ's privacy model simply didn't fit in a less private, more data-intensive, online world. For online platforms, affordances like Facebook's news feed "changed the model of privacy in a way [LJ] didn't expect," according to former staffer Abe Hassan. "These sites changed the world, but we didn't try to adapt."[104] In this world, platforms grounded in platform-wide social tagging, algorithmically driven engagement, and ubiquitous user data collection would become the dominant mode of communicating online—a shift that came with significant consequences for trans-identified users and their communities.

6

Transgender in the Platform Era

2008 saw two milestones: first, *Transgender Tapestry* released its final issue, #115, after nearly continuous publication since 1978; and, second, the user base of startup microblogging service Tumblr, founded in 2007, reached (and no doubt quickly surpassed) the half-million mark.[1] *Tapestry*'s end didn't come as a surprise to former editor Dallas Denny. In 1999, IFGE, facing "declining revenues and increasing costs," laid off the existing magazine staff and contracted Denny for both editing and layout.[2] Though Denny would continue to fill this role from 1999 to 2008, pay was intermittent throughout her tenure, due to the organization's failing health, and she would eventually resign over then–IFGE director Denise Leclair's decision to run an article initially rejected by Denny because the author had already published it online. Though two more issues of *Tapestry* (including the final one) would be published without Denny at the helm, in her view it was already clear that "IFGE was doomed."[3] Moreover, *Tapestry* wasn't the only trans-focused publication suffering. *LadyLike*, the flagship magazine of JoAnn Roberts's CDS Publications, ceased publication at the end of 2007 with issue #71. In her final message on the *LadyLike* site, Roberts presented subscribers with a bleak picture. Revenues had been falling for a variety of reasons: declining subscriptions due to the Internet, the ongoing closure of small and large distribution outlets, and a shrinking pool of advertisers willing to bet on print. In the end, printing and shipping the planned January 2008 issue would have cost 50 percent more than last year's January issue, and the funds just weren't there to cover it.[4]

For a startup like Tumblr, however, the money couldn't come fast enough. At the end of 2008, the company had collected $4.5 million in investor funding on the appeal of its core design premise, microblogging: short bits of content, shared quickly and easily with a sprawling network of followers. Early press on Tumblr emphasized its difference from existing social network sites and blogging platforms, in giving users "another way to cut through the Internet din" as well as "actually represent its users on the Web by allowing them to create an identity that Facebook and MySpace and all the other social networking and blogging sites out there can't."⁵ A 2009 *New York Times* blog post described the service as "blissfully easy," so much so that "the less you think about it, the better Tumblr works."⁶ One core element of its "blissful ease" were tags: a post could be tagged in any number of ways, ranging from simple content description (#cat) and community identification (#catlovers or #cats of tumblr) to commentary (#i KNOW shes bad but i love her anyway). Instead of having centralized communities, user posts were connected via their tags, allowing posts and user networks to sprawl across the platform. Over time, these tags become part of a platform-wide folksonomy, which classifies content based on how often and in what context certain tags are applied by users. At around the same time Tumblr was drawing attention for its ease of use, it was also attracting new queer and trans users, who had begun to migrate away from LiveJournal in 2008.⁷ Unlike LiveJournal's more siloed community structure that limited posts' wider visibility, Tumblr posts could easily be encountered and shared with other followers. Tags played a key role in linking not only content but also user communities. For trans users, tagging a post #ftm, #mtf, #nonbinary# or #trans, among many other terms, added searchable keywords linking their posts to others with similar content as well as acted as an identity claim—in effect, "I am a trans person writing about trans things."⁸ By the mid-2010s, Tumblr's trans-friendly atmosphere had begun to draw scholarly and media attention, such as a 2013 Buzzfeed article headlined "Why Tumblr Is Perfect for the Trans Community" that included an interview with well-known trans activist and artist Tourmaline praising the platform for helping her and other trans users build meaningful connections.⁹ By 2021, Tumblr claimed that its users were "193% more likely to identify as part of the LGBTQIA+ community than on *any other social media platform*" (italics in original).¹⁰

In their interviews with trans Tumblr users, Oliver Haimson and his coauthors found that their interviewees appreciated the way Tumblr's pseudonymity allowed them to safely experiment with their gender identity and presentation in a space separate from their other networks, which could provide them with the confidence needed to materialize this identity there. This was particularly important for trans users of color or working-class trans users, who came to Tumblr to connect with others whose experience of transness had been shaped by racism or classism. In addition, Tumblr's emphasis on image sharing gave trans users a platform for visualizing and eroticizing the trans body, including bodies that were often left out of mainstream representation or that failed to meet normative standards of attractiveness: trans bodies of color, disabled trans bodies, or even trans bodies with highly visible scars.[11] According to media scholars Marty Fink and Quinn Miller, as these images collected and mingled with other content, Tumblr formed "a system of simultaneous consumption and production within which pleasures of juxtaposition, repetition, and recurrence are frequent and fastpaced."[12] The open freedom of tagging, which allows users to mix and match tags on a post in any combination, meant that different concepts could intermingle as users connected their transness to non-trans aspects of their identity.[13] In comparison to other nascent social media platforms at the time, Tumblr was by no means unique in its embrace of tags; journal and community-specific tags had also been present on LiveJournal and similar blogging services. However, the increased use of tags came alongside a larger shift toward semantic search, wherein algorithms draw not only on simple word incidence on a given web page but also a variety of other systems and metadata schema, including user folksonomies, to address user queries. Whereas users could initially only use a single tag to search, the feature later expanded to include searching via multiple tags and post content, as well as related blogs and post type filters. The search page reflects the modular logic of the underlying system: each element must be largely self-sufficient while still able to maintain links between elements that can be severed if necessary. By their very nature, metadata schema work best when they remain modular, able to be mixed and matched as needed to meet the needs of a given developer, who can trust that that schema is maintained by a group of subject experts.[14] As users received what seemed to them to be more and more accurate, tailored results, the search engine and its underlying algorithm began to play an increasingly important role as an information source for questioning and newly out trans individuals.

All of these changes represented a profound shift in how trans users experienced the Internet, often in ways that constrained trans users' increasing freedom described in the previous chapters. This chapter, then, shifts its focus to contemporary platforms to explore how two common systems, tagging and search algorithms, systemically transform one of the most important tools for trans self-representation, language, into the fuel powering the contemporary Internet: data. Both systems understand language as, first and foremost, modular data often divorced from the specific, contextual nuance of common use. Moreover, language as data often also functions as a commodity, wherein a given term's primary value lies in how effectively users can reproduce dominant understandings at increasingly large scales. This datafication of language thereby shapes the current trans user's experience of not only the Internet but also what it means to be trans. In order to understand the profound impact of these changes, this chapter will examine how each of these systems is implemented on a different platform—tagging on Tumblr and Google's search engine results page (SERP)—in the context of two major shifts discussed in previous chapters: first, the push to develop and define new community identity terminology, and, second, the shifting ways trans individuals use identity terminology to acquire information, particularly in the early stages of transition. This analysis will be supplemented by interviews conducted in 2014 with trans individuals about their Internet usage. Though the specifics of the platforms discussed by the interviewees have shifted in the intervening years, the interviews provide firsthand insight into how trans individuals experienced the early stages of this shift toward language as data. The first section will locate Tumblr users' efforts to develop and define new terminology within the longer history of community debates around terminology. Whereas earlier spaces limited both the participants and audiences for these debates, terminological debates on Tumblr are technically open to the entire platform. However, this openness can be a double-edged sword. It allows more voices to contribute to the discussion, with no outside editorial influence to limit individuals' self-definition; at the same time, the platform's reliance on open systems–specifically the folksonomy–means that user debate about terminology becomes embedded within the infrastructure, encouraging users to laterally police others' tag usage, lest the platform prioritize the "wrong" definition.

The second section shifts focus from definition to application by algorithmic systems—in this case, their representation on the SERP, which has become the dominant mode for interaction with the Web, including searching for information, identifying items or services for purchase, and shortcutting to a specific section of a larger website. Yet behind the SERP lies a complex database intimately shaped by dominant hegemonic norms which are then reproduced in what it presents to users on the SERP. As Safiya Noble argues, search engine results represent "an information reality, while the operations [that lie behind it] are rendered increasingly invisible."[15] For those who lie outside these norms, the information reality they encounter reinforces existing cultural biases against them while using their search queries as fuel to further power the engine's true goal: profit. As Noble extensively documents in *Algorithms of Oppression*, representations of Black women and girls were frequently reduced in early Google search results to little more than pornography, creating a feedback loop that fueled existing biases.[16] For trans individuals, particularly those who are exploring their identity or newly out, the SERP serves as a key information resource for locating resources and community. Thus, the People Also Ask (PAA) widget, designed to help address other, sometimes unstated, aspects of a user's query, represents an important site for exploring Google's "information reality." As in Noble's work, the PAA's reality, drawn from existing search results and shaped by user behavior, either reinforces existing cultural biases or actively distorts the trans experience.

The final section combines definition and application to look at a second SERP widget: the dictionary definition. Much like the PAA question, the widget's reliance on contextual examples drawn from existing linguistic corpora opens room for cultural biases and negative associations to become embedded within a term's definition. This issue also arises in several other trans-related definitions in the online dictionary Lexico, whose host company, Oxford Languages, provides the definitions for the widget. When these terms are then input into Google's AdWords and AdSense systems, they undergo a full transmutation from an identity term to a commodity, available to the most effective bidder. When faced with such large-scale use, trans individuals have limited agency to shape the very terms employed to describe their existence—a concerning development, given trans individuals' hard-fought historical efforts to challenge medical authorities' linguistic dominance.

Developing a Modern Transgender Lexicon

As noted in the introduction, defining shared terminology for the community and then pushing for the widespread adoption of this lexicon were core issues for trans activism throughout the 1980s and 1990s. These discussions were often conducted in counterpublic enclaves, such as private listservs, community BBSes, or community periodicals, before being introduced to wider publics. Participants were focused primarily on maintaining connection to the community, and their language use reflected this collective orientation. Authors' assumed audience was largely limited to other presumed community members. Debate around Virginia Prince's proposed identity, "bigenderist," and its accompanying umbrella term "bigenderal," is an excellent example. Prince by far was the most visible opponent to adopting "transgender" as a collective identity term, and her initial proposal for "bigenderist" ran under different titles in *Tapestry*, *Cross-Talk*, *Renaissance News*, and the *Femme Mirror*, as well as other smaller club newsletters, from late 1991 to early 1992, which led to the proposal's subsequent publication to alt.transgendered on Usenet.[17] Part of this Usenet thread would be republished in the September 1992 issue of *Cross-Talk*, further increasing its reach.[18] Though, ultimately, few participants found Prince's arguments persuasive—one widely quoted response began by implying that most folks were likely to read the term as "big-ender"[19]—their very access to the enclave allowed them to safely engage in "lively debate" among themselves, as well as plan strategies for future action.[20] Even as most transgender discourse moved online, many online spaces covered in previous chapters remained semienclaved counterpublics: on LiveJournal, for instance, a single user post could not be cross-posted across groups—cross-posting required manual duplication of a post in each target group—and members had a very granular level of control over who could see their posts. Thus, nongroup members may have had few opportunities to be exposed to a group's content. Within LiveJournal communities, for example, shifts in terminology, such as an increased preference for "trans" over "transgender," the adoption of "cisgender," and the increasing prominence of "nonbinary" as an umbrella term, occurred gradually throughout the early 2000s.[21]

On social media platforms driven by social tagging and search, in contrast, language shifts and associated debates both happen on the platform *and* inform its wider infrastructure. In both print and earlier digital fora, community terminology initially remained confined to these spaces before beginning to circulate elsewhere—the gradual adoption of cisgender, as discussed in chapter 3, is a prime example. On a social media platform, however, tagging integrates this terminology into the platform infrastructure from the very first use. These tags form the basis for the platform-wide folksonomy, defined by designer Thomas Vander Wal as "the result of personal free tagging of information and objects (anything with a URL) for one's own retrieval," done in "a social environment (shared and open to others)." The folksonomy's value lies in being "derived from people using their own vocabulary and adding explicit meaning."[22] Ideally, folksonomies are emergent and iterative collections that resist concretization and "guarantee a much broader access to [resources] . . . which is independent of the guardian [infrastructure]."[23] One of the folksonomy's great advantages is how it shifts definitional power from dominant authorities to users. Unlike controlled vocabularies such as the Library of Congress Subject Headings (LCSH), where changes are governed by determination of literary warrant or use of certain terms in authoritative sources, social tagging systems are collaborative systems primarily constructed by users, and users' tagging practices reflect their personal relationship with terminology.[24] So, while a user may add "trans," "transgender," or other associated terms to the folksonomy with their first post, "transgender" did not enter the LCSH as an independent category (as opposed to a referent for transsexuality) until 2007.[25] Generally, folksonomies don't compensate for lexical conflict or anomalies and can even open room for new knowledge to enter the system. In her research on trans tagging on book-storing site LibraryThing, scholar Melissa Adler found that trans users' tags not only added information but also "[provided] a means to negotiate norms of gender expression through categories or labels."[26]

This freedom to explore self through language can also exist in contrast to other aspects of the platform infrastructure, which are built on binary logics of M or F (and sometimes O). These classification systems pose a variety of risks for trans users as they attempt to translate social norms and lived experience into acceptable data that can be validated by a technical system.[27] As was the case in the UK in the 1960s and 1970s, when used by the state, such systems instantiate static sex and gender categories and continual state surveillance.[28] On social media platforms, in contrast, advertisers' preference for gender-driven advertising necessitates a binary gender system, though a third more customizable option was at times available. However, this third option then becomes its own alternate category, "partition[ed] . . . away from the normalized binary."[29] In some cases, system administrators do not actually alter the database's binary classifications of sex and gender, but instead obscure the system's core binaristic division from users.[30] Thus, while users may present their gender on a platform in a variety of ways, the platform itself retains either a binary or tripartite system. Such systems may also prioritize ideals of "authenticity" over user freedom, as seen in Facebook's "real name" policy, first challenged in 2014.[31]

Self-description through language, then, offers trans users the freedom to explore different forms of self-expression using methods legible to the database. A post tagged "#queer #girlslikeus #trans #transition #transgender #transfem #enby #nonbinary" more accurately reflects the differing aspects of an individual's own gender identity and expression. In addition, through tagging users can unobtrusively make their transness relevant in personal, quotidian moments that draw attention to their other interests, desires, and experiences.[32] For a trans woman who tags a selfie wearing her Seahawks jersey "#alwaysbe12ing #seahawks #nflplayoffs #mtf #trans* #Transwoman #transgirl #transgender," her tagging draws attention to both her trans identity and her sports fandom. Alternately, trans identity can serve as a site of creative potential, as fans reimagine characters as transgender or show off their "#crossplay" (a neologism combining "cosplay" and "cross-dressing"). Instead of understanding trans terminology as a specialized lexicon that requires a detailed glossary, these users' tagging practices position trans terms as everyday and commonplace. The use of social tagging as identity markers offers increased visibility for what seem, according to the archival record, relatively rare terms such as "bigender," as well as the development of new identity terminology, including "genderfluid" and "agender." In most cases, use of these terms is further elaborated through other user practices such as posts or biographical boxes.[33] In his work with LGBTQ Polish migrants to the UK, media scholar Lukasz Szulc discovered that access to a more expansive lexicon, particularly via a digital platform, allowed individuals room to more safely explore their gender identity and performance through disidentification: a sense of "this is me, but."[34] This growing lexicon, Brady Robards and his coauthors argue, reflects "a complex process of re-working language to suit individual experiences that are not confined to singular pre-existing categories."[35]

Notably, this process of disidentification and subsequent exploration via language has a longer history within transgender discourse: Writing in the September 1990 issue of *Cross-Talk*, Kymberleigh Richards described how she was first prompted to seek out alternative community terminology when asked by a student in a human sexuality class, "What do you call yourself?" To her surprise, she found this question difficult to answer, because, as she went on to explain, she disidentified with all of the major identity terms within the community.[36] However, Richards's search was constrained by her emphasis on terms that could be legible to those outside the community. She and others writing during this period were primarily concerned not with delineating between interior definitions but with having a recognizable face for the exterior "masses." In her first column following *Tapestry*'s switch to Transgender from TV-TS in 1995, IFGE executive director Alison Laing made an effort to note that, while the change reflected dominant community trends, it remained important to respect others' self-identifications: "Each of us can still exercise our right to ask that we be called whatever we want. However, we should do so politely, as the current proliferation of the terms has many people legitimately confused, within and without the community." In her view, terminology was at best a distraction from larger issues, as "in these days of concern about political correctness, it is one thing to be sensitive but it is another to become offended by minor semantic variation. There are more important things to deal with than labels. I guess I come from the old school, 'You can call me what ever you want. Just don't call me late for dinner.'"[37]

In contrast, on contemporary social media platforms like Tumblr or Instagram, a given user is primarily focused on, first, developing an internal sense of self, which is in part expressed through new terminology and other linguistic innovations. In their work on identity labeling among asexual, queer, and trans (AQT) youth online, psychologists Zach Schudson and Sari van Anders argue that self-labeling "facilitates relationally oriented ways of being that incorporate care and understanding for others into individuals' self-concepts."³⁸ The new terminology produced in these spaces "articulate subjectivities that are harmed by [hegemonic] systems and spark creative forms of political and relational thinking."³⁹ Associated tags, such as #genderfluid and #agender, become safe spaces to build community.⁴⁰ Over time, these terms enter the platform's trans lexicon through users' tagging practices, such as tagging a post "#nonbinary #genderfluid #androgynous #trans." Even with such freedom, though, the content of a folksonomy remains heavily informed by preestablished subcultural vocabularies. The "exploration" of subject positions within folksonomies, scholar Patrick Keilty contends, is always constrained by a logic requiring instantly recognizable cues, regularized under the conventions of the particular subculture. In fact, socialization within it relies on such regulatory strictures, just as effective information retrieval relies on control.⁴¹ In other words, the most widely adopted or visible terms eventually emerge as "stable consensus" choices with similarly static definitions, around which most conversation centers.⁴² Ultimately, despite transgender's umbrella status, the "consensus" understanding of "trans" centers a normative image: individuals, largely middle-class and white, who actively experience bodily dysphoria and aim to alleviate it by transitioning from one end of the binary to the other. Once established, this definition then becomes a tool for boundary drawing when those who, in one way or another, fail to fit this consensus definition use the tag as a marker of their own trans identity. As Patrick Keilty argues of identity tags on XTube, "These terms are deeply personal and social, such a part of one's identity in relation to others that one feels the need to intervene into others' self-understanding when confronted with difference."⁴³ This is a particular issue for nonbinary individuals, who can frequently find their claims to transness rejected on the grounds that they're not "trans enough."⁴⁴ Tag policing and subsequent charges of tag "misuse" illustrate the stakes embedded in tag definition. For those policing tags, individuals who they believe wrongly use—and thus wrongly identify with—trans tags represent an existential threat.⁴⁵ In these encounters, personal identity, terminology, and platform affordances collapse individual, counterpublic, and systemic contexts in ways that highlight what happens when language becomes data. At these moments, it "becomes volatile and invasive; its effects spreading more widely and more quickly, than the printed word."⁴⁶ In search engines and social tagging-centered platforms, speech, writing, and code collide, an encounter from which, as N. Katherine Hayles points out, "they do not emerge unchanged."⁴⁷

Terminology as Commodity

No set of systems have datafied language quite as effectively as the search engine and its attendant tools. From their earliest iterations, search engines and their underlying algorithms relied on linguistic queries, whose effectiveness was determined in part by how accurate the results seemed to the user. Early search was often an inexact affair, as most engines had few methods for defining content relevance in relation to a search query and proved susceptible to manipulation or being overwhelmed by spam.⁴⁸ Directory-based search engines offered more specific results, but they were often compiled by those outside the community, and these editors didn't have contextual knowledge of the topics they were compiling. In response, some sites developed community-specific, directory-driven search engines, including Gayscape (gayscape.com), RainbowQuery (rainbowquery.com), and the Susan's Place Transgender Resources Search Engine, which in 1997 claimed to have indexed 11,104 pages. However, the emergence of Google in 1998 transformed the search engine market. Bolstered by its innovative page-ranking system and Netscape distribution deal, Google quickly began to overtake its competitors; by 2005, it was used for 46.3 percent of all US searches.⁴⁹ Key to Google's financial success was its embrace of web advertising, which shifted search engines' core business model from selling advertisers on the size of a search engine's mass audience to selling them the click of a "definite visitor," who was shown an ad based on their search terms.⁵⁰ In effect, a search engine's core commodity has become the way they direct the flow of web traffic in particular ways based on the user's specific query. These framing effects increase with the use of different widgets, such as dictionary definitions, biographical boxes, and answers to common related questions. The SERP has now become "an interactive, radically open and distributed artifact that" mediates the interaction between "human actors and the cultural records they wish to access."⁵¹

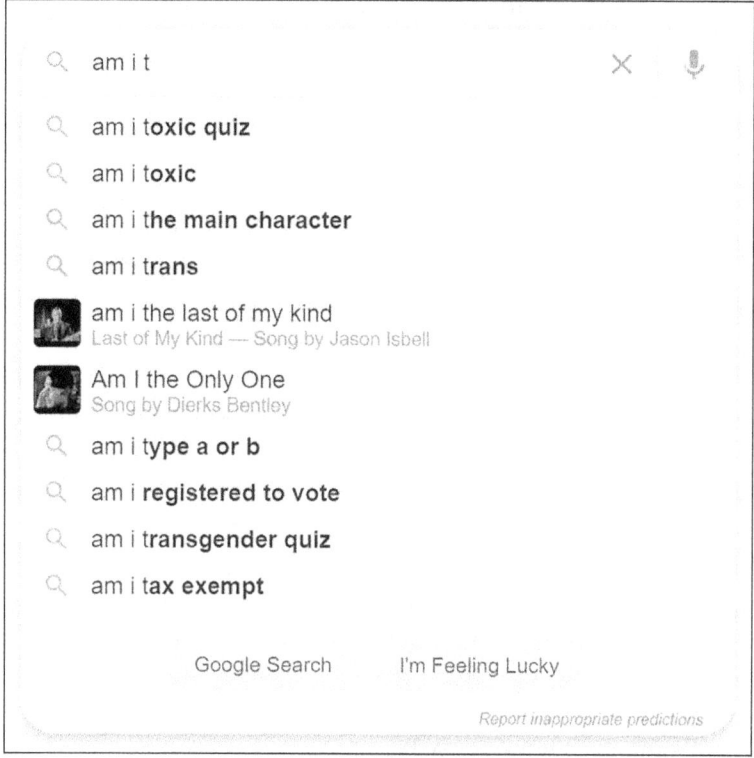

Figure 6.1. Google autocompletion results for "am i t." Screenshot taken December 17, 2020.

Though such mediation affects all users, it takes on greater meaning when the user is questioning if they might be trans, a process increasingly driven by search engines. In 2020, the fourth and ninth autocomplete suggestions for "am i t" both reference being trans (fig. 6.1), suggesting that the question is submitted with some regularity. Interviewees frequently referenced using search engines (often through a generic reference to "googling" something) as part of their initial research into trans identity. Often, they described starting out using basic keywords such as "transgender," "MTF," or "FTM" and then branching out to include more specific terms as they learned them, which they would first encounter in their search results. One interviewee knew no trans people when he came out, so Google played a "huge" role in his information gathering: "It was pretty much all just Google and figure out what comes up." Through Google, he learned the key terms he needed in order to find more information about hormone replacement therapy and chest-binding. When users lacked even these terms, the blank search box allowed questioning individuals, as scholar Vanessa Kitzie has found, to "express a natural language query specific to [their] experience," like, "I was born a boy and wanted to be a girl" or "Feel male, but only inside."[52] Search engines were also seen as more effective for information seeking than using print materials. Whereas looking for print texts could lead to, according to one interviewee, spending "a lot of fruitless energy looking for this stuff," in a Google search "you get 1,000 hits. And it's easier to do that. I'm not saying that it's a better way to do it, but it's easier." Identifying useful information within search also requires the user engage in self-filtering, as users encountered a variety of re-traumatizing or heteronormative results.[53] Beyond the presence of dominant norms in the SERP, though, few of my interviewees questioned algorithmic decision-making that underlay the SERP's overall structure. When asked how they make sense of Google search results, one interviewee said they relied primarily on the preview text to determine if a site looked "helpful," only going through three or four links at most, all of them on the first page. The presence of topic-negative information in a SERP, though, highlights the search algorithm's role in shaping user perceptions. Despite their corporate owners' claims to objectivity, algorithmic judgments of relevance are founded, as media scholar Tarleton Gillespie argues, in a "particular *knowledge logic* . . . built on specific presumptions about what knowledge is and how one should identify its most relevant components" (emphasis author's).[54] Ultimately, search algorithms "never *mimicked* a social process of searching information; they *created* a new system of data circulation based on algorithmically defined criteria of quantified popularity."[55] In some cases, the results this system produces reinforce users' implicit bias and present an oversimplified portrait of complex issues.[56]

Given these issues, it may be more fruitful to think of the search algorithm as not only a research tool that interprets human language but as an independent actor, with its own specific definitions and understandings of what it means to be "transgender." As Taina Bucher notes, "Algorithms do not simply change *with* the event; they also have the ability to change the event." She cites the Google flu tracker, whose reliance on search results ended up "producing the conditions it was trying to merely describe and predict."[57] For the questioning user, then, the "event" of possibly coming into a new identity may be changed by what they find on the SERP. This is especially true for the questioning user who lacks community-specific keywords, as their language acquisition is driven in part by algorithmic judgment. Even how they structure queries may not be entirely natural, as tools like Google's autocomplete "tends to transform natural language into more regular, economically exploitable linguistic subsets."[58] Yet, given the general opaqueness of the different factors that play into what appears in the SERP, how can we—as Bucher puts it—make the algorithm speak? She proposes using technography, "a way of describing and observing the workings of technology in order to examine the interplay between a diverse set of actors (both human and nonhuman)," with the aim of developing "a critical understanding of the mechanisms and operational logic of software."[59] What follows is a technographic inquiry into the operational associations the Google search algorithm makes around "transgender" as a concept through a close examination of one SERP widget: the People Also Ask feature.

People Also Ask . . .

The People Also Ask (PAA) feature debuted on Google's SERP in 2015. Drawing on a question database derived from existing user queries, the PAA widget offers a set of questions and answers, excerpted from existing web content, that may address a user's query (fig. 6.2). Using the initial query and search results, the database identifies associated "topic sets," which are developed based on what links previous users have chosen to interact with. These topic sets then determine what questions will populate the People Also Ask widget. When users expand a question to see the answer, the widget will load between two to four "associated" questions related to the one expanded. The order in which questions are loaded may or may not be based on ranking within the database, derived from how it determines answer quality. These quality determinations arise from several different factors, including a response resource's "quality score," existing search ranking, and length of the answer. When multiple possible answers are available, how often a key term is repeated may determine which answer is selected.[60] In practice,

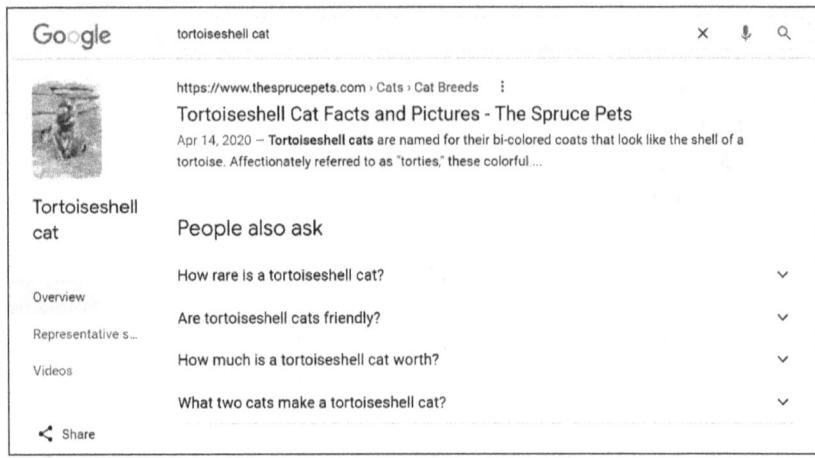

Figure 6.2. Example of a search engine results page (SERP), including People Also Ask section, for "tortoiseshell cat." Screenshot taken June 23, 2020.

the PAA seems most useful when dealing with definitional questions or diagnostic issues, where the answer includes simple definitions or identifiable symptoms. A question like "Am I transgender?," in contrast, is neither definitional nor diagnostic, but existential. Given the importance of these results, what information appears in the PAA plays an important role, as users tend to reduce the time and effort spent searching when presented with informative snippets over a list of search results.[61]

For a topic like "transgender," however, the different knowledges that construct the database's associated concepts fail to account for users' vastly differing intents, producing questions and answers that reflect a wider cultural focus on medicalization and surgery. Furthermore, the system's focus on producing helpful answers via short excerpts reduced complex questions to short snippets that don't always reflect a source's larger argument. Searching "What is transgender?" produces questions focused on definition ("What transgender means?" and "What is the difference between transgender and transvestite?"), root causes ("What is transgender and how does it happen?"), and self-identity ("How do you know if you're transgender?").[62] Drilling further down into these questions produces other questions centering surgery, such as "How do you become a transgender?" and "What is it called when a man has surgery to become a woman?" Furthermore, the answers chosen appear to offer definitive answers to what remain open questions. For the question "What causes transgender disorder?," the PAA answer cites the "Gender Dysphoria" FAQ page of Ireland's public health service as offering a clear response: malfunctioning hormones (fig. 6.3). Yet, when the full page is loaded, the section this excerpt derives from—"Causes of Gender Dysphoria"—clearly states at the beginning that "the exact cause of gender dysphoria is unknown and there is much debate over the possible causes of gender dysphoria."[63]

At times, these questions cross-pollinate with existing gendered assumptions. The question "What happens when a man becomes a woman?" directs users to an excerpt from the Wikipedia page "Sex Reassignment Surgery (Male to Female)," as well as loading "How do they turn a man into a woman?" as a related question, which leads to the same Wikipedia excerpt. However, expanding this second question loads "Do tall guys have bigger?," which includes an excerpt from an online health site with information about the relationship between height and genital size. Admittedly, it's unlikely an average user would expand such similar questions one after another, but the inclusion of the third question points to how, presumably, repeated references to genitalia generates an association between the three questions within the question database.

Furthermore, the database's preference for sites with a high "quality score" such as Wikipedia means that few of the sources chosen to be

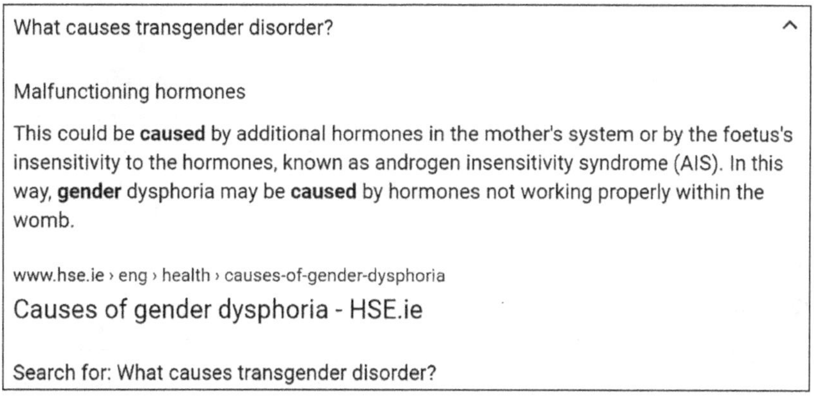

What causes transgender disorder? ^

Malfunctioning hormones

This could be **caused** by additional hormones in the mother's system or by the foetus's insensitivity to the hormones, known as androgen insensitivity syndrome (AIS). In this way, **gender** dysphoria may be **caused** by hormones not working properly within the womb.

www.hse.ie › eng › health › causes-of-gender-dysphoria
Causes of gender dysphoria - HSE.ie

Search for: What causes transgender disorder?

Figure 6.3. People Also Ask result for "What causes transgender disorder?" Screenshot taken July 23, 2020.

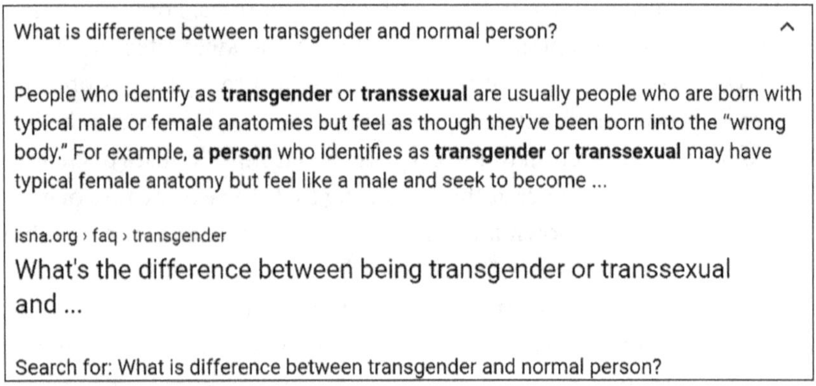

> What is difference between transgender and normal person?
>
> People who identify as **transgender** or **transsexual** are usually people who are born with typical male or female anatomies but feel as though they've been born into the "wrong body." For example, a **person** who identifies as **transgender** or **transsexual** may have typical female anatomy but feel like a male and seek to become ...
>
> isna.org › faq › transgender
> **What's the difference between being transgender or transsexual and ...**
>
> Search for: What is difference between transgender and normal person?

Figure 6.4. People Also Ask result for "What is difference between transgender and normal person?" Screenshot taken July 23, 2020.

excerpted were from trans organizations or sites beyond the National Center for Transgender Equality. Instead, the system prioritizes medical authorities, popular science and health sites, or Wikipedia. When trans or allied organizations were cited, the differences between page content and the PAA question offered a telling contrast, often misrepresenting the arguments of their trans and allied authors. For the question "What is difference between transgender and normal person?," Google cites the Intersex Society of North America's FAQ page for the question, "What's the difference between being transgender or transsexual and having an intersex condition?" (fig. 6.4). In this example, several different issues emerge. At the level of framing, the PAA question reinforces the wider cultural perception of the transgender person as "abnormal," while the ISNA question addresses an ongoing discussion within transgender and intersex communities of boundaries and allyship. In terms of page content, the ISNA page begins with a paragraph defining transgender and transsexual, which forms the basis for the PAA excerpt.[64] However, based on the use of selective emphasis, the ISNA excerpt appears not to have been selected for its discussion of transgender issues, but because it included the word "person."

A similar issue arises in the chosen source and excerpt for the question "What are all the sexes?," which pointed in June 2020 to a web-based copy of well-known trans studies scholar Aaron Devor's 1996 lecture "How Many Sexes? How Many Genders? When Two Are Not

Enough" (fig. 6.5). Devor's lecture addresses the ways dominant gender ideologies limit how individuals can express and embody gender, and the selected excerpt comes from a list entitled "The Ideology of the Dominant Gender Schema."[65] Yet this excerpt appears to have been primarily chosen for its repeated use of the word "all" (bolded in the figure). A similar issue arises for the question "How many human genders are there?," which also cites this excerpt, presumably due to its use of "there" and "genders" (fig. 6.6). In at least one case, the reliance on identifying keywords within questions creates associations with decidedly anti-trans content: in response to the questions "Is sex change surgery painful?" and "Does sex change surgery hurt?" the PAA response links to an opinion piece hosted by the Heritage Foundation opposing the informed consent model of trans-affirmative medical care. (fig. 6.6).

What are all the sexes?

3) Genders are the social manifestation of sex. There are two and only two genders: men and women, (boys and girls). **All** males are either boys or men. **All** females are either girls or women. Sep 12, 2018

web.uvic.ca › ~ahdevor › HowMany › HowMany
How Many Sexes? How Many Genders? When Two Are Not Enough

Search for: What are all the sexes?

Figure 6.5. People Also Ask result for "What are all the sexes?" Screenshot taken July 22, 2020.

How many human genders are there?

There are two and only two **genders**: men and women, (boys and girls). All males are either boys or men. All females are either girls or women. 4) All persons are either one **gender** or the other. Sep 12, 2018

web.uvic.ca › ~ahdevor › HowMany › HowMany
How Many Sexes? How Many Genders? When Two Are Not Enough

Search for: How many human genders are there?

Figure 6.6. People Also Ask result for "How many human genders are there?" Screenshot taken July 23, 2020.

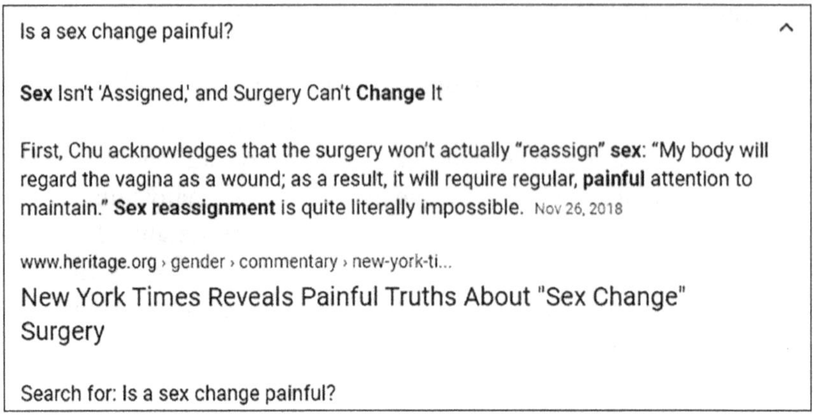

> Is a sex change painful?
>
> **Sex** Isn't 'Assigned,' and Surgery Can't **Change** It
>
> First, Chu acknowledges that the surgery won't actually "reassign" **sex**: "My body will regard the vagina as a wound; as a result, it will require regular, **painful** attention to maintain." **Sex reassignment** is quite literally impossible. Nov 26, 2018
>
> www.heritage.org › gender › commentary › new-york-ti...
> New York Times Reveals Painful Truths About "Sex Change" Surgery
>
> Search for: Is a sex change painful?

Figure 6.7. People Also Ask result for "Is a Sex Change Painful?" Screenshot taken July 23, 2020.

Defining Transgender

Such issues of misaligned algorithmic associations are not limited to question-and-answer snippets, however. Online dictionaries, which provide the definitions used in the "definition" card on the SERP, have also reemphasized popular negative associations. In her analysis of algorithmic association, scholar Pip Thornton cites the 2016 controversy over the Oxford Dictionary Online's use of "rabid feminist" as the sole contextual example in their entry for feminist, while Debbie Ging, and her coauthors found that definitions of sex- and gender-related terminology on Urban Dictionary, which relies heavily on folksonomies and user voting, were inflected by distinctly misogynistic framings common in the manosphere.[66] In the definition of "transsexual" used in Google SERP definition widget, sourced from Oxford Languages, the chosen contextual usage example for the term as an adjective until at least July 2020 was "transsexual fantasies" (fig. 6.8).

As with "rabid feminist," the contextual use examples chosen "mirror the most likely pairings or orderings of already existing words based on the semantically irrelevant factors of frequency and proximity."[67] The choice of "transsexual fantasies," as opposed to the far more benign and undoubtedly common example "transsexual women" (the adjectival example that would come to replace "transsexual fantasies"), raises questions not only about the corpora from which these examples are selected but also about their longer impact. As scholar Pip Thornton argues, Oxford's (and by extension, Google's) "reliance on algorithmically mediated samples effectively puts an extraordinary and unintended epistemic power in the hands of another private company."[68] For their part, Oxford presents their selection process for example sentences (and, presumably, contextual phrases as well) as merely representing a word's "the typical grammatical and semantic context without distracting from the essential information the definition conveys" while "[doing] our best to eliminate example sentences that contain factually incorrect, prejudiced, or offensive statements from real-life sources."[69] This assertion of avoiding prejudice and offense, however, neatly sidesteps addressing the ideological implications of these selections. Just as "rabid feminist" has clear ideological implications, "transsexual fantasies" has clear sexualized connotations, which are then reinforced when the phrase is input into Google and other search engines. The first page of search results is

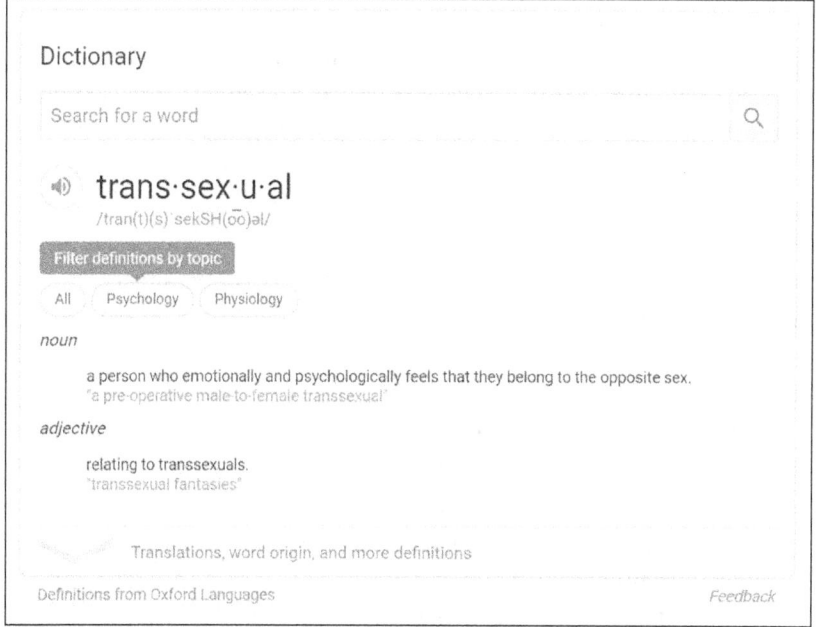

Figure 6.8. Google SERP Dictionary widget definition for "transsexual." Screenshot taken July 22, 2020.

almost entirely either erotic literature or pornographic films, not produced by trans individuals themselves, that center non-trans individuals fetishizing trans women's bodies. Other results are either now-outdated psychological research or takedowns of trans individuals' existence.

A similar disconnect between "typical context" and implication is also present in the trans-related definitions of their stand-alone Oxford Dictionary Online, rebranded in 2019 as Lexico before being shuttered in 2022. In the entry for "transgender," the "more example sentences" section includes the example sentences (taken directly from the corpus) "First, in the view of transgender advocates gender is simply a matter of individual identity" and "One can ask several questions about transgender sexuality and gender identity." On their face, the amount and variety associated words, such as "advocates," "gender," "identity," "gender identity," and "sexuality," would make both examples good candidates for a "typical" context, given how frequently these terms coappear. However, the structure of both examples carries wider ideological implications that, depending on one's reading, are often used to undermine trans individuals' sense of self. For, without their original contexts, each sentence has an implicit continuation. The first frames trans individuals' understanding of gender as one side of a debate, implying that another, equally valid view of gender exists. This view may also be one of the "several questions" raised in the second example, but, without the original context, the implication is that something about "transgender" can be questioned.

In its quotation selection, Lexico reproduces two rhetorical tactics common to the arguments of trans-exclusive radical feminists: first, the opposing viewpoints framing, which implies that two equally valid positions regarding the validity of trans existence; and, second, the implication that transgender life should be subject to question. As feminist scholar Sara Ahmed contends, these tactics are meant to functionally deny trans existence, for "when a question becomes a place you reside in, everything can be thrown into question: explanations you might have handy that allow you to make sense or navigate your way through unfamiliar as well as familiar landscapes no longer work."[70] When placed in context, at least the first example sentence bears this concern out. It originally appeared in a 2001 essay published in *off our backs* entitled "Sex, Lies, and Feminism" addressing the presence of Camp Trans outside the annual Michigan Womyn's Music Festival (MWMF). MWMF, which ended in 2015, had a long-standing policy of being a "womyn-born-womyn" space, refusing entry to anyone assigned male at birth. The 1991 expulsion of trans woman Nancy Burkholder inspired the creation of Camp Trans, an opposition demonstration held outside the festival's gates throughout the mid-1990s and into the mid-2000s.[71] Many of the debates surrounding MWMF were precursors to contemporary debates around trans inclusion within feminism. In "Sex, Lies, and Feminism," author Charlotte Croson argues that Camp Trans protesters, in her view, not only attempt to define women's interests for attendees but are also, "to put it simply, on the wrong side. In opposition to feminism."[72] In the section where the example sentence appears, Croson does in fact take the "opposing viewpoints" framing to argue that trans individuals' understanding of gender reinforces existing patriarchal constructions.[73] Throughout her article, she implicitly questions or undermines trans individuals' identities, using scare quotes around words like "become" (as in "become" women), framing trans men as women first ("FTM remain women and, as such, targets of male violence."), and misgendering well-known trans author Pat Califia.[74]

In other trans-related definitions, example sentences include decontextualized references to otherwise settled debates. One of the "more example sentences" in Lexico's definition of "transsexual" contains the example "According to the authors, these professionals are ignorant of the homosexual versus autogynephilic typology of transsexuals." This sentence appears in Walter O. Bockting's 2005 review of J. Michael Bailey's controversial 2003 book, *The Man Who Would Be Queen: The Science of Gender-Bending and Transsexualism*, which asserted that some trans women are motivated to transition by autogynephilia, or erotic attraction to the image of themselves as women. Though autogynephilia as a theory pre-dates Bailey's book, it drew popular attention to the idea. When it was published, *The Man Who Would Be Queen* was vociferously critiqued by trans women, and Bockting's review questions Bailey's endorsement of autogynephilia and cites several different trans critiques.[75] The theory has seen little adoption beyond psychological and sexological circles—so little, in fact, that the word "autogynephilia" doesn't even appear in Lexico or the *Oxford English Dictionary*. However, the inclusion of this quote lacks any meaningful context, requiring the curious reader to research the term and, in the process, strengthening the links between these concepts. "Genderqueer," as the newest term, has examples that largely reflect contemporary usage, though, again, their decontextualization raises more questions than answers.[76]

While all of these examples except for "transsexual fantasies" appear "below the fold" and require users to click on an expandable box to view, their existence highlights how relying on mathematical models that understand language primarily as data can have serious implications. Moreover, it's not clear what kind of content makes up Oxford's corpus, which they described in 2016 as containing "a vast bank of more than 1.9 million example sentences (around 38 million words) of real English, extracted from the world's newspapers and magazines, academic journals, fiction, and blogs," or how often it's updated.[77] All three of the example sentences discussed here appear in a 2016 archived copy of their definitions. Given the contemporary debate around both the place of trans individuals within feminism as well as challenges to youth claiming a trans identity, there's a considerable possibility that these viewpoints may enter into the corpus, long after the actual debates have become outdated. While the 2016 explanation of example sentences includes the disclaimer that "opinions and views expressed in the usage examples are the views of the individuals concerned and are not endorsed by Oxford University Press," the concern isn't that lexicographers are, by implication, transphobic, but that using mathematical models to identify examples obscures their temporal and cultural context. Just as Oxford's corpus creates a direct connection back to both the debates regarding trans exclusion from MWMF and the controversy over Bailey's book, future corpus additions could revive disputed psychological concepts such as "rapid onset gender dysphoria," which at its core seeks to undermine the autonomy of trans youth.

Linguistic Capitalism and Buying Trans

If the case of Lexico's corpus raises questions about the impact of decontextualized language, Google's AdWords and AdSense transmute parts of the trans lexicon from simple descriptors or identity markers to economic and social commodities with calculable monetary value. Using Google AdWords Keyword Planner, users can identify the average monthly searches for keywords on Google, competition for ad placement, and the amount advertisers in your geographic area are paying to appear in search results.[78] Prospective advertisers submit an ad, as well as a set bid for specific combinations that (if selected to appear in search results) they pay Google each time an individual clicks on their ad, also known as the cost per click (CPC). Whether or not Google will run an ad is determined by multiplying the bid price and the ad's Google-assigned "quality score."[79] This structure means that advertisers face "no cost or disadvantage to placing bids on uncommon or unlikely words," encouraging advertisers to engage in, in Richard Graham's words, "a kind of linguistic land grab."[80] The AdWords system reflects Google's larger investment in what digital humanities scholar Frédéric Kaplan defines as "linguistic capitalism," which functions in an "economy of expression," whose primary goal is "not to catch the users' gaze but to develop intimate and sustainable linguistic relationships with the largest possible number of users in order to model linguistic change accurately and mediate linguistic expression systematically." Kaplan hypothesizes that, within this economic model, it's possible "natural languages could progressively evolve to seamlessly integrate the linguistic biases of algorithms and the economical constraints of the global linguistic economy."[81] Under linguistic capitalism, trans individuals' ability to define terms in the trans lexicon risks being constrained by Google's drive to reach the widest possible audience. Using "transgender" as a starting keyword in the AdWords Planner, the most in-demand related search terms with over one thousand average monthly searches centered transness as an identity to be consumed, though the manner of consumption varied.[82] The most competitive, "trans pride" (top of CPC bid range at the time of this writing: $3.57), is topped with ads for all manner of clothing in the trans pride flag colors or with trans-related sayings, an extension of the algorithmically generated, targeted T-shirts frequently advertised on Facebook. The next most competitive, "mtf transgender" (top of CPC bid range: $5.00), includes ads for all manner of items culturally associated with transness, from natural testosterone blockers and local therapists to "raunchy" lingerie and sex toys. The final competitive keyword combination, "transgender near me" (top of CPC bid range: $2.84), includes ads for either health-care providers or trans-specific hookup and dating sites. The presence of these sites, as well as erotic items in ads attached to results for "mtf transgender," suggests the other kind of trans-related consumption: consuming trans bodies. On the one hand, digital spaces allow more trans individuals space to explore their sexuality and bodies in a positive, supportive environment, as well as produce and distribute independent, trans-positive erotic material.[83] Yet this content exists alongside professionally produced material that primarily centers trans bodies as fetish objects.

The presence of both uses can, in response, drive user behavior. In her 2016 analysis of nonbinary gender presentation on Tumblr, scholar Abigail Oakley reports that she initially attempted to collect sample data from the #lesbian tag but found it to be primarily populated by explicit content instead of posts by lesbian-identified users. These users, she found, used the #girlswholikegirls tag, presumably in response to the presence of such pornographic content. For similar reasons, trans users on Tumblr in 2016 tended to tag using #trans or #trans instead of #transgender, which was at the time primarily dominated by commercial fetish pornography.[84] In both cases, the commodity value is apparent when considered in terms of scale: the number of posts in a given tag required to generate economic value dwarfs the visibility and influence of individual users.[85] Nevertheless, the overwhelming presence of fetishistic imagery in the #transgender tag is not reason to argue that the correct (or even effective) response is banning such content, as Tumblr did in 2018. Exploration of sex and sexuality has long played a key role in trans individuals' lives, and such widespread deplatforming has serious consequences for users' mental health and economic stability.[86] Instead, users' avoidance of these terms is a prime example of how the transformation of words into commodities reduces their capacity to hold personal or contextual meaning.

In contrast to their economic value, trans terms can be used by non-trans individuals as social commodities in order to acquire appropriate social and cultural capital. The choice by non-trans individuals to add "cisgender" to their vocabulary is one example of this effect. Finn Enke argues that, as the visibility of "cisgender" increased in the late 2000s, non-trans individuals' use of the term within educational spaces became a key part in performing trans allyship.[87] Yet, as noted in chapter 3, "cisgender" was always intended to be used as a political tactic aimed not at defining trans individuals but at creating a distinct binary; therefore, adoption by non-trans individuals was an inherent goal. The term "Latinx," however, is a prime example of a term as social commodity, where widespread adoption, driven by non-trans individuals, came at the expense of trans individuals. Initially, "Latinx" was primarily used by genderqueer, nonbinary, and gender nonconforming individuals of Latin American descent as a way to signify their individual differing gender identities. As the term was adopted by largely non-trans-identified academics and activists, the definition that entered public discourse positioned the term as a linguistic method for representing the many different gender identities within *Latinidad*.[88] In the process, "Latinx" as an identity reflecting individuals' different senses of self becomes subsumed by "Latinx" as an umbrella term. Once positioned as the "inclusive" choice, "latinx" as umbrella is reproduced through users' tagging practices, where using #latinx is a marker of one's commitment to diversity, thus generating social and cultural value.

Conclusion: Where We Go from Here

No technological shift has had as many far-reaching effects on trans life as the datafication of language. Compared to their presence in the earlier digital eras discussed in previous chapters, trans users are now fully embedded in the infrastructural fabric of contemporary platforms. Such visibility has clear benefits, especially for young and newly out users: information about trans life can be accessed with relative ease, and there are many different possible outlets to find social support. It's also easier for non-trans individuals to see and encounter affirming trans narratives, including those that explicitly challenge the ideal of the binary-identified "good trans subject." Technological affordances like social tagging allow trans users to make transness visible as part of their everyday experience and encourage users' linguistic innovation to develop terminology that exceeds the limitations of official taxonomies.

All of this visibility, however, remains contingent on the continued support, explicit or implicit, of a platform's corporate owners. No event made this as clear as the 2018 "Tumblrpocalypse," which followed an announcement by Tumblr CEO Jeff D'Onofrio on December 3, 2018, that the company would be banning 'adult content,' including 'photorealistic imagery or photography—images, videos, or GIFs—with real humans that include exposed genitals or female-presenting (yeah, we know you hate this term) nipples or depict sex acts.'"[89] The adult content ban directly contradicted these aspects and clearly demarcated Tumblr as being Not For Them. Trans and queer artists and sex workers, who used Tumblr to promote their work and connect with clients, were hit particularly hard.[90] Yet migrating away from Tumblr may be equally difficult: not only did platform affordances disincentivize users migrating away but there was also not a "good enough" alternative platform available.[91] However, the history of trans community periodicals may offer us a model for what a "good enough" platform could be.

Conclusion

Owning Our History

In June 2014, *Time Magazine* ran a full-page cover story featuring well-known trans actress, producer, and activist Laverne Cox next to the headline "The Transgender Tipping Point: America's Next Civil Rights Frontier." Since publication, this piece has become an oft-cited exemplar of positive media coverage of trans individuals as well as a wider embrace of visibility politics. Throughout the 2010s, trans individuals were visible on-screen in shows like *Orange Is the New Black*, *Sense 8*, or *Pose*, alongside other events such as Caitlyn Jenner's heavily documented coming out. Steinmetz's piece contains all the requisite elements: a celebrity interview (Cox), a recap of modern trans history for unfamiliar readers, an overview of current political issues, and (most important for this book) a discussion of the Internet's role in all of this. Midway through the article appears a now familiar anecdote: trans folks, both young and old, praising the Internet as a key resource in their coming out and transition. To author Katy Steinmetz, their stories serve as "a reminder that the Internet has been a revolutionary tool for the trans community, providing answers to questions that previous generations had no one to ask, as well as robust communities of support," as well as "helped expose the broader culture to trans people."[1] As proof, Steinmetz contrasts the experience of Rose Hayes, an engineering director at Google who'd only recently come out in "early middle age," and twenty-five-year-old Teagan Widmer:

> Hayes is certain she could have had a completely different life if she had been born later. "If the Internet had existed, in any meaningful sense, when I was 21, I would have figured it out," she says. That alternate reality sits opposite Hayes in a tank top and short purple hair. Teagan Widmer, 25, grew up a pastor's son in Northern California and now

lives as a programmer in Berkeley, where she designed an app called Refuge Restrooms to map gender-neutral, "safe" bathrooms around the world. As with many other millennial trans people, Widmer's transition started with search results. As a middle schooler who had secretly experimented with wearing women's clothes, she queried, "How do I hide my penis?" That was the beginning of an education that led to Widmer's coming out in graduate school.[2]

Missing from this "generation gap" narrative, of course, are the historical and political forces that made Widmer's search possible. That, in part, was the task of this book: filling in the historical gaps between Hayes's and Widmer's experiences. Early gender community BBSes showed users the inherent possibility of digital communications, both socially and politically. It would be commercial services, however, where most members of what was rapidly becoming the transgender community would first communicate online. Just as the walled garden changed how individuals communicated, the World Wide Web transformed how they accessed and published information. Information circulation, once a task requiring a large investment of time and physical resources, could now be accomplished with a single website, which you might not even have to pay for, if an organization chose to use one of the numerous ad-supported web-hosting services that began popping up. These services also ushered in a brand-new, individualized format: the home page. On the home page, users could explore their identity outside of group settings, both online and offline. Many common elements of the home page have since become essential to contemporary social media. Now most trans socialization and political activism happens online.

Yet, for all the Internet's lauded importance, far fewer folks have yet addressed an equally important issue: How do we preserve not only this history, but also the history that's happening now? While some may dismiss the idea that anything from the mid-1990s on counts as "history," these years are rapidly receding. As historian Ian Milligan points out, students will soon be completing (if they haven't completed already) research projects on "the September 11, 2001, attacks, the dot-com boom, the Clinton administration, and maybe even a cultural phenomenon such as the Tamagotchi pocket pet craze." Yet, "without using a web archive, any of the above research questions would either be impossible or poorly done."[3] For trans research, the web archive is even more essential: while any of the topics Milligan mentions received wide coverage within mass media, discussion of trans issues were almost entirely confined to community periodicals and occasional coverage in the LGB press. Web archives, in contrast, have a wealth of information to supplement these sources—and more information is entering them every day.

Looking Back, Looking Forward

Throughout the process of writing this book, I often reflected on a comment made in 2014 by one of my interviewees (which were also referenced in chapter 6): a thirty-six-year-old genderqueer individual who, in their words, felt caught in-between trans communities and age cohorts, forced to "choose between angry young kids or 50-year-old crossdressers." They attributed this reality to "the timeline of Internet progression" and being part of an age group that "kind of missed the train a little bit"—neither an early adopter nor an individual who had grown up with Internet access. However, this location also gave them an interesting perspective on trans life online:

> Message boards are much more of an older generation than things like Tumblr or Twitter. I think Facebook has become too big to talk about in any kind of generalities. But Tumblr and Twitter definitely seem to have captured the interest of the generation younger than mine, and I think that is so interesting because message boards, as far as archival purposes and being able to go back and find information, they may be as timeless enough to be useful five to ten years out. . . . I'm kinda curious what we're gonna see years from now, because a lot of what is happening online is happening in a more ephemeral and abbreviated way. And I wonder ten years from now, will it be harder to search stuff, or will it be things changed so quickly that you don't need to go online and search about all this stuff because it will have already passed people.

Part of my attraction to this quote is no doubt personal: much of my youth was spent on message boards, which played a formative role in my identity. Yet all of these boards have long since closed, and few traces of them are left online, outside of the Internet Archive. The other attraction, however, lies in their argument for the value in both message boards and social media. While Twitter and Tumblr are more popular with young users, message boards have an archival value that clearly sets them apart from "ephemeral" social media. In this moment, they express concerns not all that different from Linda Phillips's, as discussed in chapter 5: the "sobering experience," as she said, of "[becoming] obsolete in your own lifetime."

However, the different events that prompted each of their reflections highlight just how technology changed trans life. Phillips's sense of her own obsolescence arose from her fear that the contributions of heterosexual cross-dressers like Virginia Prince were being written out of history, with no one to preserve her legacy. Yet Prince's body of work, along with that of many others, *was* being preserved by groups such as the National Transgender Library and Archives, a division of AEGIS founded by Dallas Denny in 1992. The NTL&A continued to amass materials until 2000, when it was donated to the Labadie Collection at the University of Michigan in 2000. Much of chapters 1, 2, and 4 draw on periodicals held in this collection.

For my interviewee, in contrast, there is a sense that these message boards (and their attached websites) are "archival," but what it means to preserve them is unclear. Web archives, most notably the Internet Archive's Wayback Machine, present one possible solution, but they also raise several different issues. First, mass web archiving fails to address the complicated ethical issues of preserving web content. Second, as noted in the introduction, an archived website isn't just the site itself but consists of five different layers: the text and images on a page; one part of the larger collection of pages that make up a website; a site's shared topical web sphere; and, finally, the wider Web when the site was live.[4] Any one of these elements is impossible to preserve with total fidelity, as pages can vanish prior to archiving, or links to images or other sites break down over time. Certain elements of a site, once essential to its functioning, may become defunct with technological change; such was the fate of Adobe Flash, a once indispensable web development tool discontinued in December 2020. Web browser design matters as well, as new affordances change how sites are structured. Ultimately, no replication is a perfect re-creation, since any attempt "to make a defunct site historically accurate from the perspective of a user" may require

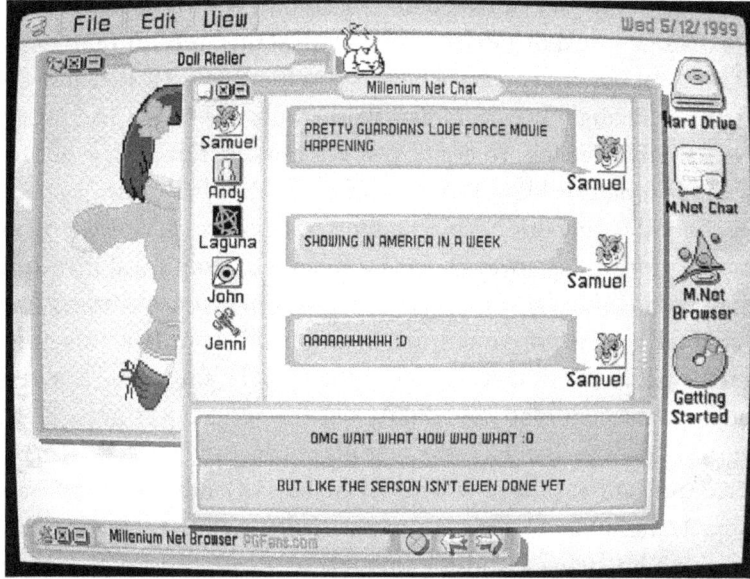

Figure c.1. Screenshot from *Secret Little Haven*, which purposely emulates a Y2K-era personal computer, from the visual aesthetics to the simulated software.

the host to "deform the source" to make it function in a contemporary browser.[5] Beyond technical re-creation, there's also the affective experience of using the web, particularly the sense of unstructured exploration so typical of the early Web. At best, this feeling can be simulated, as in the video game/visual novel *Secret Little Haven*, where players explore the computer of not-yet-out teen trans girl Alex Cole in 1999 (fig. c.1). Unlike a single narrative, *Secret Little Haven* encourages the player to explore all of the features of the computer, from an AIM-esque chat client and fandom message board to dollmaker software. In interviews, creator Victoria Dominowski has described being inspired by her own experiences "browsing old fan forums on my 1999 pink, translucent iMac," exploring the "federated archipelago of hamlets" that made up the Web in the mid to late 1990s—which, in Dominowski's view, offered far more opportunities for intimate connection and freeform exploration than the current Web's "select few bustling cities."[6]

The contrast between the Internet of *Secret Little Haven* and the contemporary Net also speaks to another point: the increasingly centralized nature of discussion online, and the risks it poses for preservation. Though we didn't discuss it in depth at the time, my interviewee's clear contrast between message boards and Facebook, Twitter, and Tumblr felt increasingly prescient as I worked on this book. The message board's archival feeling, I'd argue, owes not to the format's age but to its independent nature: like a BBS (its earliest ancestor), the message board is not bound to any one corporate master. In contrast, content on corporate platforms has always been contingent on continued investment in maintaining the platform. This reality informed much of my research for chapter 2, as most content from early walled gardens was purged when the platforms shut down. More recently, the 2019 closure of Yahoo Groups posed a similar issue. Early on, the service was popular with many LGBT groups; in fact, the first place I met (virtually) other trans folks in my state was the now-defunct Alabama Gender Alliance's Yahoo Group. Transgender individuals in particular took advantage of Yahoo Group's photo sharing and file hosting to create private groups, like ftmsurgeryinfo, that became well-known resources for information on medical procedures. Over time, these groups' age increased their value to members, as they contained a wide variety of information collected over many years. Some Yahoo Groups themselves became resources, like the transgendernews group, which reposted trans-related news pieces for approximately twenty years. Unlike an archive of "official" sources like Lexis-Nexis, transgendernews collected content from all over the Web, including now-defunct advocacy organizations and sites that didn't count as mainstream news sources. While some groups were able to be preserved, the ease with which such content could be wiped from the Net raises real questions about what it means that so much trans knowledge and history appears to live on borrowed time.

A Space of Our Own

In the dedication program for the NTL&A, Dallas Denny describes realizing, not long after she came out, that "the transgender community had little sense of its history." In the late 1980s and early 1990s, "there seemed to be no libraries, archives, or repositories for material about transsexualism and other transgender behavior; few of the national transgender organizations even maintained file copies of their own publications.

A few organizations and individuals had been wise enough to donate archival materials to universities and nonprofits, but for the most part transgender historical materials were being discarded and destroyed on a daily basis."[7] Born-digital transgender documents, in the contemporary moment, face a similar cycle of creation and destruction, especially as their presence on platforms like Tumblr is diminished or erased entirely. Simply preserving already produced content, however, doesn't solve the problem at the heart of the cycle: ownership. Ultimately, corporate platforms' emphasis on profitability and shareholder-friendly monetization will put marginalized users at risk unless a platform is, by design, interested and invested in their needs.

Historically, when faced with corporate indifference, silencing, or co-option, marginalized communities have sought out alternative means of publication, from gay and lesbian periodicals like *One* or the *Ladder* to the Women in Print movement.[8] In a similar vein, gender community groups and small presses developed and released their own publications, both books and periodicals, in order to help make a world where they could share their thoughts, feelings, and goals. Though often limited by small staffs and shoestring budgets, they played a key role in keeping the community together. Most importantly, though, they were fully owned and run by gender community members who were invested in the community's ongoing well-being. As scholar Oliver Haimson and his coauthors argue, these same features must be present in any future "trans technology": "A real trans technology would be designed specifically by and for trans people, outside of capitalist frameworks, with features enabling trans experiences and policies allowing trans content in the service of intersectional community building, regardless of how "pornographic" that content may appear to outsiders. Trans technologies do not need to be social media sites, but may be any sort of technology that accounts for the complexities of trans experiences and aims to solve trans community challenges."[9]

A site like Archive of Our Own (archiveofourown.org, commonly referred to as AO3) offers a possible model. AO3 and its host organization, the nonprofit Organization for Transformative Works (commonly referred to as OTW), were founded in 2007 following LiveJournal's mass deletion of accounts listing interests in "adult" content (known in fandom lore as Strikethrough).[10] The event, which came without warning or recourse, galvanized fans and clarified the importance of community ownership. As one early AO3 rallying cry put it, "I Want Us to Own the Goddamned Servers."[11] AO3 functions as a nonprofit, noncommercial, fan-based alternative to corporate platforms, centering core "feminist values" like "agency, inclusivity, diversity, and empowerment."[12] AO3's development team not only consistently emphasizes user involvement, but they also foreground their own investment as community members. These commitments and values are evident in the site's design, such as allowing multiple pseudonyms for one account, building in a variety of warning tags and visibility filters, allowing users to "orphan" (or abandon) content they no longer want associated with the account, and using intermediary "tag wranglers" to manage the site's complex folksonomy. Ongoing maintenance for AO3 is funded through donations to the OTW. Notably, AO3 has also not come without critique from fans of color for the ways its infrastructure "reproduce[s] the unmarked white defaults that allow racism to flow unchecked."[13] Yet the community-oriented infrastructure of AO3 has existing affordances built within it, fandom scholars Alexis Lothian and Mel Stanfill contend, that can be used to begin systemically addressing this racism, as well as a community culture with the capacity to be reoriented toward antiracist struggle and abolition.

All of these would be necessary elements of any future trans platform: a commitment to serving users' needs and actively involving them in site decisions, while also designing for long-term sustainability and preservation. Most importantly, from the outset this platform could plan ahead for possible closure and archiving. By design, it would include a variety of granular privacy and anonymity controls, allowing users to determine what content or attached metadata might be archived, if they wanted any of it preserved at all. Similar to AO3, this platform would ideally be overseen by a cooperatively governed organization, not unlike the many smaller, regional organizations discussed in this book. Long-term sustainability would come via access to a variety of funding streams, such as donations, grants, and sliding-scale memberships. This differentiation (member versus user) is key: users often have limited input in developing and implementing tools they use, while members are part of a larger decision-making collective where they can exert agency. Cooperative-style governance, with clearly designated access points for member participation, would ensure that the platform stays focused on empowering the site's primary demographic: trans and queer individuals.

Right now, this platform is, at best, a modest proposal. Yet it speaks to one of the central challenges throughout the history of trans life online: the need for safe spaces *we* own. In these battles, control of both hosting and platform governance have played a key role. When users had both, as they did on BBSes, Usenet, and websites, these spaces could thrive, and discussion flourished. In cases where they lacked direct access, as in walled gardens, trans spaces remained contingent on the continued largess of a platform's corporate host. If trans life is to not only truly thrive but also be preserved for future generations, then trans individuals, like fans, must "own the goddamned servers."

ACKNOWLEDGMENTS

This book would never have been possible without an amazing network. It took many years and much input from many different people to get to this final version. First, I want to thank the people, both named and pseudonymous, whose writing and activism made it possible to be trans online. I hope this book, however small, honors their legacy of labor and their faith in a better future for trans people everywhere. So much of this work has been shaped by my mentors and colleagues: Jason Farman, who always encouraged me to follow my instincts, even when I didn't always know where I was going; Katie King who pushed me to see beyond what was right in front of me to find the wider networks of power across history; and Alexis Lothian, who provided invaluable support and insight throughout my career and never stopped encouraging me. I also benefited immensely from the guidance of my other committee members, Kristy Maddux and Kari Krauss. Jess River Vooris was always willing to help me talk through an issue and challenge me when I needed it. And I owe special thanks to the other scholars who have supported me in ways big and small, including Kevin Driscoll, Cait McKinney, K. J. Rawson, Oliver Haimson, Davin Heckman, Ian Milligan, and Camille Paloque-Bergès.

I also want to thank the institutional sponsors whose support made this book possible. The University of Michigan Library's William P. Heidrich Visiting Research Fellowship allowed me to explore the treasure trove of materials held in the National Transgender Library and Archive, part of the Joseph A. Labadie Collection. Chapter 3 wouldn't be possible without the support of the Maryland Institute for Technology in the Humanities (MITH), who provided me with not just financial support during my dissertation, but time, space, and community. Ed Summers always had a second to talk through a coding issue, and it was my earliest conversations with Purdom Lindblad that helped lay the foundation for the Queer Digital History Project. This book could not have happened without the amazing resources held in the Digital Transgender Archive, and I hope it lives up to the project's commitment to making transgender history accessible to all. Thank you also to the individuals who were willing to share their memories and perspectives. Gwendolyn Ann Smith was not only willing to answer my many, many questions but also provided the amazing archival images included in chapter 2. Juno Salazar Parrenas offered invaluable insight into what it was like to be a queer teen on AOL in the 1990s.

I'm grateful for the invaluable feedback and guidance my series editors, Amanda Phillips, Bo Ruberg, and micha cárdenas provided throughout the writing process, as well as the incisive critiques of my two readers. Lastly, this book wouldn't be what it is without the support of my family and friends, especially my spouse, Cassy Dame-Griff. Even when I doubted myself, she never did, and was often willing to listen with bemused patience as I geeked out on the ins and outs of thirty-year-old Internet gossip. My life would be so much less without you.

NOTES

INTRODUCTION

1. Driscoll and Paloque-Berges, "Searching for Missing 'Net Histories.'"
2. Driscoll and Paloque-Berges, 10.
3. Hill, "As a Man I Exist."
4. Stryker, *Transgender History*.
5. Nownes, *Organizing for Transgender Rights*.
6. The choice to include "gender" instead of "transgender" in the organization's name would prove prophetic of Wilchins's later split with transgender organizations, as discussed in chapter 4.
7. McKinney, *Information Activism*, 8.
8. McKinney, 3.
9. Hill, "Before Transgender."
10. Functionally, there was little practical difference in the terms, so much so that the glossary published by Ariadne Kane's Human Outreach and Achievement Institute listed "bigenderist" as a synonym of "androgyne."
11. J. Nance, "From the Closet to Academia."
12. "New Glossary for Better Understanding." Even among English-language gender community publications, glossaries were sometimes required: the *Tartan Skirt*, a magazine for the Scottish gender community, included a "wordlist" for readers who might be going to American community events or reading American magazines, for while they may "manage to understand one another reasonably well; but from time to time jargon will rear its ugly head and get in the way of mutual understanding." See Forrester, "Parliamo Americano?"
13. Blackwood, "Why Terms Are Necessary"; Richards, "Needing a New Term."
14. Beecroft, "Executive Director's Page"; Jones, "Dictionary Project." While Jones would get interest from major trans organizations like IFGE and AEGIS, the project appears to have never officially gotten off the ground.
15. Wilchins, "What's in a Name." In an ironic twist, this piece would be published in the issue where the publication switched from *TV-TS Tapestry* to *Transgender Tapestry*. It's also worth noting that, were Wilchins to launch a campaign promoting the single-s "transexual" with the #transexual hashtag on (for example) Twitter, her content would be sorted not similar English-language posts but posts in Spanish, which uses the single-s spelling. In effect, she would be unwittingly advocating colonizing another community's space.

16 Bolin, *In Search of Eve*.
17 Sarah, "New Terminology!?!"
18 Kane, "Glossary for Understanding Gender Diversity"; Prince, "Proposing a New Terminology."
19 Boswell, "Transgender Alternative."
20 Feinberg, *Transgender Liberation*.
21 Denny, "Vision 2001."
22 Westbrook, "Becoming Knowably Gendered."
23 Reflecting the changes in community politics over the intervening years, "genderqueer" in particular was framed as not just an identity but an explicitly political term critiquing gender policing. In a 1995 essay describing the terminology she used, Riki Wilchins framed "genderqueer" as an explicitly political term that highlighted how "being 'queer,' i.e. being gay or lesbian or bi or drag or intersexed or trans is fundamentally about policing gender." However, early use of "genderqueer" in particular differs significantly from the modern definition, functioning both as a noun "genderqueers" and an adjective, as in "genderqueer youth." Wilchins and other contemporaneous activists primarily used the term as an umbrella noun, "genderqueers," which encompassed, in her words, "diesel dykes and stone butches, leatherqueens and radical fairies, nelly fags, crossdressers, intersexed, transsexuals, transvestites, transgendered, transgressively gendered, intersexed, and those of us whose gender expressions are so complex they haven't even been named yet" ("Note from Your Editrix"). This nounal use reflected contemporaneous arguments, such as Kate Bornstein's work in *Gender Outlaw* (1994), around rethinking gender binarism and norms. It would appear alongside the adjectival "genderqueer" into the late 1990s, eventually fusing with the adjectival form as use of genderqueer evolved to represent a spectrum of nonbinary identifications.
24 Wilchins.
25 Smith, "History Lesson."
26 Venkatesh, Shih, and Stolzoff, "Longitudinal Analysis of Computing."
27 Venkatesh, "Computers and Other Interactive Technologies."
28 Vitalari, Venkatesh, and Gronhaug, "Computing in the Home."
29 Pollack, "Ruling May Not Aid Videotex."
30 Delwiche, "Early Social Computing."
31 Driscoll, *Modem World*, 3.
32 Driscoll, 121.
33 National Telecommunications and Information Administration, "Falling through the Net."
34 Times Mirror Center for the People and the Press, *Technology in the American Household*, 14.
35 Venkatesh, "Computers and Other Interactive Technologies."
36 Venkatesh and Vitalari, "Emerging Distributed Work Arrangement."
37 Dedrick and Kraemer, "Market Making," 294.

38 National Telecommunications and Information Administration, "Falling through the Net"; Greene, "Discovering the Divide." As Greene details, such "digital divide" literature often ignored or downplayed larger social and economic issues that made gaining access to this "vault" so difficult in the first place.
39 Times Mirror Center for the People and the Press, *Technology in the American Household*; Venkatesh, Shih, and Stolzoff, "Longitudinal Analysis of Computing."
40 Ankerson, *Dot-Com Design*.
41 Pew Research Center, "Internet News Audience Goes Ordinary."
42 Pew Research Center, "Americans' Internet Access."
43 Rose, "Gender Support."
44 Pow, "Trans Historiography of Glitches and Errors."
45 "Appendix D"; Docter and Prince, "Transvestism."
46 Schwartz and Sherman, *All Dressed Up*; Giardina, "Oral History"; Wilchins, "Riki Wilchins."
47 Driscoll and Paloque-Berges, "Searching for Missing 'Net Histories.'"
48 Brügger, *Archived Web*.
49 Ankerson, "Writing Web Histories."
50 McKinney, "Printing the Network."
51 For further discussion of the complications of working with Usenet, see Dame-Griff, "Herding the 'Performing Elephants.'"
52 Milligan, *History in the Age of Abundance?*, 57.
53 Leong et al., "Question Concerning (Internet) Time."
54 Goodnight, "Queenspeak."
55 Bodkin, "Networking."
56 Giardina, "Oral History."
57 Nownes, *Organizing for Transgender Rights*.
58 Glover, "I Know What I Am," 124.
59 Sutherland, "Trans Enough."
60 Glover, "I Know What I Am," 98–99.
61 Bornstein, *Gender Outlaw*; Gabriel, "Fool's Paradox." Notably, Kate Bornstein in *Gender Outlaw* discusses reading such erotica early on and locates it as an important aspect of her self-discovery. However, the gap in community attitudes was apparent in an interview in *TransSisters*, where interviewer Davina specifically notes her disidentification with such texts.

1. DIALING INTO THE REVOLUTION

1 Carr, "Type Dirty to Me," 174.
2 Squires, "Rethinking the Black Public Sphere."
3 Brenda P., "Notice."
4 Meeker, *Contacts Desired*; Beins, *Liberation in Print*.
5 Hill, "As a Man I Exist."
6 Hall, "Performativity."
7 Stryker, *Transgender History*, 2017.

8   IFGE, *1st Annual*, 7.
9   IFGE, 72; "Boulton & Park Library."
10 Michaels, "Star Date," 10.
11 IFGE, *1st Annual*, 35.
12 Dyrud, "Exploration of Gender Bias," 35.
13 Dillon, "Clipart Images as Commonsense Categories."
14 "Eveolution."
15 Jackie, "So You Think."
16 IFGE, *1st Annual*.
17 Richards, "Kymberleigh's Clipboard: How Best to Reach Out?"
18 IFGE, *1st Annual*, 34.
19 IFGE, 72.
20 Driscoll, *Modem World*.
21 Delwiche, "Early Social Computing," 36.
22 Driscoll, *Modem World*.
23 McCloskey, *Crossing*.
24 Delwiche, "Early Social Computing," 43.
25 Driscoll, *Modem World*, 3.
26 "GGA Introduces Gendernet."
27 "Paula Elizabeth Keiser."
28 "GENDERNET News," *TV-TS Tapestry*, 1985, DTA, 68.
29 Delwiche, "Early Social Computing"; Friedman, *Interpreting the Internet*.
30 David Lowe, "Computerized Networks of Hate."
31 Berlet, "When Hate Went Online," 9.
32 Berlet, 4.
33 Berlet, 9.
34 Kohn, "Bulletin Boards for Gay Computer Hackers."
35 "Trial Balloon Gay BBS Listing—1989."
36 Driscoll, *Modem World*, 158.
37 McKinney, "Printing the Network."
38 Brewster and Ruberg, "Survivors."
39 Haas, "State OKs Proposal."
40 Hilty, "This Sister Oughta Be Famous"; Sister Mary Elizabeth, "Letter to the Editor."
41 IFGE, *IFGE's 1st Annual*.
42 Roberts, "From the Editor's Pen."
43 Wells, "Proposal from Jennifer Wells."
44 Turner, *From Counterculture to Cyberculture*.
45 Turner; Dahlberg, "Libertarian Cyber-Utopianism."
46 Brophy, "Developing a Corporeal Cyberfeminism."
47 Turner, *From Counterculture to Cyberculture*, 146.
48 Turner, 147.
49 "Announcing the Formation."

50 "US TOO to Be Up and Running."
51 Raeder, "Editorial: All Systems, Go."
52 "Americans With Disabilities Act. S.722."
53 "Americans With Disabilities Act. S.722."
54 Colker, "Homophobia, AIDS Hysteria." In fact, the ADA includes two different sections specifically excluding "transvestites" from coverage, the first coming from an earlier amendment by Senator Jesse Helms. See Cokler for a longer discussion of the legal decisions that led to Helms' proposed amendment.
55 Raeder, "Get Involved!"
56 As further support for her argument, Raeder excerpts several posts from a longer conversation between Sister Mary Elizabeth of J2CP and Anne Ogborn, a trans activist who would coordinate the first incarnation of Camp Trans in 1991 and later founded Transgender Nation, the influential if short-lived transgender focus group of Queer Nation.
57 Raeder, "Editorial: 'Tis the Season!"
58 Bolin, "In Search of Eve."
59 Stephanie Rose, "Gender Support," 21.
60 Carr, "Type Dirty to Me," 174.
61 Bolin, "In Search of Eve."
62 "Paula Elizabeth Keiser."
63 "Paula Elizabeth Keiser."
64 "GENDERNET News."
65 Rose, "Gender Support," 21.
66 Carr, "Type Dirty to Me," 175.
67 Cummins and Cummins, "Tri-Ess Computer Bulletin Board System."
68 McCloskey, *Crossing*, 17.
69 McCloskey, 21.
70 McCloskey, 21. The appearance of such large telephone bills is indicative of the one-way online communication could risk outing a BBS user. Many users saved money by downloading messages to read offline, composing responses, and then dialing back in to upload them. However, this could prove a more technical process that required assistance for less technically skilled users like McCloskey. She felt unable to request assistance from a expert because "then [she] would be known. It was like the library."
71 Frederickson, "Editor's Corner: Up the Road."
72 Rose, "Gender Support," 22.
73 Stone, "Will the Real Body Please Stand Up?"
74 McCloskey, *Crossing*, 56.
75 Kimberly Ann N., "To All My New Friends."
76 IFGE, *IFGE's 1st Annual*, 66.
77 McCloskey, *Crossing*.
78 IFGE, *IFGE's 1st Annual*, 65.
79 IFGE, 66.

80 Marlene, "Library Outreach."
81 Bolin, "In Search of Eve," 64.
82 Driscoll, *Modem World*, 99.
83 Rose, "Gender Support."
84 Driscoll, *Modem World*, 100.
85 Richards, "Information Highway and You."
86 IFGE, "Atlanta Action Update."
87 Friedman, *Interpreting the Internet*, 98.
88 McKinney, "Printing the Network."
89 In some cases, content would be published and republished in the same publication, based on what platform the editor preferred. Dallas Denny's essay "Tripping the Light Fantastic: Staying Sane and Whole While in Transition," initially published in *Our Sorority*, no. 25 (1991), was also uploaded to the Genderline forum on Compuserve. From there, it was downloaded and republished in the November/December 1991 issue of *XX: Newsletter of Twenty Club*. The same essay would be later published, under a different editor, in the November/December 1994 issue of *XX*, but credited to the America OnLine Gender Group. The essay continued to be available via the nonprofit that Denny founded, AEGIS, and would be republished again on the GenderWeb site by Julie Case in early 1997. Its final print publication was in the newsletter of the Gender Centre in Sydney, Australia, *Polare* (edition 18) in 1997.
90 "National Gender News"; Gardner, "News Beat and Reminder."

2. OUT OF THE CYBERCLOSET, INTO THE CYBERSTREETS

1 McCullough, "She Gave the World."
2 McCullough.
3 Allbritton, "America Online."
4 Habib and Cornford, "Computers in the Home."
5 Sender, *Business, Not Politics*.
6 Maya, "1994.'"
7 Kasey et al., *What the Heck's the Net?*
8 Untitled Prodigy Commercial.
9 Roberts, "Hot Buzz"; Marla Louise, "In the Middle,", 21.
10 Rose, "TG Community and the Internet"; Linda, "Linda's Corner."
11 Thomas, "Computer Chronicles," 61.
12 Alicia, "Transgenderism and the Information Superhighway."
13 Carmichael, "Out of Focus."
14 Anya, "Transgendered Computing"; Anya, "Computing and the Transgendered."
15 Jenifer, "Jenifer's Juxtaposition: Net Surf'n."
16 Gardner, "News Beat and Reminder."
17 Jenifer, "Jenifer's Juxtaposition: New Found Freedom."
18 By 1995, many groups began publishing lists of member email addresses, as a way to facilitate communication outside of regular meetings. The earliest list came as a

part of Tri-Ess's existing Pen Pal program: in 1993, newsletter editors collected and published Prodigy members' numbers for Tri-Ess members who wanted to talk to other trans users on the service. At its height, the list had thirty-two members, including the organization's president, Carol Beecroft.

19. Wells, "Letter: T.G.I.F. [*Sic*] NEWS."
20. Main, "Girl at Heart," 17.
21. Main, 17.
22. Louise, "In the Middle."
23. Marla Louise, "Bird on a Wire."
24. Batterson, "Subject: File 2."
25. Prior to the passage of the Communications Decency Act, two cases were particularly influential: *Cubby, Inc. v. CompuServe Inc.*, which established that services could not be held liable for the posting of content that had not been previously reviewed, and *Stratton Oakmont, Inc. v. Prodigy Services Co.*, which established that Prodigy's "conscious choice" to review content prior to publication meant that the service could be held liable for content published on Prodigy.
26. De Luca, "Computer Network."
27. Dowd and Herbek, "Computer Bulletin Board Systems."
28. Outland, "Sears' Queers."
29. Outland, "Sears Discontinues Sexy Prodigy Board."
30. Sugawara, "Computer Networks and the 1st Amendment."
31. Swisher, *AOL.Com*, 94.
32. "Censorship, Online Services.'"
33. It's worth noting that this terminology ban was at times applied to advertisers as well. In a 1995 ACLU media release (republished in Computer Underground Digest), Jeff Satkin, owner-operator of New Jersey–based mail-order gay video store ATKOL Gay Videos, reported receiving a request from AOL managers to censor a substantial number of the title listings in his text-only catalog so that his advertisement would have "the look and feel that best fits our environment," the small business forum Downtown AOL. Not only did the request catch Satkin off-guard, given that the full catalog had already been available for a month, but he also couldn't fully understand their specific criteria for removal. While titles like *Advanced Disrobics* and *Gayracula* were to be censored, *Gay Tarzan* and *Bung Hole Buddies* were allowed to remain. See Computer Underground Digest, "AOL Censors."
34. Laermer, *Get On with It*.
35. Hill, "As a Man I Exist."
36. Attorney General's Commission on Pornography and US Department of Justice, *Final Report*.
37. "Letters: Member Essay Feature."
38. The piece's author doesn't clarify if Kadzin is an AOL-approved "guide," who would have the authority to censure TV chat participants, or a regular user.
39. Schwartz, "Caution."

40 Much of the details in this section come from Melanie Anne Phillips's writings, as well as her webzine, *The Subversive*. However, while the text-based version of *The Subversive* posted to AOL was dated in the filename, the web version is undated. As such, I draw heavily from this timeline, developed by Gwendolyn Ann Smith in 1999, to identify approximate date ranges for the events described here. See Smith, "AOL's Banned Words."
41 Phillips, "*Subversive* #25: Explorations."
42 Phillips, "*Subversive* #32: The Last *Subversive*!"
43 Phillips, "*Subversive* #15: Updates."
44 Phillips, "*Subversive* #17: Updates and Useful Information."
45 Leveque, *Trans / Active*.
46 Phillips, "*Subversive* #10: Explorations."
47 Leveque, *Trans / Active*, 21.
48 Phillips, "*Subversive* #32: The Last *Subversive*!"
49 Smith, "AOL's Banned Words."
50 Smith, personal communication, December 11, 2018.
51 Cassel, "Re: Sex on AOL."
52 Swisher, *AOL.Com*, 102–3.
53 "*Subversive* #13: Letters to the Editor," 13.
54 Phillips, "*Subversive* #17: Updates and Useful Information."
55 Dahir, "Online Computer Service."
56 Dahir.
57 Phillips, "*Subversive* #15: Updates"; Phillips, "*Subversive* #32: The Last *Subversive*!"
58 Phillips, "*Subversive* #15: Updates."
59 Murib, "LGBT."
60 "*Subversive* #13: Letters to the Editor."
61 Weise, "Gay and Lesbian Net Surfers."
62 "*Subversive* #13: Letters to the Editor."
63 Phillips, "*Subversive* #26: Explorations," 26.
64 In an excerpt from a 1995 guide training session, the trainer instructs trainees that "cross dressing transvestite, transsexual . . . are ALL allowed and are NOT TOS Violations." See Holyoak, "AOL's Secret Dirty Word List."
65 Nangeroni, "Gender Outlaws."
66 Javier, "Welcome."
67 Sontag, "Once a Pariah."
68 Leveque, *Trans / Active*, 30.
69 Smith, sersonal communication, December 11, 2018.
70 Laermer, *Get On with It*.
71 Kloehn, "Lesbians, Gays March for Pride."
72 Laermer, *Get On with It*, 92–93.
73 AdRespect, "Print Ad Library."
74 Weise, "Gay and Lesbian Net Surfers"; Lewis, "Planet Out."
75 "Planetout Debuts"; Smith, personal communication, December 11, 2018.

76 "Pride! Universe"; Pride Media, "Virtual Reality World."
77 Silberman, "Gay.Net Launch Challenges AOL."
78 Napoli, "Feeling Abandoned by America Online."
79 Hu and Yamamoto, "AOL's Squeeze Play."

3. POLITICS AND "PETTY USELESS BICKERING"

1 Brunton, *Spam*.
2 Gene Spafford, "Gene Spafford's Personal Pages: Quotable Spaf," accessed April 10, 2019. spaf.cerias.purdue.edu.
3 Pfaffenberger, "Standing Wave."
4 Barr, "So You Want." Unsurprisingly, the alt.* hierarchy was frequently prone to spin-off or joke newsgroups, such as "alt.swedish.chef.bork.bork.bork."
5 Whittaker et al., "Dynamics of Mass Interaction"; Brunton, *Spam*.
6 Grossman, *Net.wars*; Pfaffenberger, "Standing Wave."
7 Raymond, "September That Never Ended."
8 Grossman, *Net.wars*.
9 Kelly, "Netskills Corner."
10 Grossman, *Net.wars*, 33–34.
11 Gilster, *Mosaic Navigator*.
12 Engst, *Internet Starter Kit*; Grossman, *Net.wars*.
13 Smith, "Invisible Crowds in Cyberspace."
14 Whittaker et al., "Dynamics of Mass Interaction," 84.
15 Baym, *Tune In, Log On*; Whittaker et al., "Dynamics of Mass Interaction."
16 Pfaffenberger, "Standing Wave."
17 Pfaffenberger, 21.
18 Burnett and Bonnici, "Beyond the FAQ."
19 Baym, *Tune In, Log On*.
20 Baym, 187.
21 Kayany, "Contexts of Uninhibited Online Behavior."
22 Lee, "Behavioral Strategies for Dealing with Flaming."
23 Lee, 399.
24 Raymond, "Jargon File Resources."
25 Whittaker et al., "Dynamics of Mass Interaction," 81.
26 Whittaker et al.
27 The inexactness of this date comes from *The Subversive*'s publishing practices, as discussed in chapter 2: none of the "issues" are dated, so getting an exact publication date is difficult. However, the survey had been published prior to when the webzine's home page was archived by the Internet Archive for the first time in 1997, making it possible to estimate a date.
28 Phillips, "*Subversive* #16: Transgender Survey."
29 Kaye, "TG Net News."
30 Roberts, "Hot Buzz," 12.
31 Rachel, "Murder in the Magnolia State."

32 Nownes, *Organizing for Transgender Rights*, 139–41; Davidson, "Seeking Refuge under the Umbrella."
33 Dame, "Making a Name for Yourself."
34 Richmond, "Queen's Throne," July 1996.
35 Wilson, "Soc.Support.Transgendered FAQ."
36 Matthews, "Charter—Alt.Fashion.Crossdressing."
37 In fact, the level of contention was so high among regular posters to alt.support.srs that it spurred several efforts between 1997 and 2004 to reestablish the newsgroup as a moderated one. However, because members could not agree on just who would be able to serve as an impartial moderator, these efforts ultimately failed.
38 Usenet Historical Collection.
39 Matthews, "Alt.Fashion.Crossdressing."
40 Martin, "Freegan, Yarn Bombing." The 2015 addition was not the first made by OED staff, according to Sunnivie Brydum: "cisgender" had been available in the *OED*'s online public-facing dictionary, OxfordDictionaries.com (rebranded as Lexico in 2019), since 2013. Brydum, "True Meaning."
41 Aviance, "I Am NOT Cisgendered"; Sisto, "Cis-Ridiculous."
42 Goldberg, "What Is a Woman?"
43 For a more detailed discussion of how whiteness intertwines with the concept of cisgender, see Bey, *Cistem Failure*.
44 Blank, "Will 'Cisgender' Ever Go Mainstream?"
45 Savage, "Will 'Cisgender' Survive?"
46 Use of a cis-/trans binary first appears in the early 1900s: sexologist Ernst Burchard uses the term "cisvestitismus," defined as "the inclination to put on the clothing of other ages, classes, or professions and the same gender for the purpose of sexual recreation," as an antonym of "transvestitismus" (or "transvestitism") in his 1914 book *Lexikon des gesamten Sexuallebens* [Lexicon of the entire sex life]. The first more contemporary usage—in this case the variant term "cissexual"—comes in German sexologist Volkmar Sigusch's two-part 1991 article "Die Transsexuellen und unser nosomorpher Blick" [Transsexuals and our nosomorphic view] (Sigusch 1998). See Williams, "So, I Hear"; and Sigusch, "Neosexual Revolution."
47 James, "MTF Glossary"; Annie, "Annotated Glossary of Terms." James's dismissive attitude could be partially attributed to her overall low opinion of Usenet, of which she declared that "anyone posting there should be considered unreliable and unstable, and possibly dangerous. These are support group rejects who have proven they are unable to play nice with others." See James, "Transgender Forum List."
48 Enke, "Education of Little Cis."
49 Defo0008, "Talk," 1. An unregistered user claims below Defosse's comment to have coined "cisgendered" in 1994 as a term "to describe those who move from one mode of masculinity or femininity to another," which they later used in publicity materials for GLQSOC-L, the Gay, Lesbian, Queer Social Science listserv. While it is difficult to determine the validity of this claim, the term is used

amongst a list of other deviant categories on the listserv's landing page, which was last updated in 1999. Its contextual placement, then, implied a very different meaning from its current one. "Comment from 1994 user of the term cisgender," 2007; "Gay/Lesbian/Queer Social Science List."

50 Carolmooredc, "Several Questionable Sources."
51 "Cisgender."
52 Matthews, "Definitions."
53 Koyama, "Cissexual/Cisgender."
54 Serano, "Whipping Girl FAQ."
55 In some cases, posters used the noun "cisgenders"; simply using "cis" was fairly uncommon until the mid-to-late 2000s.
56 By the time my analysis begins, this format had been widely established as the standard for quoting on Usenet.
57 For a more in-depth discussion of the technical and ethical aspects of this work, see Dame-Griff, "Herding the 'Performing Elephants.'"
58 Matthews, "Welcome to Nowhere"; Blake, "TransEqual Collection."
59 Blake, "TransEqual Collection."
60 Ontario Human Rights Commission, "Discussion Paper"; Masters, "New Canadian Human Rights Commission."
61 Smith, personal communication, September 25, 2021.
62 Like Masters, Blake would be interviewed as an expert transgender activist for articles in several Canadian newspapers and magazines, such as *now* Magazine in Toronto and the *Winnipeg Free Press*, throughout the early 1990s. See Wheeler, "Sex Role Revolt"; and Davis, "Life's a Drag."
63 Blake's pugnacious tone, however, would emerge in her letters to the editor, often when she disagreed with a specific individual. She took a particular dislike to prominent activist Phyllis Frye and dismissed her attempt to have transgender individuals recognized at Stonewall 25 as "sheer lunacy! Ms Frye desperately needs to grow up!" See Masters, "Mailbag."
64 Masters, "Achieving Equality," 56.
65 In 2000, Blake also claimed without evidence that the term was in "*common* use in many parts of the transcommunity as well as in human rights work." She closed her comment noting that "if this is the first time you've encountered it, I can only suggest you are at least 5 years out of date." However, based on the Buijs creation narrative she regularly presented, the term would have had to rocket to popularity within months of its creation.
66 Matthews, "Definitions."
67 Blake's position on transsexuality also inspired a rule of the "Laura Blake Drinking Game:" "At any point in the game anyone can be required to take the 'Transsexual Challenge' by someone rising up, pointing to the person being challenged and shouting 'Internalized Transphobia!' The person being challenged must then say the words 'Cisgender Ideal' three times fast. If she fails to do so then she must take a drink, If successful the challenger must take two drinks."

68 This practice was anecdotally confirmed when I received the copy I requested via InterLibrary Loan, which had a Tri-Ess donation sticker on the back inside cover.
69 Enke, "Education of Little Cis."
70 Matthews, "Crossdressing and Society."

4. ALWAYS ON

1 Greenstein, *How the Internet Became Commercial*, 229n1.
2 Greenstein, 228.
3 Chris Nerney, "Net Buzz."
4 Near the end of January, AOL would reach a settlement with the attorney generals for thirty-six states, ensuring that subscribers would be eligible for refunds up to $39.90 (approximately $69 adjusted for inflation). AOL's competitors also rushed to capitalize on the debacle: that year, CompuServe spent a million dollars for a thirty-second Superbowl ad comparing AOL's failure—symbolized by a fifteen-second recording of a modem trying and failing to successfully dial in—to their own "dependable Internet access." See CNN, "CompuServe Takes Aim."
5 Karen Kaplan, "AOL Ads Wanting?"
6 Streeter, *Net Effect*, 127.
7 Devor and Matte, "Building a Better World."
8 Holly, "Letter From Holly."
9 "Library Project."
10 Denny, "Impact of Emerging Technologies."
11 Denny.
12 Denny.
13 Denny and Xavier, "On the Future," 5.
14 Smith, "Remembering Our Dead."
15 Cheung, "Home on the Web"; Fletcher, "Internet Atrocity!"
16 Ankerson, *Dot-Com Design*.
17 "Local Advertising."
18 "Metroplex CrossDressers Club."
19 Motavalli, *Bamboozled at the Revolution*.
20 Prosser, *Second Skins*.
21 Bolin, "In Search of Eve."
22 Gamson, *Freaks Talk Back*.
23 Streeter, *Net Effect*.
24 Ankerson, *Dot-Com Design*.
25 Wolfe, " (Second Phase of the) Revolution."
26 Prosser, *Second Skins*.
27 Vanessa Edwards, "TG Tidbits."
28 Casey, "Web Rings."
29 Surkan, "Passing Rhetorics."
30 "Vanity Club Welcome—Version 5.1."

31. "Vanity Club Membership Information—Version 5.0"; Gardner, "Profile."
32. "Our Beginnings"; "Vanity Club Membership Information—Version 5.0."
33. For a detailed case study of how the neighborhood model fostered community, see Milligan, *History in the Age of Abundance?*, chap. 5.
34. Elmer-Dewitt, "On a Screen Near You."
35. Marwick, "To Catch a Predator?"
36. Chun, *Control and Freedom*.
37. Crabtree, "E-Mail Links Strangers."
38. Roberts, "HotBuzz." Notably, Roberts fails to mention that she, as one of the primary financial beneficiaries of TGForum, stood to lose the most financially from the passage of the CDA.
39. "Queer Resources Directory Affidavit."
40. Gay and Lesbian Alliance Against Defamation, "Access Denied"; "CYBERsitter Site Filtering."
41. "GeoCities Guidelines FAQ."
42. Murib, "Transgender."
43. Blanton, "George I. Sanchez, Ideology, and Whiteness"; Beauchamp, "Artful Concealment and Strategic Visibility."
44. When such content began to reappear in the AOLGG's attached newsletter, *The Subversive*, Melanie Phillips began a second newsletter specifically for it. See Phillips, "Subversive #26: Explorations."
45. McKinney, "Crisis Infrastructures."
46. "ACLU Intervenors' Complaint."
47. "Document: Opinion."
48. Certainly, this move no doubt facilitated the closure of many such publications, which charged significantly more to publish photos alongside ads.
49. Gardner, "Editorial." At times, the relationship with chasers could be framed (from the chaser perspective) as mutually beneficial. Kevin, the head of Transgender Website Support, a free service offering preformatted templates as well as custom web design services to trans women, was a self-described chaser who claimed to be "one of the biggest TV-admirers on this Big Blue Marble!" However, TWS also served as a funnel for Kevin's other site, the Transgendered Models Site. Kevin himself admonished other "admirers" emailing models to "please show some common courtesy towards the ladies," as "most of them are not interested in getting nasty email containing foul language . . . treat them with the utmost respect; they deserve it." Yet the disclaimer used in the TWS homepage template (fig. 4.17) was by far the most legalistic, implicitly framing the trans homepage as sexualized.

5. BECOMING "OBSOLETE IN YOUR OWN LIFETIME"

1. Johnson, "Keynote Address," 67.
2. Johnson, 67.
3. Johnson, 68.
4. Gardner, "Talkin' with Sarah Thomas," 9.

5   Gardner, "Editorial," 1999.
6   Gardner, "Profile: Amanda Richards," 6–7.
7   Roberts, "On My Mind . . ."
8   Yarborough, "California Unity '97," 27.
9   Peo, "People of Color."
10 "Appendix D."
11 Beyond surveys and conference sessions on issues related to people of color, the archival record offers an incomplete picture of the place of people of color within in the gender community at a more granular level; groups' focus on member privacy makes identifying possible people of color within the archival record particularly challenging. Beyond a lack of membership rolls, this is most prevalent in newsletters, where many authors used only chosen femme first names (and possibly the first letter of a last name). This practice makes identifying racially or ethnically specific names difficult, instead rendering individuals as part of more generalized, deraced "femininity."
12 Frye, "IFGE in Portland, Oregon." Frye also maintained this commitment for the annual conference she chaired, International Conference on Transgender Law and Employment Policy (ICTLEP). The 1996 conference would feature a highly publicized session on the issues of transgender people of color, which discussed these issues in more depth, as well as panelists' own experience with racism within the transgender community.
13 Though leaders would urge audiences to engage in outreach, groups at the national level rarely prioritized it, instead focusing on public education or lobbying aimed at a mainstream, middle-class white audience. In a 1995 essay for Canadian zine *gendertrash from hell*, transgender activist and social worker Christine Tayleur highlighted this contrast in describing her experience at the 1989 IFGE Convention in San Francisco: hearing speeches about "federalism and liberty" delivered to an audience of "power-brokers . . . [and] staying in a deluxe hotel and eating prime rib" while, in the community she served—transgender people living in the Tenderloin—"these ideas meant nothing to people who were worried about where they were going to sleep or eat that night." See Tayleur, "Racism and Poverty."
14 Wilchins, "How to Dilute Your Focus." In this column, Wilchins would also hint at the new focus GenderPAC would take in 2000 (discussed later in this chapter), citing the shared discrimination around "gender perception" and homophobia shared between gay, lesbian, and transgender individuals. This shared experience led her to believe that "maybe a gender movement is a much more powerful, inclusive, and broad thing than we ever dared hope."
15 Whittle, "Trans-Cyberian Mail Way," 405.
16 Whittle, 399.
17 Dae, "Rose by Any Name"; "More Hints about Choosing A Name"; "'Rules' for Playing the Name Game."
18 "More Hints about Choosing A Name"; Dae, "Rose by Any Name."
19 Nakamura, *Cybertypes*.

20 Tamara, "Mexico," 26.
21 tamara, 27.
22 Israel, "Column: Gianna E. Israel."
23 "Termination of Carolyn's Place BBS."
24 Richards, "Open Letter to the Community."
25 Though the Internet facilitated the creation and founding of groups, no comparable work has been done around group dissolution—assuming they even formally dissolved. As with many historical projects, the archival record prioritizes those groups who had the resources necessary to regularly produce and circulate newsletters. For more precarious groups, there may be little to no record of their existence outside mentions in a newsletter or inclusion on a mailing list.
26 Roberts, "On My Mind . . ."
27 Keller, "Future of CIGA."
28 Cresap, "Is the Internet Killing All the Support Groups?"
29 Phillips, "TV Tech."
30 Phillips's approval of Internet use was, in fact, contingent on offline embodiment—her only positive mentions of the Internet after 1995 came when she noted "over a hundred people" attended the Texas "T" Party because they learned about it online.
31 Phillips, "In the Gender Groove."
32 Phillips, "Dear Mr. Schneider."
33 Phillips, "Are You Ever Gonna Go Out?"
34 Phillips, "Writers in Gender World"; Phillips, "Gender Newsletter."
35 Ms. High Heels, "That Long Trip." Though the author is pseudonymous, Phillips had written previously as Ms. High Heels for both *Gender Euphoria* and *Cross-Currents*. Both Phillips and her wife Cynthia regularly used pseudonyms when they didn't receive enough content from contributors.
36 Hubbard, "Michelle's Ramblings," December 1998; Hubbard, "Michelle's Ramblings," April 1999.
37 Phillips, "the Gender Groove."
38 Phillips, "Last."
39 Phillips, "Editorial: The End."
40 Phillips, "Who Was the One?"
41 Smith, "History Lesson."
42 Gill-Peterson, *Histories of the Transgender Child*, 150–54.
43 Stryker, *Transgender History*.
44 Gill-Peterson, *Histories of the Transgender Child*, 206.
45 Barbara Jean, "Insight #48."
46 Richards, "Kymberleigh's Clipboard: What about Teenaged Transgendered?"
47 Kirk, "Youth Research Project."
48 Sheila Kirk, "There Is Help," 23.
49 Kirk, 24.
50 Kirk, 24.

51 Richmond, "Queen's Throne."
52 Peo, "Roger's Notebook #30: Teenage Crossdressers."
53 Silberman, "We're Teen, We're Queer."
54 Silberman.
55 Juno Salazar Parrenas, personal communication, June 16, 2022.
56 Affidavit of Rheana Parrenas in *ACLU et al. v. Reno*.
57 Affidavit of Hunter Allen in *ACLU et al. v. Reno*.
58 Affidavit of Christine Soto in *ACLU et al. v. Reno*.
59 Silberman, "We're Teen, We're Queer"; Batterson, "AOL Chat Rooms."
60 Batterson.
61 Kielwasser, "GLAAD Media Watch."
62 Batterson, "AOL Chat Rooms."
63 Batterson; Gwendolyn Ann Smith, personal communication, September 17, 2021.
64 Richards, "Kymberleigh's Clipboard: What about Teenaged Transgendered?"
65 Addison and Comstock, "Virtually Out."
66 *Oral History*; "Origin of This Newsgroup."
67 Juno Salazar Parrenas, personal communication, June 16, 2022.
68 Staff, "Updata."
69 "More about the TransBoy Resource Network."
70 "Home Page."
71 "IFGE Begins Youth Outreach Program."
72 "PFLAG TNET—About."
73 Giordano, "Volunteers Reach Out."
74 Roberts, "Hot Buzz," February 1996.
75 Xavier, "On the Future of the TG Community."
76 Dale, "Transgender Fund."
77 Dale.
78 Dale.
79 "Letters: Letter from Krista."
80 Denny's choice to suggest GSLEN as a resource is indicative of a wider inattention to youth concerns, as GSLEN's target demographic is students in K–12 schools—far too young to assist a twenty-two-year-old college student.
81 Powell and Porch, "Averies."
82 Gender Education and Advocacy, "Gender Variance."
83 Davidson, "Seeking Refuge."
84 Stryker, "Transgender History, Homonormativity, and Disciplinarity"; Stryker, *Transgender History: The Roots of Today's Revolution*.
85 Valentine, "Calculus of Pain."
86 Davidson, "Seeking Refuge."
87 "Youth Advocacy."
88 Davidson, "Seeking Refuge," 72.
89 Davidson, 73.
90 Davidson.

91 Tapestry Staff, "Coming Together 2004."
92 "YGP."
93 See Dallas Denny's editorial, "Disaster, Deceit, and Betrayal" for an in-depth discussion of the changing status of IFGE.
94 GenderPAC would close its doors in 2009, citing the variety of other groups doing similar work. In an implicit admission of the generic nature of the organization's mission, GenderPAC transferred GenderYOUTH's functions to Choice USA, a reproductive justice youth organization founded by Gloria Steinem.
95 Lynam, "Chicago Gender Society."
96 John, "Sharing and Web 2.0."
97 Dym and Fiesler, "Generations, Migrations, and the Future."
98 Busker, "On Symposia."
99 Driver, "Virtually Queer Youth Communities," 242.
100 Driver, 243.
101 For a more detailed narrative account of posting to birls in the early 2000s, see Brager, "LiveJournal Made Me Gay."
102 Driver, "Virtually Queer Youth Communities," 240.
103 Liedtke, "Blogging Pioneers Six Apart."
104 Wright, "Linux of Social Media."

6. TRANSGENDER IN THE PLATFORM ERA

1 Kafka, "Who Said Web 2.0 Was R.I.P.?"
2 Kowalska, "Heroines of My Life."
3 Kowalska.
4 Roberts, "*LadyLike* Magazine Ceases Publication."
5 Shafrir, "Would You Take a Tumblr?"
6 Boutin, "Tumblr Makes Blogging Blissfully Easy."
7 Zimman and Hayworth, "How We Got Here."
8 Dame, "Making a Name for Yourself."
9 McBee, "Why Tumblr Is Perfect."
10 thequeerestplaceontheinternet, "♥ ♥ ♥ ♥ ♥."
11 Haimson et al., "Tumblr Was a Trans Technology." In *Misogynoir Transformed*, scholar Moya Bailey argues Tumblr specifically gave these users space to have conversations that "[created] the networks needed to address this anti-Black racist misogyny both on- and offline." For example, Bailey's interviewees, Danielle Cole and Antoinette Luna Myers, each described how Tumblr served as a useful tool for facilitating in-person connection at events such as the Allied Media Conference.
12 Fink and Miller, "Trans Media Moments," 614.
13 Fink and Miller, 622.
14 Duval et al., "Metadata Principles and Practicalities."
15 Noble, *Algorithms of Oppression*, 147.
16 Noble.

17 Prince, "Proposing a New Terminology."
18 "Re: Terminology for the Crossdressing Community."
19 Tere Frederickson, "Re: 'Terminology.'"
20 Squires, "Rethinking the Black Public Sphere."
21 Zimman and Hayworth, "How We Got Here."
22 "Folksonomy: Vanderwal.Net."
23 Peters, *Folksonomies*. It's worth noting that most research on categorization systems uses datasets from bookmarking services or sites primarily geared toward information organization like Delicious or LibraryThing. While users may connect using these sites' social tools, the tagging system does not form part of the backbone supporting social interaction.
24 Barité, "Literary Warrant"; Macgregor and McCulloch, "Collaborative Tagging."
25 Johnson, "Transgender Subject Access."
26 Adler, "Gender Expression in a Small World."
27 Johnson, "Information Systems."
28 Hicks, "Hacking the Cis-Tem."
29 Bivens and Haimson, "Baking Gender into Social Media Design."
30 Hicks, "Hacking the Cis-Tem"; Bivens, "Gender Binary."
31 Haimson and Hoffmann, "Constructing and Enforcing."
32 Dame, "Making a Name for Yourself."
33 Oakley, "Disturbing Hegemonic Discourse."
34 Szulc, "Digital Gender Disidentifications."
35 Robards et al., "Twenty Years of 'Cyberqueer.'"
36 Richards, "Need for a New Term." Richards would continue to write about her search for an appropriate term for several years, before finally settling on "transgenderist" as the most functional compromise choice. Even so, she made a point to note that this use continued to conflict with her view of "transgender" as an umbrella term.
37 Laing, "Label by Any Other Name."
38 Schudson and van Anders, "You Have to Coin New Things," 363.
39 Schudson and van Anders, 365.
40 Oakley, "Supporting One Another."
41 Keilty, "Sexual Boundaries and Subcultural Discipline."
42 Golder and Huberman, "Usage Patterns of Collaborative Tagging Systems."
43 Keilty, "Sexual Boundaries and Subcultural Discipline," 427.
44 Garrison, "On the Limits of 'Trans Enough'"; Darwin, "Challenging the Cisgender/Transgender Binary"; Scheuerman et al., "Safe Spaces and Safe Places."
45 Dame, "Making a Name for Yourself."
46 Thornton, "Geographies of (Con)Text."
47 Hayles, *My Mother Was a Computer*, 39.
48 Halavais, *Search Engine Society*.
49 Van Couvering, "History of the Internet Search Engine," 202.
50 Van Couvering, 196.

51 Kallinikos et al., "Theory of Digital Objects."
52 Kitzie, "That Looks Like Me"; Huttunen et al., "Uncomfortable in My Own Skin."
53 Kitzie, "That Looks Like Me."
54 Gillespie, "Relevance of Algorithms," 168.
55 Couldry and Van Dijck, "Researching Social Media."
56 Noble, *Algorithms of Oppression.*
57 Bucher, *If . . . Then,* 28.
58 Kaplan, "Linguistic Capitalism and Algorithmic Mediation," 60.
59 Bucher, *If . . . Then,* 60–61.
60 Matias et al., "Generating Related Questions."
61 Pothirattanachaikul et al., "Analyzing the Effects."
62 It should be noted that, because of the algorithmic nature of the PAA system, the questions highlighted in search may change based on the date, time, or location of the searcher, making reproducing individual results difficult.
63 "Causes of Gender Dysphoria."
64 Intersex Society of North America, "What's the Difference?"
65 Devor, "How Many Sexes?"
66 Thornton, "Geographies of (Con)Text"; Ging et al., "Neologising Misogyny."
67 Thornton, "Geographies of (Con)Text."
68 Thornton.
69 "Oxford Languages and Google."
70 Ahmed, "Affinity of Hammers."
71 Stryker, *Transgender History.*
72 croson, "Sex, Lies And Feminism."
73 croson.
74 croson.
75 Bockting, "Biological Reductionism Meets Gender Diversity."
76 In particular, the example sentence "Okay the term was first coined for othering the genderqueer from the people of transsexual history, but it gained new and positive meaning in the nineties" has questionable historical accuracy. Though the sentiment that nonbinary individuals were rarely represented within trans spaces prior to the 1990s is accurate, the assertion that "genderqueer" was used in a derogatory fashion is not supported within the English language archive.
77 "Example Sentences."
78 This approach to researching language value is inspired by Pip Thornton's "[poem].py," which applies AdWords pricing to poetry to question how we value language. See Thornton, "{poem}.py."
79 Kaplan, "Linguistic Capitalism and Algorithmic Mediation."
80 Graham, "Google and Advertising."
81 Kaplan, "Linguistic Capitalism and Algorithmic Mediation."
82 "Trans barbie" and "barbie transgender" appear to be anomalies whose presence on the list is driven not by the presence of "trans," but by "barbie," as the vast

majority of ads at the top of the search results redirect to either Mattel's website or other major American retailers such as Target and JCPenney.

83 Bronstein, "Pornography, Trans Visibility"; Haimson et al., "Tumblr Was a Trans Technology."
84 Oakley, "Disturbing Hegemonic Discourse"; Dame, "Making a Name for Yourself."
85 The commodity value of queer tags is a long-standing issue on Tumblr: in 2013, following Tumblr's sale to Yahoo!, efforts to flag content as "Safe" or "Not Safe For Work" lead the #gay tag to be blocked in the Tumblr mobile app due to the the overwhelming presence of NSFW content. See "Tumblr Staff."
86 Byron, "'How Could You Write Your Name"; Haimson et al., "Tumblr Was a Trans Technology."
87 Enke, "Education of Little Cis."
88 Dame-Griff, "What Do We Mean." While the adoption of "Latinx" shares some features with "transgender"—notably, increased use by institutional actors—their path to adoption was markedly different. Prior to being promoted outside of the community, the use of "transgender" as an umbrella was widely debated and discussed in community periodicals, and publications made a clear effort to advocate for its adoption by community members. "Latinx," in contrast, was only subject to widespread debate *after* it had begun to be used in umbrella form. Most notably, those arguing against Latinx-as-umbrella were not individuals who'd used "Latinx" as an individual label, as was the case for early opponents of transgender, but non-trans Latina/o individuals arguing that the current term was itself already inclusive.
89 D'Onofrio, "Better, More Positive Tumblr."
90 Craven, "Tumblr Is Betraying."
91 Fiesler and Dym, "Moving across Lands"; Edwards and Boellstorff, "Migration, Non-Use, and the 'Tumblrpocalypse.'"

CONCLUSION

1 Steinmetz, "Transgender Tipping Point."
2 Steinmetz.
3 Milligan, "How Can We Be Ready?," 1347.
4 Brügger, *Archived Web*.
5 Milligan, *History in the Age of Abundance?*, 65.
6 Caitlin Galiz-Rowe, "Making Playgrounds, Not Toys."
7 "NTL&A Dedication Ceremony Program Book (2004)."
8 Meeker, *Contacts Desired*; Travis, "Women in Print Movement."
9 Haimson et al., "Tumblr Was a Trans Technology."
10 "Strikethrough and Boldthrough."
11 Fiesler, "Surprise Hugo Nomination."
12 Fiesler et al., "Archive of Their Own," 2574–75.
13 Lothian and Stanfill, "Archive of Whose Own?"

BIBLIOGRAPHY

LIST OF ABBREVIATIONS

DTA   Digital Transgender Archive, www.digitaltransgenderarchive.net.

JNTC   Jean-Nickolaus Tretter Collection in Gay, Lesbian, Bisexual, and Transgender Studies, University of Minnesota.

L&CP   Linda and Cynthia Phillips Papers, University of Texas at San Antonio.

NTLA-JALC   National Transgender Library and Archive, Joseph A. Labadie Collection, University of Michigan.

"ACLU Intervenors' Complaint." Accessed July 4, 2020. www.techlawjournal.com.

Addison, Joanne, and Michelle Comstock. "Virtually Out: The Emergence of a Lesbian, Bisexual, and Gay Youth Cyberculture." In *Generations of Youth: Youth Cultures and History in Twentieth-Century America*, edited by Joe Alan Austin and Michael Willard, 367–78. New York: NYU Press, 1998.

Adler, Melissa. "Gender Expression in a Small World: Social Tagging of Transgender-themed Books." *Proceedings of the American Society for Information Science and Technology* 50, no. 1 (2013): 1–8.

American Civil Liberties Union. Affidavit of Christine Soto in *ACLU, et al. v. Reno*. Accessed June 7, 2022. www.aclu.org/.

———. Affidavit of Hunter Allen in *ACLU, et al. v. Reno*. Accessed June 7, 2022. www.aclu.org/.

———. Affidavit of Rheana Parrenas in *ACLU, et al. v. Reno*. Accessed June 7, 2022. www.aclu.org/.

———. Queer Resources Directory Affidavit in *ACLU, et al. v. Reno*. Accessed June 29, 2020. www.aclu.org/.

Ahmed, Sara. "An Affinity of Hammers." *Transgender Studies Quarterly* 3, nos. 1–2 (2016): 22–34.

Alicia. "Transgenderism and the Information Superhighway." *Transmission Line*, February 1995. NTLA-JALC.

Allbritton, Chris. "America Online Tops 10 Million Subscribers." *Washington Post*, November 18, 1997. www.washingtonpost.com/.
Americans With Disabilities Act. S.722. Congressional Record, 101st Cong., 1st sess. webarchive.loc.gov.
Ankerson, Megan Sapnar. *Dot-Com Design: The Rise of a Usable, Social, Commercial Web*. New York: NYU Press, 2018.
———. "Writing Web Histories with an Eye on the Analog Past." *New Media & Society* 14, no. 3 (2012): 384–400.
Annie. "Annotated Glossary of Terms." Annie's Place, May 7, 1999. web.archive.org.
"Announcing the Formation of the Sunday Society." *TV-TS Tapestry* 52, 1988. DTA.
Anya. "Computing and the Transgendered." *Powder & Pearls*, September 1997. NTLA-JALC.
———. "Transgendered Computing." *Powder & Pearls*, August 1997. NTLA-JALC.
"Appendix D: The Large 'n', Non-Clinical Surveys of Boulton & Park Society." International Conference on Transgender Law and Employment Policy, August 1994. DTA Transgender Archive.
Attorney General's Commission on Pornography and US Department of Justice. *Final Report*. Washington, D.C.: U.S. Dept. of Justice, 1986.
Aviance, J. Nelson. "I Am not Cisgendered." Huffington Post, July 18, 2014. www.huffingtonpost.com/.
Bailey, Moya. *Misogynoir Transformed: Black Women's Digital Resistance*. New York: New York University Press, 2021.
Barbara Jean. "insight #48." *Cross-Port InnerView*, March 1994. DTA.
Barité, Mario. "Literary Warrant (IEKO)." *Knowledge Organization* 45, no. 6 (2018): 517–36.
Barr, David. "So You Want to Create an Alt Newsgroup." faqs.org. Accessed March 23, 2017. www.faqs.org/.
Batterson, David. "AOL Chat Rooms (In Re: CuD 6.40)." Computer Underground Digest, May 15, 1994. computer-underground-digest.org/.
———. "Subject: File 2—Personal E-Mail-Networking W/OutLANs; Gay on-Line Services." Computer Underground Digest, January 13, 1994. computer-underground-digest.org/.
Baym, Nancy K. *Tune in, Log on: Soaps, Fandom, and Online Community*. Thousand Oaks, CA: Sage, 2000.
Beauchamp, Toby. "Artful Concealment and Strategic Visibility: Transgender Bodies and US State Surveillance after 9/11." *Surveillance & Society* 6, no. 4 (2009): 356–66.
Beecroft, Carol. "Executive Director's Page." *Femme Mirror*, Fall 1992. NTLA-JALC.
Beins, Agatha. *Liberation in Print: Feminist Periodicals and Social Movement Identity*. Atlanta: University of Georgia Press, 2017.
Berlet, Chip. "When Hate Went Online." Paper presented at the Northeast Sociological Association Spring Conference, April 28, 2001, Sacred Heart University, Fairfield, Connecticut.

Bey, Marquis. *Cistem Failure: Essays on Blackness and Cisgender*. Durham, NC: Duke University Press, 2022.
Bivens, Rena. "The Gender Binary Will Not Be Deprogrammed: Ten Years of Coding Gender on Facebook." *New Media & Society* 19, no. 6 (2017): 880–98.
Bivens, Rena, and Oliver L. Haimson. "Baking Gender into Social Media Design: How Platforms Shape Categories for Users and Advertisers." *Social Media + Society* 2, no. 4 (2016): 1–12.
Blackwood, Anne. "Why Terms Are Necessary." *Cross-Talk: The Gender Community's News & Information Monthly*, November 1991. DTA.
Blake, Laura. "The TransEqual Collection." Donna's Hideout. Accessed March 23, 2017. cydathria.com.
———. "TransEqual: HomePage." November 24, 2001. web.archive.org.
Blank, Paula. "Will the Word 'Cisgender' Ever Go Mainstream?" *Atlantic*, September 24, 2014. www.theatlantic.com/.
Blanton, Carlos K. "George I. Sanchez, Ideology, and Whiteness in the Making of the Mexican American Civil Rights Movement, 1930–1960." *Journal of Southern History* 72, no. 3 (2006): 569–604.
Bockting, Walter O. "Biological Reductionism Meets Gender Diversity in Human Sexuality." *Journal of Sex Research* 42, no. 3 (August 2005): 267–70.
Bodkin, Vern. "Networking." *FTM Newsletter*, February 1994.
Bolin, Anne. *In Search of Eve: Transsexual Rites of Passage*. Hadley, MA: Bergin & Garvey, 1988.
Bornstein, Kate. *Gender Outlaw: On Men, Women, and the Rest of Us*. New York: Vintage, 1994.
Boswell, Holly. "The Transgender Alternative." *Chrysalis Quarterly*, Summer 1991. DTA.
"Boulton & Park Library: Other Newsletters/Journals/Magazines We Receive." *Gender Euphoria: Newsletter of the Boulton & Park Society*, May 1992. JNTC.
Boutin, Paul. "Tumblr Makes Blogging Blissfully Easy." Gadgetwise Blog, March 13, 2009. gadgetwise.blogs.nytimes.com/.
Brager, J. B. "LiveJournal Made Me Gay." The Nib, June 7, 2019. thenib.com.
Brenda P. "Notice." *XX: Newsletter of Twenty Club*, April 1992. DTA.
Brewster, Kathryn, and Bonnie Ruberg. "Survivors: Archiving the History of Bulletin Board Systems and the AIDS Crisis." *First Monday* 25, no. 1 (2020). journals.uic.edu.
Bronstein, Carolyn. "Pornography, Trans Visibility, and the Demise of Tumblr." *Transgender Studies Quarterly* 7, no. 2 (2020): 240–54.
Brophy, Jessica E. "Developing a Corporeal Cyberfeminism: Beyond Cyberutopia." *New Media & Society* 12, no. 6 (2010): 929–45.
Brügger, Niels. *The Archived Web: Doing History in the Digital Age*. Cambridge, MA: MIT Press, 2018.
Brunton, Finn. *Spam: A Shadow History of the Internet*. Cambridge, MA: MIT Press, 2013.
Bucher, Taina. *If . . . Then: Algorithmic Power and Politics*. Oxford: Oxford University Press, 2018.

Burnett, Gary, and Laurie Bonnici. "Beyond the FAQ: Explicit and Implicit Norms in Usenet Newsgroups." *Library & Information Science Research* 25, no. 3 (2003): 333–51.

Busker, Rebecca Lucy. "On Symposia: LiveJournal and the Shape of Fannish Discourse." *Transformative Works and Cultures* 1 (August 2, 2008). journal.transformativeworks.org/

Carolmooredc. "Several Questionable Sources." Wikipedia Talk Page: Cisgender, June 21, 2014. en.wikipedia.org.

Carolyn. "Termination of Carolyn's Place BBS." *Transmission Line*, August 1995. NTLA-JALC.

Carr, Robert E. "Type Dirty to Me." *Playboy*, March 1985, n.p.

Casey, Carol. "Web Rings: An Alternative to Search Engines." *College & Research Libraries News* 59, no. 10 (1998): 761–63.

Cassel, David. "Re: Sex on AOL: Cover-up, Part II!" aolwatch.com, May 1, 1996. aolwatch.com/.

Cheung, Charles. "A Home on the Web: Presentations of Self on Personal Homepages." In *Web Studies: Rewiring Media Studies for the Digital Age*, edited by David Gauntlett, 43–51. London: Arnold, 2000.

Chun, Wendy Hui Kyong. *Control and Freedom: Power and Paranoia in the Age of Fiber Optics*. Cambridge, MA: MIT Press, 2008.

"Cisgender." In *Oxford English Dictionary*. Oxford: Oxford University Press, June 2015. www.oed.com/.

CNN. "CompuServe Takes Aim—Jan. 24, 1997." Accessed June 10, 2021. money.cnn.com/.

Colker, Ruth. "Homophobia, AIDS Hysteria, and the Americans with Disabilities Act." *Journal of Gender, Race & Justice* 8 (2004): 33–56.

Computer Underground Digest. "AOL Censors Gay Video Titles—'Buns' Ok, 'Studs' Not!" December 6, 1995. computer-underground-digest.org/.

Couldry, Nick, and Jose Van Dijck. "Researching Social Media as If the Social Mattered." *Social Media + Society* 1, no. 2 (2015): 1–7.

Crabtree, Penni. "E-Mail Links Strangers with Shared Interests; If You Have Internet Access, You Can Reach Just about Anyone Who's On-Line across the Globe." *San Diego Union-Tribune*, August 20, 1995, special section ("Digital Age"), 4.

Craven, Julia. "Tumblr Is Betraying The Sex Workers And NSFW Artists Who Relied On The Platform." Huffington Post, December 4, 2018. www.huffpost.com/.

Cresap, Jayne. "Is the Internet Killing All the Support Groups?" *Dresseret News, Newsletter of Alpha Rho Chapter of Tri-Ess*, September 1997. NTLA-JALC.

croson, charlotte. "Sex, Lies and Feminism." *off our backs* 31, no. 6 (2001): 6–9.

Cummins, Rachel, and Kathy Cummins. "Tri-Ess Computer Bulletin Board System." *Femme Mirror*, Spring 1991. NTLA-JALC.

"CYBERsitter Site Filtering." December 6, 1998. web.archive.org.

Dae. "A Rose by Any Name." *Femme Mirror*, Winter 1998. DTA.

Dahir, Mabarak. "Online Computer Service 'Cyberclosets' Transvestites." *Philadelphia Daily News*, March 22, 1994, 26.

Dahlberg, Lincoln. "Libertarian Cyber-Utopianism and Global Digital Networks." In *Globalization and Utopia: Critical Essays*, edited by Patrick Hayden and Chamsy El-Ojeili, 176–89. London: Springer, 2009.

Dale, Diane. "The Transgender Fund: What Are We Doing for Our Youth?" *LadyLike*, 2000. DTA.

Dame, Avery. "Making a Name for Yourself: Tagging as Transgender Ontological Practice on Tumblr." *Critical Studies in Media Communication* 33, no. 1 (2016): 23–37.

Dame-Griff, Avery. "Herding the 'Performing Elephants' Using Computational Methods to Study Usenet." *Internet Histories* 3, nos. 3–4 (2019): 223–44.

Dame-Griff, E Cassandra. "What Do We Mean When We Say 'Latinx?': Definitional Power, the Limits of Inclusivity, and the (Un/Re) Constitution of an Identity Category." *Journal of International and Intercultural Communication* 15, no. 2 (2022): 119–31.

Darwin, Helana. "AOL Chat Rooms (In Re: CuD 6.40)." Computer Underground Digest, May 15, 1994. computer-underground-digest.org/

———. "Challenging the Cisgender/Transgender Binary: Nonbinary People and the Transgender Label." *Gender & Society* 34, no. 3 (2020): 357–80.

Davidson, Megan. "Seeking Refuge under the Umbrella: Inclusion, Exclusion, and Organizing within the Category Transgender." *Sexuality Research and Social Policy* 4 (2007): 60–80.

Davis, Tony. "Life's a Drag." *Winnipeg Free Press*, October 31, 1993, n.p.

Delta Chapter Newsletter. "Eveolution; Eve-Olution." n.d. NTLA-JALC.

De Luca, Nancy. "Computer Network Axes Lesbian/Gay 'Club.'" Gay Community News, December 30, 1986. Internet Archive. archive.org.

Dedrick, Jason, and Kenneth L Kraemer. "Market Making in the Personal Computer Industry." In *The Market Makers: How Retailers Are Reshaping the Global Economy*, edited by Benjamin Senauer, Gary G. Hamilton, and Misha Petrovic, 291–310. Oxford: Oxford University Press, 2011.

Defo0008. "Comment from 1994 User of the Term Cisgender." Wikipedia Talk Page: Cisgender, July 6, 2006. en.wikipedia.org.

Delwiche, Althea. "Early Social Computing: The Rise and Fall of the BBS Scene (1977–1995)." In *The Sage Handbook of Social Media*, edited by Jean Burgess, Alice Marwick, and Thomas Poell, 35–52. London: Sage, 2018.

Denny, Dallas. "Disaster, Deceit, and Betrayal at the International Foundation for Gender Education." Transgender Forum, June 27, 2011. tgforum.com/.

———. "The Impact of Emerging Technologies on One Transgender Organization." Accessed September 13, 2022. dallasdenny.com/.

———. "NTL&A Dedication Ceremony Program Book (2004)." Accessed January 4, 2021. dallasdenny.com/.

———. "The Origin of the National Transgender Library & Archive." Accessed November 28, 2022. dallasdenny.com/.

———. "Vision 2001: A Gender Odyssey—Part III." *AEGIS News*, September 1996. DTA.

Denny, Dallas, and Jessica Xavier. "On the Future of the TG Community." *AEGIS News*, April 1998. DTA.

Devor, Aaron. "How Many Sexes? How Many Genders? When Two Are Not Enough." September 7, 2019. web.archive.org.

Devor, Aaron, and Nicholas Matte. "Building a Better World for Transpeople: Reed Erickson and the Erickson Educational Foundation." *International Journal of Transgenderism* 10, no. 1 (2007): 47–68.

Diane Kaye. "TG Net News." *The Pinnacle: A Publication of Delta Chi Educational Association, D.C.E.A.*, October 1996. NTLA-JALC.

"Digest of Education Statistics, 1995 (Table 19: Household Income and Poverty Rates, by State: 1990 and 1993)." National Center for Education Statistics, 1995. nces.ed.gov/.

Dillon, George L. "Clipart Images as Commonsense Categories." *Visual Communication* 5, no. 3 (2006): 287–306.

Docter, Richard F., and Virginia Prince. "Transvestism: A Survey of 1032 Cross-Dressers." *Archives of Sexual Behavior* 26, no. 6 (1997): 589–605.

"Document: Opinion in Loudoun Library Filtering Software Case, 11/23/98." Accessed July 4, 2020. www.techlawjournal.com/.

D'Onofrio, Jeff. "A Better, More Positive Tumblr." Tumblr Staff. Accessed January 29, 2019. staff.tumblr.com.

Dowd, Jennifer R., and Dale A. Herbek. "Computer Bulletin Board Systems and the First Amendment: The Common Carrier Solution." In *Proceedings of the Annual Meeting of the Association for Education in Journalism and Mass Communication*, 364–96. Kansas City, Missouri, 1993. archive.org.

Driscoll, Kevin. *The Modem World: A Prehistory of Social Media*. New Haven, CT: Yale University Press, 2022.

Driscoll, Kevin, and Camille Paloque-Berges. "Searching for Missing 'Net Histories.'" *Internet Histories* 1, nos. 1–2 (2017): 47–59.

Driver, Susan. "Virtually Queer Youth Communities of Girls and Birls: Dialogical Spaces of Identity Work and Desiring Exchanges." In *Digital Generations*, edited by David Buckingham and Rebekah Willett, 229–45. London: Routledge, 2013.

Duval, Erik, Wayne Hodgins, Stuart Sutton, and Stuart L Weibel. "Metadata Principles and Practicalities." *D-Lib Magazine* 8, no. 4 (2002): 1–10.

Dym, Brianna, and Casey Fiesler. "Generations, Migrations, and the Future of Fandom's Private Spaces." *Transformative Works and Cultures* 28 (2018). journal.transformativeworks.org.

Dyrud, Marilyn A. "An Exploration of Gender Bias in Computer Clip Art." *Business Communication Quarterly* 60, no. 4 (1997): 30–51.

Edwards, Emory James, and Tom Boellstorff. "Migration, Non-Use, and the 'Tumblrpocalypse': Towards a Unified Theory of Digital Exodus." *Media, Culture & Society*, November 4, 2020. journals.sagepub.com.
Electronic Frontier Foundation. "Censorship, Online Services: AOL's 'Secret TOS Policy.'" n.d. web.archive.org.
Elmer-Dewitt, Philip. "Online Erotica: On A Screen Near You." *Time*, July 3, 1995, n.p.
Elizabeth, Sister Mary. "Letter to the Editor." *FTM Newsletter*, January 1992. NTLA-JALC.
Engst, A. C. *Internet Starter Kit for Macintosh*. Indianapolis: Hayden, 1996.
Enke, A. Finn. "The Education of Little Cis." In *Transfeminist Perspectives in and beyond Transgender and Gender Studies*, 60–80. Philadelphia: Temple University Press, 2012.
Delta Chapter Newsletter. "Eveolution; Eve-Olution." n.d. NTLA-JALC.
"Example Sentences—Oxford Dictionaries." August 28, 2016. web.archive.org.
Feinberg, Leslie. *Transgender Liberation: A Movement Whose Time Has Come*. New York: World View Forum, 1992.
Fiesler, Casey. "Why This Fan Fiction Site's Surprise Hugo Nomination Is Such a Big Deal." Slate, April 9, 2019. slate.com/.
Fiesler, Casey, and Brianna Dym. "Moving across Lands: Online Platform Migration in Fandom Communities." *Proceedings of the ACM on Human-Computer Interaction* 4, no. CSCW1 (2020): 1–25.
Fiesler, Casey, Shannon Morrison, and Amy S. Bruckman. "An Archive of Their Own: A Case Study of Feminist HCI and Values in Design." In *Proceedings of the 2016 CHI Conference on Human Factors in Computing Systems*, San Jose, California, May 7–12, 2016, 2574–85.
Fink, Marty, and Quinn Miller. "Trans Media Moments: Tumblr, 2011–2013." *Television & New Media* 15, no. 7 (2014): 611–26.
Fletcher, Dan. "Internet Atrocity! GeoCities' Demise Erases Web History." *Time*, November 9, 2009. content.time.com/.
"Folksonomy: Vanderwal.Net." Accessed December 19, 2019. vanderwal.net/.
Forrester, Anne. "Parliamo Americano? A Crossdresser's American-English Wordlist." *The Tartan Skirt*, July 1992. DTA.
Frederickson, Tere. "Editor's Corner: Up the Road." *Gender Euphoria: Newsletter of the Boulton & Park Society*, January 1991. JNTC.
———. "Re: 'Terminology for the Crossdressing Community' (January '92)." *Cross-Talk: The Gender Community's News & Information Monthly*, September 1992. DTA.
Friedman, Elisabeth Jay. *Interpreting the Internet: Feminist and Queer Counterpublics in Latin America*. Berkeley: University of California Press, 2016.
Frye, Phyllis Randolph. "IFGE in Portland, Oregon." *TV-TS Tapestry*, Summer 1994. DTA.
Gabriel, Davina Anne. "Fool's Paradox: An Interview with Kate Bornstien." *TransSisters: The Journal of Transsexual Feminism*, Summer 1994. DTA.

Galiz-Rowe, Caitlin. "Making Playgrounds, Not Toys: A Discussion With 'Secret Little Haven' Dev Tori Rose." Your Geeky Gal Pal, June 24, 2018. www.yourgeekygalpal.com/.
Gamson, Joshua. *Freaks Talk Back: Tabloid Talk Shows and Sexual Nonconformity*. Chicago: University of Chicago Press, 1998.
Gardner, Angela. "Editorial." *LadyLike*, 1999. DTA.
———. "Editorial." *LadyLike*, 1999. DTA.
———. "News Beat and Reminder." *Renaissance News & Views*, February 1994. DTA.
———. "News Beat and Reminder." *Renaissance News & Views*, July 1996. DTA.
———. "Profile: Amanda Richards." *LadyLike*, 1999. DTA.
———. "Talkin' with Sarah Thomas." *LadyLike*, 1999. DTA.
Garrison, Spencer. "On the Limits of 'Trans Enough': Authenticating Trans Identity Narratives." *Gender & Society* 32, no. 5 (2018): 613–37.
Gay & Lesbian Alliance Against Defamation. "Access Denied." December 2, 1997. web.archive.org.
"Gay/Lesbian/Queer Social Science List." July 1999. www.qrd.org.
Gender Education & Advocacy, Inc. "Gender Variance: A Primer." *Transgender Tapestry*, Spring 2003. DTA.
"Gendernet News." *TV-TS Tapestry* 45, 1985. DTA.
"GeoCities Guidelines FAQ." April 25, 1998. web.archive.org.
"GGA Introduces Gendernet." *TV-TS Tapestry* 42, 1984. DTA.
Giardina, Henry. "An Oral History of the Early Trans Internet." Gizmodo, July 9, 2019. gizmodo.com/.
Gillespie, Tarleton. "The Relevance of Algorithms." In *Media Technologies: Essays on Communication, Materiality, and Society*, edited by Tarleton Gillespie, Pablo J. Boczkowski, and Kirsten A. Foot, 167–93. Cambridge, MA: MIT Press, 2014.
Gill-Peterson, Jules. *Histories of the Transgender Child*. Minneapolis: University of Minnesota Press, 2018.
Gilster, Paul. *The Mosaic Navigator: The Essential Guide to the Internet Interface*. Hoboken: NJ: John Wiley & Sons, 1995.
Ging, Debbie, Theodore Lynn, and Pierangelo Rosati. "Neologising Misogyny: Urban Dictionary's Folksonomies of Sexual Abuse." *New Media & Society* 22, no. 5 (2020): 838–56.
Giordano, Scott A. "Volunteers Reach Out to Transgender Youth." *Philadelphia Gay News*, August 2, 1996. John J. Wilcox Jr. LGBT Archives. digital.wilcoxarchives.org.
Glover, Alexie Moira. "'I Know What I Am and What I Am Not': Heterosexual Male Cross-Dressing in Postwar America, 1960–1990." Master's thesis, University of Victoria, 2018.
Goldberg, Michelle. "What Is a Woman?" *New Yorker*, July 28, 2014. www.newyorker.com/.
Golder, Scott A., and Bernardo A. Huberman. "Usage Patterns of Collaborative Tagging Systems." *Journal of Information Science* 32, no. 2 (2006): 198–208.
Goodnight, Joan. "Queenspeak." *Girl Talk*, August 1998. DTA.

Graham, Richard. "Google and Advertising: Digital Capitalism in the Context of Post-Fordism, the Reification of Language, and the Rise of Fake News." *Palgrave Communications* 3, no. 1 (December 12, 2017): 45.

Greene, Daniel. "Discovering the Divide: Technology and Poverty in the New Economy." *International Journal of Communication* 10 (2016). ijoc.org.

Greenstein, Shane. *How the Internet Became Commercial*. Princeton, NJ: Princeton University Press, 2015.

Grossman, Wendy. *Net.wars*. New York: NYU Press, 1997.

Haas, Robert. "State OKs Proposal on High-Tech Data Service." *San Francisco Sentinel*, July 18, 1985. San Francisco Bay Area Gay and Lesbian Serials, University of California, Berkeley.

Habib, Laurence, and Tony Cornford. "Computers in the Home: Domestication and Gender." *Information Technology & People* 15, no. 2 (2002): 159–74.

Haimson, Oliver L., and Anna Lauren Hoffmann. "Constructing and Enforcing 'Authentic' Identity Online: Facebook, Real Names, and Non-Normative Identities." *First Monday* 21, no. 6 (2016). journals.uic.edu.

Haimson, Oliver L, Avery Dame-Griff, Elias Capello, and Zahari Richter. "Tumblr Was a Trans Technology: The Meaning, Importance, History, and Future of Trans Technologies." *Feminist Media Studies* 21, no. 3 (2021): 345–61.

Halavais, Alexander. *Search Engine Society*. Hoboken, NJ: John Wiley & Sons, 2017.

Hall, Kira. "Performativity." *Journal of Linguistic Anthropology* 9, no. 1–2 (1999): 184–87.

Hayles, N. Katherine. *My Mother Was a Computer: Digital Subjects and Literary Texts*. Chicago: University of Chicago Press, 2010.

Hicks, Mar. "Hacking the Cis-Tem." *IEEE Annals of the History of Computing* 41, no. 1 (2019): 20–33.

Hill, Robert. "Before Transgender: Transvestia's Spectrum of Gender Variance, 1960–1980." In *Transgender Studies Reader 2*, edited by Susan Stryker and Aren Aizura, 364–79. London: Routledge, n.d.

Hill, Robert S. "'As a Man I Exist; as a Woman I Live': Heterosexual Transvestism and the Contours of Gender and Sexuality in Postwar America." PhD diss., University of Michigan, 2007.

Hilty, Wyn. "This Sister Oughta Be Famous." *OC Weekly*, May 6, 1999. www.ocweekly.com.

Holly. "A Letter from Holly." *XX: Newsletter of Twenty Club*, October 1991. DTA.

Jordanne Holyoak. "AOL's Secret Dirty Word List." AfterNoon, March 31, 1996. web.archive.org.

HSE.ie. "Causes of Gender Dysphoria." Accessed August 21, 2020. www.hse.ie/.

Hu, Jim, and Mike Yamamoto. "AOL's Squeeze Play." CNET. Accessed December 16, 2019. www.cnet.com/.

Hubbard, Michelle. "Michelle's Ramblings . . ." *Gender Euphoria: Newsletter of the Boulton & Park Society*, December 1998. Gender Euphoria 1995–99, MS 38, box 2, folder 2, L&CPP.

———. "Michelle's Ramblings . . ." *Gender Euphoria: Newsletter of the Boulton & Park Society*, April 1999. Gender Euphoria 1995–99, MS 38, box 2, folder 2, L&CPP.

Huttunen, Aira, Noora Hirvonen, and Lotta Kähkönen. "Uncomfortable in My Own Skin—Emerging, Early-Stage Identity-Related Information Needs of Transgender People." *Journal of Documentation* 76, no. 3 (2020): 709–29.

International Foundation for Gender Education (IFGE). "Atlanta Action Update," March 17, 1995. DTA.

———. "IFGE Begins Youth Outreach Program." *IFGE Newsletter*, Fall 1996. DTA.

———. *IFGE's 1st Annual "Coming Together-Working Together" Convention: Book of Program Transcripts*. International Foundation for Gender Education, 1987. DTA.

Intersex Society of North America. "What's the Difference between Being Transgender or Transsexual and Having an Intersex Condition? | Intersex Society of North America." Accessed August 21, 2020. isna.org/.

Israel, Gianna E. "Column: Gianna E. Israel." *Transgender Tapestry*, Summer 1998. DTA.

J. Nance. "From the Closet to Academia." *Outreach Newsletter*, Spring/Summer 1986. DTA.

Jackie. "So You Think You Don't Need a Post Office Box." *Femme Mirror*, Summer 1990. NTLA-JALC.

James, Andrea. "MTF Glossary." TS Road Map, August 13, 2001. web.archive.org.

———. "Transgender Forum List." TS Road Map. Accessed March 23, 2017. web.archive.org.

Javier, Loren. "Welcome to the Virtual Transgender Community Center." *GLAAD Images Newsmagazine*, Summer 1997. web.archive.org.

Jenifer. "Jenifer's Juxtaposition: Net Surf'n." *Devil Woman*, March 1995. NTLA-JALC.

———. "Jenifer's Juxtaposition: New Found Freedom." *Devil Woman*, May 1995. NTLA-JALC.

John, Nicholas A. "Sharing and Web 2.0: The Emergence of a Keyword." *New Media & Society* 15, no. 2 (2013): 167–82.

Johnson, Bette Lee. "Keynote Address (Transcript): Texas T-Party (San Antonio, Texas; February 24, 1990)." *TV-TS Tapestry*, 1990. DTA.

Johnson, Jeffrey Alan. "Information Systems and the Translation of Transgender." *TSQ: Transgender Studies Quarterly* 2, no. 1 (February 1, 2015): 160–65.

Johnson, Matt. "Transgender Subject Access: History and Current Practice." *Cataloging & Classification Quarterly* 48, no. 8 (2010): 661–83.

Jones, Billie Jean. "The Dictionary Project." 1992. DTA.

Kafka, Peter. "Who Said Web 2.0 Was R.I.P.? Microblog Tumblr Raises $4.5 Million, Expectations." All Things Digital. Accessed December 15, 2020. allthingsd.com/.

Kallinikos, Jannis, Aleksi Aaltonen, and Attila Marton. "A Theory of Digital Objects." *First Monday* 15, no. 6 (2010).

Kane, Ariadne. "A Glossary for Understanding Gender Diversity." *Journal of Gender Studies*, Winter/Spring 1995. DTA.

Kaplan, Frederic. "Linguistic Capitalism and Algorithmic Mediation." *Representations* 127, no. 1 (2014): 57–63.

Kaplan, Karen. "AOL Ads Wanting?: Everything at America Online." *Los Angeles Times*, February 17, 1997. www.latimes.com/.

Kasey, Trish., Deb. Roum, Moms on the Net, and Mommy Times. *What the Heck's the Net?* Springfield, MO: Mommy Times, 1997.

Kayany, Joseph M. "Contexts of Uninhibited Online Behavior: Flaming in Social Newsgroups on Usenet." *Journal of the Association for Information Science and Technology* 49, no. 12 (1998): 1135–41.

Keilty, Patrick. "Sexual Boundaries and Subcultural Discipline." *Knowledge Organization* 39, no. 6 (2012). www.nomos-elibrary.de.

Keller, Teddy. "The Future of CIGA." *Finesse, Newsletter of the Central Illinois Gender Association*, October 1999. NTLA-JALC.

Kelly, Brian. "Netskills Corner." *Ariadne*, 1996. Accessed September 13, 2022. www.ariadne.ac.uk/.

Kielwasser, Al. "GLAAD Media Watch." *Bay Area Reporter*, June 9, 1994. Internet Archive.

Kiki Carmichael. "Out of Focus." *Chi Tribune*, March 1996. DTA.

Kimberly Ann N. "To All My New Friends." *TV-TS Tapestry*, 1988. DTA.

Kirk, Sheila. "There Is Help for the Teenaged Transgendered!" *Cross-Talk: The Gender Community's News & Information Monthly*, March 1996. DTA.

———. "Youth Research Project." *TV-TS Tapestry*, 1989. DTA.

Kitzie, Vanessa. "'That looks like me or something i can do': Affordances and Constraints in the Online Identity Work of US LGBTQ+ Millennials." *Journal of the Association for Information Science and Technology* 70, no. 12 (2019): 1340–51.

Kloehn, Steve. "Lesbians, Gays March for Pride." *Chicago Tribune*, July 1, 1996. www.chicagotribune.com/.

Kohn, Arthur. "Bulletin Boards for Gay Computer Hackers." *Advocate*, September 18, 1984. NTLA-JALC.

Kowalska, Monika. "The Heroines of My Life: Interview with Dallas Denny." *The Heroines of My Life*, April 1, 2014. theheroines.blogspot.com/.

Koyama, Emi. "Cissexual/Cisgender: Decentralizing the Dominant Group." eminism.org—Interchange, June 7, 2002. www.eminism.org.

Krista. "Letters: Letter from Krista." *Transgender Tapestry*, Spring 2001. DTA.

Laermer, Richard. *Get On with It: The Gay and Lesbian Guide to Getting Online*. New York: Broadway, 1997.

Laing, Alison. "A Label by Any Other Name Might Stick." *Transgender Tapestry*, Winter 1995. DTA.

Lee, Hangwoo. "Behavioral Strategies for Dealing with Flaming in an Online Forum." *Sociological Quarterly* 46, no. 2 (2005): 385–403.

Leong, Susan, Teodor Mitew, Marta Celletti, and Erika Pearson. "The Question Concerning (Internet) Time." *New Media & Society* 11, no. 8 (2009): 1267–85.

"Letters: Member Essay Feature." *CompuServe Magazine*, February 1992. archive.org.

Leveque, Sophia Cecelia. *Trans / Active: A Biography of Gwendolyn Ann Smith*. Winston-Salem, NC: Library Partners, 2017.

Lewis, Peter H. "Planet Out: 'Gay Global Village' of Cyberspace." *New York Times*, August 21, 1995. www.nytimes.com/.
"Library Project . . . Share the Information." *Renaissance News*. March 1988. DTA.
Liedtke, Michael. "Blogging Pioneers Six Apart, LiveJournal to Break Apart." Associated Press Financial Wire, December 3, 2007.
Linda. "Linda's Corner." *Cross-Port InnerView*, January 1993. DTA.
"Local Advertising." *TGIC News*, November 1992. DTA.
Lothian, Alexis, and Mel Stanfill. "An Archive of Whose Own? White Feminism and Racial Justice in Fan Fiction's Digital Infrastructure." *Transformative Works and Cultures* 36 (2021). journal.transformativeworks.org.
Louise, Marla. "In the Middle of the Superhighway." *Cross-Talk: The Gender Community's News & Information Monthly*, June 1994. DTA.
Lowe, David. "Computerized Networks of Hate: An ADL Fact Finding Report." Anti-Defamation League of B'nai B'rith, 1985. Internet Archive. archive.org/.
Lynam, Rowan. "The Chicago Gender Society Is a Vital Resource for Trans Women, By Trans Women." them. Accessed December 17, 2019. www.them.us/.
Macgregor, George, and Emma McCulloch. "Collaborative Tagging as a Knowledge Organisation and Resource Discovery Tool." *Library Review* 55, no. 5 (2006): 291–300.
Main, Terri. "A Girl at Heart." *Compuserve Magazine*, December 1991, n.p.
Marla Louise. "Bird on a Wire." *Delta Chapter Chatter*, November 1993. NTLA-JALC.
——. "Bird on a Wire." *Delta Chapter—Colorado Chapter of Tri-Ess*, n.d. NTLA-JALC.
——. "In the Middle of the Superhighway." *Cross-Talk: The Gender Community's News & Information Monthly*, June 1994. DTA.
Marlene. "Library Outreach." *Femme Mirror*, Summer 1990. NTLA-JALC.
Martin, Katherine Connor. "Freegan, Yarn Bombing, and the Surprisingly Long History of Twerk: New Words in the OED." OxfordWords, June 25, 2015. blog.oxforddictionaries.com/.
Marwick, Alice E., "To Catch a Predator? The MySpace Moral Panic." *First Monday* 13, no. 6 (2008). firstmonday.org.
Masters, Laura. "Achieving Equality." *TV-TS Tapestry* 65, 1993. DTA.
——. "Mailbag: Throwing Stones." *TV-TS Tapestry* 69, Fall 1994, 20. DTA.
Matias, Yossi, Dvir Keysar, Gal Chechik, Ziv Bar-Yossef, and Tomer Shmiel. "Generating Related Questions for Search Queries." June 13, 2017. patentimages.storage.googleapis.com.
Matthews, Donna Lynn. "Alt.Fashion.Crossdressing." Accessed December 18, 2019. cydathria.com.
——. "Charter—Alt.Fashion.Crossdressing." Donna's Hideout. Accessed March 23, 2017. cydathria.com.
——. "Crossdressing and Society." Donna's Hideout, October 1997. cydathria.com.
——. "Definitions." Donna's Hideout, October 4, 2000. web.archive.org.
——. "Welcome to Nowhere: Field Notes from the Outskirts of Gender." Accessed September 13, 2022. cydathria.com.

Maya, Felipe. "1994: Couric, Gumbel on 'What Is the Internet?'" CBS News, January 31, 2011. www.cbsnews.com/.

McBee, Thomas Page. "Why Tumblr Is Perfect For The Trans Community." BuzzFeed, May 31, 2013. www.buzzfeed.com/.

McCloskey, Deirdre N. *Crossing: A Memoir*. Chicago: University of Chicago Press, 2000.

McCullough, Brian. "She Gave The World A Billion AOL CDs—An Interview with Marketing Legend Jan Brandt." Internet History Podcast. Accessed December 16, 2019. www.internethistorypodcast.com/.

McKinney, Cait. *Information Activism: A Queer History of Lesbian Media Technologies*. Raleigh, NC: Duke University Press, 2020.

———. "Printing the Network: AIDS Activism and Online Access in the 1980s." *Continuum* 32, no. 1 (January 2, 2018): 7–17.

Meeker, Martin. *Contacts Desired: Gay and Lesbian Communications and Community, 1940s-1970s*. Chicago: University of Chicago Press, 2006.

"Metroplex CrossDressers Club." December 5, 1998. web.archive.org.

Michaels, Michelle Anne. "Star Date: The Voyage Continues; Rising of the Moons." 1991. NTLA-JALC.

Milligan, Ian. *History in the Age of Abundance?: How the Web Is Transforming Historical Research*. Montreal: McGill-Queen's University Press, 2019.

———. "How Can We Be Ready to Study History in the Age of Abundance? A Response." *American Historical Review* 125, no. 4 (2020): 1347–49.

"More about the TransBoy Resource Network." TransBoy Resource Network, September 28, 1998. web.archive.org.

"More Hints about Choosing a Name." *Twenty Minutes*. May 1991. DTA.

Motavalli, John. *Bamboozled at the Revolution: How Big Media Lost Billions in the Battle for the Internet*. New York: Viking, 2002.

Ms. High Heels. "That Long Trip." In *Gender Euphoria: Newsletter of the Boulton & Park Society*, April 1997. Gender Euphoria 1995–1999, MS 38, box 2, folder 2, L&CPP.

Murib, Zein. "LGBT." *Transgender Studies Quarterly* 1, nos. 1–2 (2014): 118–20.

———. "Transgender: Examining an Emerging Political Identity Using Three Political Processes." *Politics, Groups, and Identities* 3, no. 3 (2015): 381–97.

Nakamura, Lisa. *Cybertypes: Race, Ethnicity, and Identity on the Internet*. London: Routledge, 2013.

Nangeroni, Nancy Reynolds. "Gender Outlaws: Kate Bornstein with David Harrison." *TV-TS Tapestry*, Summer 1994. DTA.

Napoli, Lisa. "Feeling Abandoned By America Online." *New York Times*, February 2, 1998. www.nytimes.com/.

National Telecommunications and Information Administration. "Falling through the Net." National Telecommunications and Information Administration, 1995. Accessed September 13, 2022. www.ntia.doc.gov/.

"New Canadian Human Rights Commission." *Gender Mosaic's Notes from the Underground*, Spring 1993, n.p.

Nerney, Chris. "'Net Buzz." *Network World*, January 20, 1997, 60.
"A New Glossary for Better Understanding." Human Outreach and Achievement Institute. DTA.
NGLTF's Youth Institute. "Home Page," March 1, 1997. web.archive.org.
Noble, Safiya Umoja. *Algorithms of Oppression: How Search Engines Reinforce Racism.* New York: NYU Press, 2018.
Nownes, Anthony J. *Organizing for Transgender Rights: Collective Action, Group Development, and the Rise of a New Social Movement.* Albany, NY: SUNY Press, 2019.
Oakley, Abigail. "Disturbing Hegemonic Discourse: Nonbinary Gender and Sexual Orientation Labeling on Tumblr." *Social Media + Society* 2, no. 3 (2016): 1–12.
———. "Supporting One Another: Nonbinary Community Building on Tumblr." In *Sex in the Digital Age*, edited by Paul G. Nixon and Isabel K. Düsterhöft, 101–12. London: Routledge, 2017.
Ontario Human Rights Commission. "Discussion Paper: Toward a Commission Policy on Gender Identity." October 1999. Accessed September 13, 2022. www.ohrc.on.ca/.
Oral History with Mary L. Gray and Kalev Hunt. Spokane, Washington, 2021.
"Origin of This Newsgroup." Soc.Support.Youth.Gay-Lesbian-Bi, October 14, 1999. www.modemac.com.
"Our Beginnings." Vanity Club, June 27, 2009. web.archive.org.
Outland, Orlando. "Sears Discontinues Sexy Prodigy Board." *Bay Area Reporter*, February 1993. Internet Archive.
———. "Sears' Queers." *Bay Area Reporter*, January 1993. Internet Archive.
"Oxford Languages and Google—English | Oxford Languages." Accessed September 28, 2020. languages.oup.com/.
"Paula Elizabeth Keiser." Geni. Accessed December 13, 2019. www.geni.com.
Peo, Roger. "People of Color in the CD Community." *Femme Mirror*, Summer 1993. NTLA-JALC.
———. "Roger's Notebook #30: Teenage Crossdressers." *TV-TS Tapestry*, 1989. DTA.
Peters, Isabella. *Folksonomies: Indexing and Retrieval in Web 2.0.* München: KG Saur Verlag Gmbh, 2009.
Pew Research Center. "Americans Internet Access: Percent of Adults 2000–2015." Pew Research Center: Internet, Science & Tech, June 26, 2015. www.pewresearch.org/.
———. "The Internet News Audience Goes Ordinary." Pew Research Center—U.S. Politics & Policy, January 14, 1999. www.pewresearch.org/.
Pfaffenberger, Bryan. "'A Standing Wave in the Web of Our Communications': Usenet and the Socio-Technical Construction of Cyberspace Values." In *From Usenet to CoWebs*, edited by Christopher Lueg and Danyel Fisher, 20–43. London: Springer, 2003.
PFLAG Transgender Network. "PFLAG TNET—About." November 27, 2003. web.archive.org.
Phillips, Linda. "Are You Ever Gonna Go Out?" *Gender Euphoria: Newsletter of the Boulton & Park Society*, October 1998. Gender Euphoria 1995–99, MS 38, box 2, folder 2, L&CPP.

———. "Dear Mr. Schneider." n.d. Correspondence, 1991–97 and undated, MS 38, box 4, folder 2, L&CPP.

———. "Editorial: The End." *Gender Euphoria: Newsletter of the Boulton & Park Society*, April 1999. Gender Euphoria 1995–99, MS 38, box 2, folder 2, L&CPP.

———. "In the Gender Groove." *Gender Euphoria: Newsletter of the Boulton & Park Society*, October 1997. Gender Euphoria 1995–99, MS 38, box 2, folder 2, L&CPP 0.

———. "The Gender Newsletter, Is It Doomed?" *Gender Euphoria: Newsletter of the Boulton & Park Society*, August 1996. Gender Euphoria 1995–99, MS 38, box 2, folder 2, L&CPP.

———. "The Last Word . . . : Well Tonto, It Looks Like Our Work Here Is Finished." *Gender Euphoria: Newsletter of the Boulton & Park Society*, April 1999. Gender Euphoria 1995–99, MS 38, box 2, folder 2, L&CPP.

———. "TV Tech." *Cross Currents, Newsletter of Publication of Heart of Texas TV*, 1989. Cross Currents, 1989–93, MS 38, box 2, folder 4, L&CPP.

———. "Who Was the One?" *Gender Euphoria: Newsletter of the Boulton & Park Society*, April 1999. Gender Euphoria 1995–99, MS 38, box 2, folder 2, L&CPP.

———. "Writers in Gender World." *Gender Euphoria: Newsletter of the Boulton & Park Society*, April 1996. Gender Euphoria 1995–99, MS 38, box 2, folder 2, L&CPP.

Phillips, Melanie Anne. "*The Subversive* #10: Explorations." *The Subversive*. Accessed December 16, 2019. web.archive.org.

———. "*The Subversive* #15: Updates." *The Subversive*. Accessed December 16, 2019. web.archive.org.

———. "*The Subversive* #16: Transgender Survey." *The Subversive*. Accessed December 18, 2019. web.archive.org.

———. "*The Subversive* #17: Updates and Useful Information." *The Subversive*. Accessed December 16, 2019. web.archive.org.

———. "*The Subversive* #25: Explorations." *The Subversive*. Accessed December 16, 2019. web.archive.org.

———. "*The Subversive* #26: Explorations." *The Subversive*. Accessed December 16, 2019. web.archive.org.

———. "*The Subversive* #32: The Last *Subversive!*" *The Subversive*. Accessed December 16, 2019. web.archive.org.

PRNewswire. "Planetout Debuts; New Online Service Targets Gay Men and Lesbians Worldwide." August 21, 1995. web.archive.org.

Pollack, Andrew. "Ruling May Not Aid Videotex." *New York Times*, September 15, 1987. www.nytimes.com/.

Pothirattanachaikul, Suppanut, Takehiro Yamamoto, Yusuke Yamamoto, and Masatoshi Yoshikawa. "Analyzing the Effects of 'People Also Ask' on Search Behaviors and Beliefs." From *Proceedings of the 31st ACM Conference on Hypertext and Social Media, Virtual Conference*, July 13–15, 2020, 101–10.

Pow, Whitney. "A Trans Historiography of Glitches and Errors." *Feminist Media Histories* 7, no. 1 (2021): 197–230.

Powell, Avery Jasper, and Avery John Porch. "Averies." *Transgender Tapestry*, Winter 2002. DTA.
Pride Media. "Pride! Universe." Accessed December 16, 2019. web.archive.org.
———. "Virtual Reality World Opens Its Doors to Gays, Lesbians, Bisexuals and Transgenders on CompuServe." Pride Media, 1996. Accessed September 13, 2022. web.archive.org.
Prince, Virginia. "Proposing a New Terminology for the Crossdressing Community." *Renaissance News*, February 1992. DTA.
"Print Ad Library: Time Warner—AOL—Keyword GLCF." AdRespect, 1996. www.adrespect.org/.
Prosser, Jay. *Second Skins: The Body Narratives of Transsexuality*. New York: Columbia University Press, 1998.
Raymond, Eric. "Jargon File Resources." Accessed March 23, 2017. www.catb.org/.
———. "September That Never Ended." Accessed March 23, 2017. www.catb.org/.
Raeder, Louise L. "Editorial: All Systems, Go!" *Trans-World Bulletin: Newsletter of the Sunday Society*, October 1989. NTLA-JALC.
———. "Editorial: 'Tis the Season!' Plan a Happy New Year!" *Trans-World Bulletin: Newsletter of the Sunday Society*, December 1989. NTLA-JALC.
———. "Get Involved! 'Lift a Finger!'" *Trans-World Bulletin: Newsletter of the Sunday Society*, November 1989. NTLA-JALC.
Renaissance News. "National Gender News." July 1989. DTA.
———. "'Rules' for Playing the Name Game." April 1991. DTA.
Richards, Eileen. "The Information Highway and You: My Local BBS." *Cross-Talk: The Gender Community's News & Information Monthly*, September 1994. DTA.
Richards, Kymberleigh. "The Need for a New Term." *Cross-Talk: The Gender Community's News & Information Monthly*, September 1990. DTA.
———. "Needing a New Term: The Sequel." *Cross-Talk: The Gender Community's News & Information Monthly*, November 1990. DTA.
———. "Kymberleigh's Clipboard: How Best to Reach Out?" *Cross-Talk: The Gender Community's News & Information Monthly*, May 1994. NTLA-JALC.
———. "Kymberleigh's Clipboard: What about Teenaged Transgendered?" *Cross-Talk: The Gender Community's News & Information Monthly*, December 1994. DTA.
———. "An Open Letter to the Community." *Renaissance News & Views*, September 1997. DTA.
Richmond, Marisa. "The Queen's Throne." Tennessee Vals Newsletter: On-Line Edition, July 1996. Queer Digital History Project. queerdigital.com/.
"Riki Wilchins." Lean In. Accessed June 27, 2022. leanin.org/.
Robards, Brady, Brendan Churchill, Son Vivienne, Benjamin Hanckel, and Paul Byron. "Twenty Years of 'Cyberqueer.'" In *Youth, Sexuality, and Sexual Citizenship*, edited by Peter Aggleton, Rob Cover, Deana Leahy, Daniel Marshall, and Mary Lou Rasmussen, 151–67. London: Routledge, 2018.
Robbins, Rachel. "Murder in the Magnolia State Episode 1: The Ice Pick Cometh." TGForum, 1996. queerdigital.com/.

Roberts, JoAnn. "From the Editor's Pen." *LadyLike*, 1989. DTA.
———. "Hot Buzz." *Renaissance News & Views*, September 1994. DTA.
———. "Hot Buzz." *Cross-Talk: The Gender Community's News & Information Monthly*, February 1996. DTA.
———. "Hot Buzz." *Renaissance News & Views*, October 1997. DTA.
———. "*LadyLike* Magazine Ceases Publication." *LadyLike*, December 13, 2007. web.archive.org.
———. "On My Mind . . ." *LadyLike*, 1999. DTA.
Rose. "The TG Community and The Internet." *Powder & Pearls*, March 1997. NTLA-JALC.
Rose, Stephanie. "Gender Support in the Computer Age." *Chrysalis Quarterly*, Spring 1991. DTA.
Sarah. "New Terminology!?!" *Cross-Talk: The Gender Community's News & Information Monthly*, April 1993. DTA.
Savage, Dan. "Will 'Cisgender' Survive?" The Stranger, September 24, 2014. slog.thestranger.com/.
Scheuerman, Morgan Klaus, Stacy M Branham, and Foad Hamidi. "Safe Spaces and Safe Places: Unpacking Technology-Mediated Experiences of Safety and Harm with Transgender People." *Proceedings of the ACM on Human-Computer Interaction* 2, no. CSCW (2018): 1–27.
Schudson, Zach, and Sari van Anders. "'You Have to Coin New Things': Sexual and Gender Identity Discourses in Asexual, Queer, and/or Trans Young People's Networked Counterpublics." *Psychology & Sexuality* 10, no. 4 (2019): 354–68.
Schwartz, John. "Caution: Children at Play on Information Highway." *Washington Post*, November 28, 1993. www.washingtonpost.com/.
Schwartz, Peter, dir. *All Dressed Up and No Place to Go: The Secret World of Heterosexual Crossdressing*. New York: Cajun Films, 1996.
Sender, Katherine. *Business, Not Politics: The Making of the Gay Market*. New York: Columbia University Press, 2005.
Serano, Julia. "Whipping Girl FAQ on Cissexual, Cisgender, and Cis Privilege." Whipping Girl, August 25, 2011. juliaserano.blogspot.com/.
Shafrir, Doree. "Would You Take a Tumblr with This Man?" *New York Observer*, January 21, 2008. web.archive.org.
Sigusch, Volkmar. "The Neosexual Revolution." *Archives of Sexual Behavior* 27, no. 4 (1998): 331–59.
Silberman, Steve. "Gay.Net Launch Challenges AOL." *Wired*, June 6, 1997. www.wired.com/.
———. "We're Teen, We're Queer, and We've Got E-Mail." *Wired*, November 1, 1994. www.wired.com/.
Sisto, Christine. "Cis-Ridiculous." *National Review*, May 21, 2014. www.nationalreview.com/.
Smith, Gwendolyn Ann. "AOL's Banned Words Make Use vulgar!" soc.support.transgendered, September 7, 1999. groups.google.com.

———. "History Lesson." *Transgender Tapestry*, Summer 2000. DTA.
———. Personal communication, December 11, 2018.
———. Personal communication, September 25, 2021.
———. "Remembering Our Dead: Behind the Website." *Transgender Tapestry*, Summer 1999. DTA.
Smith, Marc A. "Invisible Crowds in Cyberspace." In *Communities in Cyberspace*, edited by Marc Smith and Peter Kollock, 195–218. London: Routledge, 1999.
Sometimes, Natasha. "AOL's Banned Words Make Use vulgar!—Google Groups." Soc.Support.Transgendered, September 6, 1999. groups.google.com.
Sontag, Deborah. "Once a Pariah, Now a Judge: The Early Transgender Journey of Phyllis Frye." *New York Times*, August 29, 2015. www.nytimes.com/.
Spafford, Gene. "Gene Spafford's Personal Pages: Quotable Spaf." Accessed April 10, 2019. spaf.cerias.purdue.edu/.
Squires, Catherine R. "Rethinking the Black Public Sphere: An Alternative Vocabulary for Multiple Public Spheres." *Communication Theory* 12, no. 4 (2002): 446–68.
Steinmetz, Katy. "The Transgender Tipping Point." *Time*, June 9, 2014. time.com/.
Stone, Allucquere Rosanne. "Will the Real Body Please Stand Up?" In *Cyberspace: First Steps*, edited by Michael Benedikt, 81–118. Cambridge, MA: MIT Press, 1991.
Streeter, Thomas. *The Net Effect: Romanticism, Capitalism, and the Internet*. New York: NYU Press, 2011.
"Strikethrough and Boldthrough." Fanlore. Accessed January 5, 2021. fanlore.org/.
Stryker, Susan. "Transgender History, Homonormativity, and Disciplinarity." *Radical History Review* 2008 (Winter 2008): 145–57.
———. *Transgender History: The Roots of Today's Revolution*. 2nd ed. Cypress, CA: Seal, 2017.
"*The Subversive* #13: Letters to the Editor." *The Subversive*. Accessed December 16, 2019. web.archive.org.
Sugawara, Sandra. "Computer Networks and the 1st Amendment: Advanced Technology Raises New Questions and Concerns about an Age-Old Issue." *Washington Post*, October 26, 1991, A12.
Surkan, Karl. "Passing Rhetorics and the Performance of Gender Identity: (Auto) Biographical, Visual, and Virtual Representations of Transgender Subjectivity and Embodiment." PhD diss., University of Minnesota, 2003.
Sutherland, David Kyle. "'Trans Enough': Examining the Boundaries of Transgender-Identity Membership." *Social Problems*, 2021. academic.oup.com.
Swisher, Kara. *AOL.Com*. New York: Random House, 1999.
Szulc, Lukasz. "Digital Gender Disidentifications: Beyond the Subversion versus Hegemony Dichotomy and toward Everyday Gender Practices." *International Journal of Communication* 14 (2020). ijoc.org.
Tamara, Isabel. "Mexico." *Transgender Tapestry*, Fall 2001. DTA.
Tapestry Staff. "Coming Together 2004: A Review of the 18th Annual IFGE Conference." *Transgender Tapestry*, Summer 2004. DTA.

Tayleur, Christine. "Racism and Poverty in the Transgender Community." *gendertrash from hell*, Spring 1995. DTA.

thequeerestplaceontheinternet. "♥ ♥ ♥ ♥ ♥." Tumblr, It's True! May 2021. web.archive.org.

Thomas, Brenda. "Computer Chronicles: Surfing through the TG BBs." *TV-TS Tapestry*, Fall 1995. DTA.

Thornton, Pip. "Geographies of (Con)Text: Language and Structure in a Digital Age." *Computational Culture*, no. 6 (November 28, 2017). computationalculture.net/.

———. "{poem}.py: A Critique of Linguistic Capitalism." *Pip Thornton Art & Research*, June 12, 2016. pipthornton.com/.

Times Mirror Center for the People and the Press. *Technology in the American Household: Americans Going Online . . . Explosive Growth, Uncertain Destinations*. New York: Times Mirror Center for the People and the Press, 1995.

Travis, Trysh. "The Women in Print Movement: History and Implications." *Book History* 11, no. 1 (2008): 275–300.

"Trial Balloon Gay BBS Listing—1989." Queer Digital History Project. Accessed August 14, 2018. queerdigital.com/.

"Tumblr Staff." Accessed December 8, 2020. staff.tumblr.com.

Turner, Fred. *From Counterculture to Cyberculture: Stewart Brand, the Whole Earth Network, and the Rise of Digital Utopianism*. Chicago: University of Chicago Press, 2006.

Untitled Prodigy Commercial. 1990. Prodigy, Inc. Records Collection, Charles Babbage Institute, University of Minnesota.

Usenet Historical Collection. Internet Archive. archive.org.

"US TOO to Be Up and Running This Month!," *Trans-World Bulletin: Newsletter of the Sunday Society*, August 1989. NTLA-JALC.

"Updata." *Wired*, August 1, 1995. www.wired.com/.

Valentine, David. "'The Calculus of Pain': Violence, Anthropological Ethics, and the Category Transgender." *Ethnos* 68, no. 1 (2003): 27–48.

Van Couvering, Elizabeth. "The History of the Internet Search Engine: Navigational Media and the Traffic Commodity." In *Web Search*, 177–206. New York: Springer, 2008.

Vanessa Edwards. "TG Tidbits." *Gulf Coast Transgender Community Transmission Line*, n.d. NTLA-JALC.

"Vanity Club Membership Information—Version 5.0." April 7, 2001. web.archive.org.

"Vanity Club Welcome—Version 5.1." August 2, 2002. web.archive.org.

Venkatesh, Alladi. "Computers and Other Interactive Technologies for the Home." *Communications of the ACM* 39, no. 12 (1996): 47–54.

Venkatesh, Alladi, Eric Shih, and Norman Stolzoff. "A Longitudinal Analysis of Computing in the Home." In *Home Informatics and Telematics: Information, Technology and Society*, edited by Andy Sloane and Felix van Rijn, 205–15. Boston: Springer, 2000.

Venkatesh, Alladi, and Nicholas P. Vitalari. "An Emerging Distributed Work Arrangement: An Investigation of Computer-Based Supplemental Work at Home." *Management Science* 38, no. 12 (1992): 1687–706.

Vitalari, Nicholas P., Alladi Venkatesh, and Kjell Gronhaug. "Computing in the Home: Shifts in the Time Allocation Patterns of Households." *Communications of the ACM* 28, no. 5 (1985): 512–22.

Weise, Elizabeth. "Gay and Lesbian Net Surfers: A Dream Market in the Online World." Associated Press, June 23, 1996. apnews.com/.

Wells, Jennifer. "Letter: T.G.I.F. (sic) News." *TGIC News*, August 1991. DTA.

———. "Proposal from Jennifer Wells: Gender Community BBS & Data Base." *TV-TS Tapestry*, 1989. DTA.

Westbrook, Laurel. "Becoming Knowably Gendered: The Production of Transgender: Possibilities and Constraints in the Mass and Alternative Press from 1990–2005 in the United States." In *Transgender Identities: Towards a Social Analysis of Gender Diversity*, edited by Sally Hines and Tam Sanger, 43–63. London: Routledge, 2010.

Wheeler, Glen. "Sex Role Revolt." *now Magazine*, June 11, 1992, 12–13.

Whittaker, Steve, Loen Terveen, Will Hill, and Lynn Cherny. "The Dynamics of Mass Interaction." In *From Usenet to CoWebs*, edited by Christopher Lueg and Danyel Fisher, 79–91. London: Springer, 2003.

Whittle, Stephen. "The Trans-Cyberian Mail Way." *Social & Legal Studies* 7, no. 3 (1998): 389–408.

Wilchins, Riki Anne. "How to Dilute Your Focus (Just Mix in Two Eggs and Stir)." *Transgender Tapestry*, Summer 1998. DTA.

———. "A Note from Your Editrix." *In Your Face*, Spring 1995. DTA.

———. "What's in a Name: The Politics of Gender Speak." *Transgender Tapestry*, Winter 1995. DTA.

Williams, Cristan. "So, I Hear Trans People Recently Invented This Whole Cis/Trans Thing. . . ." The TransAdvocate, August 12, 2013. www.transadvocate.com/.

Wilson, Diane. "Soc.Support.Transgendered FAQ." Firelily, January 24, 2001. web.archive.org.

Wolfe, Gary. "The (Second Phase of the) Revolution Has Begun." *Wired*, October 1, 1994. www.wired.com/.

Wright, Steven T. "'The Linux of Social Media'—How LiveJournal Pioneered (Then Lost) Blogging." Ars Technica, January 22, 2019. arstechnica.com/.

Xavier, Jessica. "On The Future of the TG Community." *AEGIS News*, April 1998. DTA.

Yarborough, Melanie. "California Unity '97: The TG Community Reaches Critical Mass." *Transgender Tapestry*, Fall 1997. DTA.

Youth Gender Project. "YGP: Resources & Events," June 7, 2004. web.archive.org.

"Youth Advocacy," GenderPAC. March 3, 2001. web.archive.org.

Zimman, Lal, and Will Hayworth. "How We Got Here: Short-Scale Change in Identity Labels for Trans, Cis, and Non-Binary People in the 2000s." *Proceedings of the Linguistic Society of America* 5, no. 1 (2020): 499–513.

INDEX

Page numbers in *italics* indicate a Figure or Table

ACLU, 141, 219n33
ACLU et al. v. Reno, 140
ADA. *See* Americans with Disabilities Act
AIDS Education Global Information System (AEGIS), 40–41, 118–19
algorithms, search, 28, 177, 193; datafied language of, 184–87; linguistic bias in, 197; misaligned associations, 191; People Also Ask, 281n62; power to change events, 186–87
Algorithms of Oppression (Noble), 178
American Educational Gender Information Service (AEGIS), 7, 118–19, 165
American Psychiatric Association, 168
Americans with Disabilities Act (ADA), 45
America Online (AOL), 20, 24, 57, 61; account terminations, 69–70; America On Hold debacle, 79; branding, 65; "churn rates," 66, 76; content management, 65–66, 67; "family orientation," 70; forum promotion issue, 76–78; free trial CD, 56; gay and lesbian community relationship change, 74–80, *75–78*; gay and lesbian space on, 63; ISPs as threat to, 79; lawsuit, 115, 224n4; message threading, 85; onQ *vs.*, 79; peak hours and dial-in failures, 115, 224n4; Phillips TOS campaign, 70–74; pricing change of 1996, 115; relaunch, 68; terms banned by, 26–27; title listing censorship by, 219n33; two campaigns, 66, 69–74, 220n64; Usenet access, 84, 89; Web access through, 115–16; Web-hosting service, 123. *See also* Transgender Community Forum
America Online Gender Group (AOLGG), 68–74, *70–74*; "good citizen" narrative and, 141, 225n44
AMNET BBS, 40
androgyne, *9, 9*, 24
AO3. *See* Archive of Our Own
AOLGG. *See* America Online Gender Group
Archive of Our Own (AO3), 207–8
archives, 202–3, 204, 206–7; privacy and, 22; proposal for future trans platform, 208–9; research method and, 21–22
Archives Unleashed Project, 19
ARPANET, 81
Aryan Liberty Net, 39–40
autogynephilia, 195

Bailey, J. Michael, 195
BBSes. *See* bulletin board systems
Beecroft, Carol, 5, 9
Benjamin, Harry, 158
bigender, 8
"bigenderist," 179, 213n10
birls, 172
Black women, Google SERP and, 178

Blake, Laura, 101–2, 223n65; "cisgender ideal" posts of, 103–13, *108*, *109*; "Coming Out FAQ" by, 104–7, 111; flame war with Leigh, 113; Frye criticized by, 223n63; trans activist organization of, 103, 223n62; "transgender" definition of, 105; on transsexuality, 111, 223n67
blogging, 173, 174, 176
Bockting, Walter O., 195
born-digital documents, 21, 22, 207
Buijs, Carl, 94, 95, 102, 103–4
bulletin board systems (BBSes), 14, 18, 24, 202; advice columns, 37; affordances, 30; anonymity afforded by, 30; benefits, 30; call time, 37; chains of access, 54; coming out as trans with, 49, 217n70; communicating methods on, 48; communication services vs, 61; computer literacy and, 54–55; content reproduction, 54, 218n89; decline of, 152–54; desire for gender-oriented, 41; disembodiment and experimentation, 50–51; false fronts use by, 47; files hosted by, 53; first, 36–38, *37*; gatekeeping methods of, 47; gay-themed, 40; GIF library on, 53; group and newsletter format replicated by, 29; hate groups use of, 39–40; independent nature advantage of, 206; listings for trans-specific, 38; maintenance of, 36; nationwide communication prior to, 29; 1980s names of, 38; 1990s, 38; online transgender identity claimed through, 46–50; political organizing through, 38–46, *44*; preservation issue and, 206; privacy afforded by, 30, 46–48, 60; prominent transgender, 61; "real" woman on community and, 156; report on "sexually-oriented," 66; rhetoric shift of, 61, 62; sharing lore through, 51–55; as source material, 20; telephone bills and, 49, 217n70; as text-based medium, 50–51; user hosting and governance, 209

"bunch of girls who'd just gone shopping," 70–74

Camp Trans, 194–95
Canadian Human Rights Commission, 102–3
CD. *See* crossdresser
CDA. *See* Communications Decency Act
CDS. *See* Creative Design Services
chasers, 142–43, 225n49
chat rooms, AOL, 65; AOLGG, 68; the Gazebo, 74, 76; guides, 68–69; sanctioned/unsanctioned, 63; terminology ban, 66, 219n33; "TV Chat," 67, 68, 71; words banned on AOL, 66, 162, 219n33
churn, 66, 76
cisgender: adoption of, 27, 82, 113–14; Blake and, 101–7; Blake on passing and, 111–12; critiques and definitions, 93–96, 95, 104, 105, 222n40; crossdressing and, 110–11; etymological record, 95; first use of cis-/trans binary, 222n46; "Laura Blake Drinking Game," 105–6, 223n67; modern definitions of, 114; "monosexual" *vs.*, 94; network of posts using, *99*, *100*, *101*; origins and creators, 94, 96, 102, 222n49; SRS and, 105; terms prior to, 94; treemap of use on Usenet, *101*; usage, 96–101, *99*, *100*, *101*, 223nn55–56; Usenet and, 82, 93, 95, 114; Usenet posts using, *99*, *100*, *101*; visibility of term in 2000s, 198–99
"cisgender ideal," Blake on, 103, *108*, 108–13; "Coming Out FAQ" on, 104–7; threads containing "cisgender rules" and, 107–10, *108*, *109*
class, social, 5–6, 25; PC ownership and, 17
Clinton administration, 1, 15
coming out: older generation and, 170; online, 3, 147–52, 164
"Coming Out FAQ" (Blake), 104–7, 111
Coming Together, Working Together (CTWT), 31, 32, 41

INDEX | 255

commercial services: ads, 58; "adult" spaces on, 64; comparison of transgender support areas of, 63–64, 67; content moderation and liability issues, 64–67, 219n25, 219n33; email lists published by, 61, 218n18; "gay-friendly" billing of, 63–64; gender community presence on, 58–60; home PCs, trans community and, 61–65; internet access and, 57; ISP fees and, 79; LGBT users marketing by, 78, *78*, 79–80; 1990s largest, 57; prior to AOL, 67–68; privacy of BBS compared to, 60; skepticism about, 60; subscriber fees and services offered by, 57. *See also specific services*
Communications Decency Act (CDA), 139–41, 161, 219n25, 225n38
community groups. *See* support groups, in-person community and
CompuServe, 57, 61, 79, 144; "adult" topics and forum format, 66
CompuServe Magazine, 63, 67
computers: BBS and, 29; "computer crossdressing," 50; home PCs, 13–15, 17, 58; LGBT market and, 57; literacy, BBS and, 54–55; trans people presence in history of, 16–17, 18; warning against using work, 60
content moderation: AOL example of, 20, 65–70; children and, 137, 139–40; commercial services of 1990s and, 64–67, 219n25, 219n33; filtering software for, 140–42, 143–44; "good citizen" status and, 141, 225n44; independent contractors for, 66; ISPs and, 57; liability and, 64, 219n25; self-rating, 144; volunteer moderators, 66
cost per click (CPC), 197
Cox, Laverne, 201
CPC. *See* cost per click
Creative Design Services (CDS), 117
Cross Connection, 61, 62, 152–53, *153*

crossdresser (CD), 5, 9, *9*; AOLGG issues for, 72–73; BBS and, 49; computer crossdressing among BBS, 50; context for history of, 24; glamour shot passion of, 53; home pages of, 126; Johnson, B., predictions for, 146–47; membership in clubs, 6; newsletter networks of, 22, 31–32; in 1980s terminology, 9; 1990s number of, 146; 1990s terminology concerns for, 10, 12; previous visibility of, 23; trans community dismissal of, 23–24
crossdressing: computer, 50; Leigh book on, 112; sexual deviancy stigma, 66
Cross-Talk, 10, *11*, 35, 58, 62; closing of, 153
CTWT. *See* Coming Together, Working Together
cyberporn. *See* pornography
"cyberutopians," 41–43

Dawn Benedict, TV Detective, 90
Defosse, Dana Leland, 94, 95, 96, 222n49
Denny, Dallas, 7, 118, 174, 218n89; response to youth inquiry, 167, 228n80; WWW and, 120
diagnoses, "transgender," 129–30
Dictionary Project, 9–10
"digital divide," 15, 215n38
Digital Transgender Archive, 21
disidentification, 182
DocTalk, 45

The Educational TV Channel (ETVC), 31
EEF. *See* Erickson Education Foundation
email: first trans-specific, 54; published lists, 61, 218n18; Usenet email addresses, 84
"The Empire Strikes Back" (Stone), 50
Enke, Finn, 95
Erickson, Reed, 117
Erickson Education Foundation (EEF), 4, 31, 41, 117
erotica. *See* trans erotica
ETVC. *See* The Educational TV Channel

Facebook, 3, 173, 181
fandom, 172, 181, 205
FAQs: Blake "cisgender ideal," 104–7, 111; newsgroup charters and, 91–92; pornography defined in, 140
femail, 61
feminism, 194–96; anti-trans, 5
FidoNet, 36, 38, 42
filtering software, 140–44
First Amendment, 137, 141, 142
flaming (flame wars), 86, 89–90, 91, 92, 113; user banned for, 102
folksonomy, 177, 180, 192, 230n23
Foundation for Personality Expression (FPE), 5, 8
Frye, Phyllis, 103, 149, 223n63, 226n12
FTM International (FTMI), 6, 23, 164

Gardner, Angela, 6, 60, 141–42, 148
Gateway Gender Alliance (GGA), 6, 37
Gay, Lesbian, and Straight Education Network (GLSEN), 167, 228n80
Gay and Lesbian Community Forum (GLCF), 63, 66, 68, 69, 77; popularity, 76; TV and CD member discomfort, 72–73; youth access to, 161, 163
the Gazebo, AOL chat room, 74, 76
GEA. *See* Gender Education and Advocacy
"gender, " efforts to replace, 10
gender community, 2; ambivalence within, 90; changing generations, 170–73; computer communication priming of, 16–17; Internet, commercial services and, 58–60; Johnson, B., predictions for 2010, 146; 1980s, 5, 9, 17–18; 1990s, 17–18, 149, 226nn11–12; 1994 percentage of whites in, 149; people of color in, 149, 226n11; publications as supporting, 7, 30; racism and, 149, 226nn11–12. *See also* terminology; trans community; *specific topics*
gender dysphoria, PAA widget and, 189, *189*

Gender Education and Advocacy (GEA), 119, 168
Gender Euphoria, 155–57
gender identity: ambivalence about shared, 90; career and, 1; gender performance and, 104–5, 114; identity labeling and, 182–83; tagging for expressing, 181–83
GenderLine, 61–62, 67
GenderNet, 29, *37*, 37–38, 66; choosing personal name for login, 47–48; email list launched by, 54; name confusion, 46–47; user self-acceptance story, 50–51
GenderPAC, 7, 149–50, 213n6; closing of, 170, 229n94; protest against broader focus of, 168–69; youth outreach program, 169
gender performance: "cisgender," gender identity and, 104–5, 114; embodiment vs, 105
"genderqueer," 12–13, 113–14, 170, 214n23; "Latinx" and, 199; in more example sentences section, 196, 231n76
"Gender Terms Mix-N-Match," 10, *11*
GenderYOUTH, 169
General Electric Network for Information Exchange (GEnie), 57
generational changes, 170–73
generation gap, 201–2; Tumblr and, 204
"Genetic Girl" (GG), 94
GEnie. *See* General Electric Network for Information Exchange
Geocities, 125, 126, 145; FAQ, 140; filtering software and, 140; pornography policy, 140, 142; WestHollywood on, 123, 135, 136, 143, 144
GG. *See* "Genetic Girl"
GGA. *See* Gateway Gender Alliance
GLCF. *See* Gay and Lesbian Community Forum
GLSEN. *See* Gay, Lesbian, and Straight Education Network

INDEX | 257

Golden Gate Girls/Guys. *See* Gateway Gender Alliance
Google: AdWords and AdSense, 196–99, 231n82; algorithm reliance, 193; autocomplete, *185*, 187; emergence and financial success, 184; information reality, 178. *See also* algorithms, search; People Also Ask; search engine results page
Gulf Coast Transgender Community Transmission Line, 132–33

history, ownership of: account deletion events and, 207–8; generation gap narrative and, 201–2; historical gaps and, 202; message board closure and, 203; obsolescence and, 204; preservation threat, 205–6; server ownership for, 208–9; trans research importance of, 203–4. *See also* net histories
HIV/AIDS, BBSes and, 40
home pages, *126*, *127*, 128; coming out on, 148, 164; Davita's, 129, *130–33*, 143; digital citizenship and, 136–45; directories of, 135; disclaimers, 136–37, 138, *139*, 142–43; without disclaimers, 143; gendering practices in design of, *134*; 1990s popularity of, 148; number of trans-related GeoCities, 125; photo gallery, *134*; self-presentation on, 116, 126, 127–33, 142; social aspect of, 133–36; social media platforms replacing, 171–73; trans memoir *vs.*, 131; trans youth, 144–45, 163–65
home PCs, 13–15, 17, 58–60; commercial services for, 57, 61–65; youth limited to, 164
hotline, 35, 123–24
HTML, 1, 129
Human Outreach and Achievement Institute, 5, 213n10
hypergendering, 132

identity labeling, 182–83
IFGE. *See* International Foundation for Gender Education
inequity, 149–50
information activism, 7
information seeking, trans: digital files and limitations in, 118; emergence of independent sites for, 121; Google keywords for, 186; in-person support groups for, 117; World Wide Web transforming, 116–20; youth Internet access for, 160; youth issues of, 167. *See also* archives; libraries
informed consent model, 191
Instagram, 18
institutional connections, youth. *See* organizations
institutional politics, trans, 168
International Foundation for Gender Education (IFGE), 31, 146, 148; youth outreach, 165, 169–70; youth study, 159–60
Internet: access, 151, 152–53, 160, 161–62; author early experience of, 1–2, *2*; blessing/curse view of, 156; browsers, 16; coming out on, 3, 147–52, 164; "digital divide," 15, 215n38; early platforms, 14; education level and, 151; English language dominance on, 151–52; "fantasy" world of, 155; instruction materials, 58, *59*; interviews on using, 177, 203; as lifeline for trans members, 2; local networks weakened by, 3; minors use of, 137, 139, 143; misinformation concern for, 156; national organizations decline blamed on, 154, 227n25; net histories, 3–4, 26; newsletters for trans Net access, 19–20; 1990s access to, 57; novice *vs.* expert views of, 60–61; panic over youth use of, 137, 139; parallel shifts role of, 27–28; Phillips, L., on offline embodiment and, 155–56, 227n30; print-and-mail *vs.*, 119;

258 | INDEX

Internet (*cont.*)
  promotion and family image of, 58; reliance on, 3; as revolutionary tool, 201–2; risk in community groups *vs.*, 154; time, 21; "transgender" and, 2–3, 13; trans youth use of, 160–65; variety of terms for, 20; walled gardens of, 57, 80, 116, 206; Web histories, methods and resources, 19–26; youth limited to family/home, 164. *See also* commercial services; home PCs; *specific platforms*
Internet Archive Wayback Machine, 204
Internet Explorer, 85, 144
Internet service providers (ISPs), 57, 79
isolation, 34
ISPs. *See* Internet service providers

J2CP Information Services, 41, 117, 217n56
James, Andrea, 95, 222n47
Janus Information Facility, 117
Jersey Shore System, 53
Johnson, Bette Lee, 146–47, 170
"Join or Die," 11
Jorgensen, Christine, 68
Journal for the International Alliance for Male Feminism, 8

Kane, Ariadne, 5, 24, 213n10
Kirk, Sheila, 159–60, 165

Ladylike, 148, 171, 174
landing pages, *121*
language: commodity value of, 197, 231n78; datafied, 177, 183–84, 196, 199; decontextualized, 196; linguistic capitalism, 196–99, 231n82, 232n85; search and tagging impact on, 180
"Latinx," 199, 232n88
"Laura Blake Drinking Game," 105–6, 223n67
law, US, 4; CDA, 139–41, 161, 219n25, 225n38; terminology and, 12

lawsuits: AOL, 115, 224n4; filtering software, 141–42
LCSH. *See* Library of Congress Subject Headings
Leigh, Lacey, 112–13
Lexico. *See* Oxford Dictionary Online
libraries: BBS GIF, 53; cataloging and bibliographies, 118; community group information, 117; library card system, 51–52; printing presses of 1980s and, 117
Library of Congress Subject Headings (LCSH), 180
LibraryThing, 180
LiveJournal (LJ), 171–73, 175, 179; account deletion, 207–8

Main, Terri, 63, 67
Mainstream Loudoun v. Loudoun County Library, 141
The Man Who Would Be Queen (Bailey), 195
Marques, Susana, 133, 135, *135*
Matthews, Donna Lynn, 96, 105, 113–14
McCloskey, Deirdre, 49, 50, 52, 217n70
medicalization, 87, 188
Meese Commission, 66
memoir, trans, 127–28, 129–31
messages: flame, 86, 89–90, 91; message boards, 203–4, 206; threading, 84–85
metadata schema, 176
Michigan Womyn's Music Festival (MWMF), 195, 196
microblogging, 174
Moms on the Net, 58
"more example sentences," search engine, 194–96, 231n76
Mosaic, 84, 85, 120, 128
MWMF. *See* Michigan Womyn's Music Festival

naming practices, 150–51
National Center for Transgender Equality, 113, 190

National Gay and Lesbian Task Force, 165
National Gender Lobbying Day, 13
national organizations, membership decline, 154, 227n25
net histories, 3–4, 26. *See also* Web histories
Netscape Navigator, 85, 144
"New Economy," 15
newsgroups: Blake posts to, 101–3; charters and FAQs, 91–92; newsreaders and, 84, 89; preservation issue, 206; Usenet transgender, 84, 87–93, *88*; user behavior on, 91
newsletter exchange network (newsletters): author names, 23; clip art, 32–34, *33*, *34*; comics published in, 32, *33*; computer workshops, instructions published in, 59; decline of, 157; demographics reflected in, 22; enclave sphere of, 29; GCLF, 68; *Gender Euphoria* demise and, 155–57; Internet and, 154–55, 227n30; making first contact through, 34–36; newsletter production, 29–30, 31; privacy issue, 23, 35; rise of, 29; serial stories in, 31–32; shared social identity through, 31; trans Net access through, 19–20
newsreaders, 84–85
New York Times, 175
Noble, Safiya, 178

obscenity, content moderation and, 64, 139
"On a Screen Near You" (Elmer-Dewitt), 137
onQ (formerly QView), *77*, 78, 79–80
Organization for Transformative Works (OTW), 207, 208
organizations: archives lacking for, 206–7; decline of national, 154, 227n25; first

youth, 158; youth connections with, 165–70. *See also specific organizations*
OTW. *See* Organization for Transformative Works
Out & About (Leigh), 112, 113
OutPride, 166
Outreach Institute for Gender Studies, 5
Oxford Dictionary Online (Lexico), 178, 192, 194, 195, 196; algorithm reliance of, 193
Oxford English Dictionary, 195; Blake post reference in, 102; cisgender entry in, 93, 95
Oxford Languages, 178

PAA. *See* People Also Ask
passing, Blake on, 111–12
People Also Ask (PAA) widget, 178, 187–92, *188–92*
people of color, 149, 161, 178, 226n11; naming practices and, 150–51
People With AIDS (PWAs), 40, 41
Philadelphia Daily News, 71
Phillips, Linda, 155–56, 204, 227n30, 227n35
Phillips, Melanie, 67–68, 69, 220n40, 225n44; reframing efforts of, 70–74
Phi Pi Epsilon. *See* Foundation for Personality Expression
photo sharing practices, Internet history influence on current, 18
PICS. *See* Platform for Internet Content Selection
PlanetOut, 78, 79
Platform for Internet Content Selection (PICS), 144
Playboy, 29, 66
political organizing (activism): first trans-specific political action committees, 7
political organizing (activism), BBSes and, 38–46; first activist networking, 41; US TOO and, 42–45, *44*

pornography (cyberporn), 24–25, 161, 178; chasers and, 142–43; definition, 140; filtering software lawsuits involving, 141–42; GeoCities policy against, 140, 142; technopanic, 137, 139; Tumblr tags and, 198

Pride Media, 78, 79

Prince, Virginia, 5, 23–24, 66, 204; "bigenderist" and, 179, 213n10; crossdressing image focus of, 30; publication risk and, 31; terminology coined by, 8, 213n10; "TV Chat" reference to, 68

privacy, 22, 23, 25, 35; BBS as affording, 30, 46–48, 60; LJ vs. Facebook, 173

Prodigy, 57, 64–65

pseudonymity, 25, 175

publications and periodicals, 29; digital vs. print, 121; first gender community, 30; glossaries in, 213n12; history ownership and, 207; Internet impact on, 147–48; Internet introduced through, 58; movement building aided by, 7; prolific publishers of videos and, 117; queer youth, 163; risk of, 31; world fitted to words through, 30–34

PWAs. See People With AIDS

Queens' Liberation Front (QLF), 4
Queer Resources Directory, 160
queer youth. See trans youth; youth, issues for queer and trans
QView, 66, 76–77, 79–80

"rabid feminist," 192
race, digital communication access and, 25
racism, 149, 176, 208, 226nn11–12
radical feminism, 5, 194
Raeder, Louise L., 43–46, 217n56
REA. See Renaissance Education Association
Recreational Software Advisory Council on the Internet (RSACi), 144

Reagan, Ronald, 15
Real ID, 141
Refuge Restrooms app, 202
Remembering Our Dead, 121–22, 122, 123
Renaissance Education Association (REA), 6, 118
Renaissance News, 54
Renaissance Transgender Association, 141–42
respectability politics, 24, 141
revolutions, two: research method, 21; Rose on, 16, 46; sources for researching, 19, 20, 21
Richards, Kymberleigh, 153, 154, 159, 160; disidentification of, 182; search for identity term, 182, 230n36; youth online viewed by, 162, 164, 165
Rimm, Marty, 137, 139
"Rising of the Moons," 31–32
Robbins, Rachel, 90
Roberts, JoAnn, 89, 117, 140, 154, 225n38; Ladylike final message of, 174; as Renaissance editor, 54
Rose, Stephanie, 16, 46
RSACi. See Recreational Software Advisory Council on the Internet

SafeSurf, 144
Savage, Dan, 94
search engine results page (SERP), Google, 177–78; dictionary definition feature, 192–96, 193; PAA feature, 187–92, 188–92; web advertising and, 184; widgets, 178
search engines: datafied language of, 184; directory-based, 184; language shifts through tagging and, 180; terminology commodification on, 184–87; "transsexual fantasies" in, 193, 193, 196; webrings compared with, 133. See also algorithms
Secret Little Haven, 205, 205–6
separatism, 103, 111

Serano, Julia, 93, 96
SERP. *See* search engine results page
servers: BBS, 36; ownership, 208–9
sex reassignment surgery (SRS), 127; "cisgender" debates and, 97; cisgender definitions and, 105; PAA (People Also Ask) results for, 188–89, 191, *192*
"sexual deviancy" stigma, 66
shared identity, ambivalence about, 90
Smith, Gwendolyn (Gwen) Ann, 69, 74, 75, 121; on digital technology, 157–58
social media platforms, 83; advertisers, 181; archival features proposal for future trans, 208–9; BBS predecessor to, 14, 18; binary divisions underlying, 181; classification systems, 180–81; ephemerality of, 204; generational change and, 171–73; home page ancestor of profile, 126; infrastructure, 180–81; new terminology produced on, 179–84; social networking on, 173; trans community shift from private sharing to, 18. *See also* tagging; *specific platforms*
Society for the Second Self. *See* Tri-Ess
SRS. *See* sex reassignment surgery
STAR. *See* Street Transvestite Action Revolutionaries
Star Trek, 43
"stealth," 36, 46
Stone, Allucquère Rosanne (Sandy), 50
Street Transvestite Action Revolutionaries (STAR), 4
The Subversive, 89, 225n44
support groups, in-person community and: dissolution of, 154, 156, 227n25; generational change and, 171; information libraries and, 117; Internet as adjunct to, 148; Internet threat to, 147; local and online, 3; Mexico-based, 151–52; Usenet vitriol inhibiting attendance at, 91; video nights hosted by, 117; youth access to, 159–60, 166;

youth-only, 167; youth view of, 171. *See also* publications and periodicals

tabloid talk shows, 128
tagging (tags), 28, 175, 176, 199; commodity value and, 198, 232n85; as identity markers, 181–83; language transformed by algorithm and, 177; LCSH compared with, 180; policing, 183; study on LibraryThing, 180
TCF. *See* Transgender Community Forum
technography, 187
technology, digital communication: biggest innovations in, 28; digital utopians, 41–43; good citizenship, 140–45, 225n44; history ownership and, 202; 1990s in-home, 57–67; print compared with, 121; race and, 25; rise of home PC ownership, 13–15; Smith on, 157–58; youth and, 137, 139. *See also* commercial services
technopanic, 137, 139, 161–62
technoutopians, 43
terminology: AOL banning trans, 26–27, 69; ban on chat, 66, 162, 219n33; coded, 67; as commodity, 184–87; experimental, 9; gender community and, 8–13, *9*, *11*; glossaries in printed publications, 213n12; goal of defining shared, 8–13, 179; 1980s, 8–9, *9*, 213n12; 1990s, 9–13, *11*, 213n15, 214n23; for non gender community members, 94; Prince efforts in, 8; Richards search for identity, 182, 230n36; turf wars, 10; 2000s shift in, 179; user agency and, 28. *See also* cisgender; *Oxford English Dictionary*; *specific terms*
Terms of Service (TOS), 66, 69; AOL 1994 update of, 74, 220n64; Phillips campaign for new, 70–74
TG. *See* transgenderist
TG Forum. *See* Transgender Forum
TGForum.com, 90

TGNet. *See* TransgenderNet
Thornton, Pip, 192
Time, 137, 201
Today Show, 58
topic sets, Google PAA, 187
trans activism: of Blake, 103, 223n62; digital corporatization and, 3; information activism and, 7; institutional politics and, 168; middle-class, 24; respectability politics and, 24; Usenet user debate on, 97; us-them semantic in, 113; Wilchins and, 168. *See also specific organizations*
trans community: crossdressers viewed within, 23–24; erotica attitude gap within, 25, 215n61; hierarchy, 23; history sense lacking in, 206–7; information seeking, 116; Internet reliance issue for, 3; linguistic capitalism and, 196–99, 231n82, 232n85; 1970s, 2, 4–6; 1980s, 5–6; 1990s, 7, 17–18. *See also* terminology
TransEqual, 102, 103
trans erotica: limited reach of 1980s/1990s, 24; rise of visibility, 25; trans community attitudes towards, 24, 25, 215n61
Transexual Menace, 7, 13, 168; Internet user profiles and, 17; 1990s terminology and, 10
"transgender": Blake definition of, 105; "cisgender" and, 114; diagnoses, 129–30; gender performance / embodiment and, 105; "genderqueer" as replacing, 113–14; Google AdWords Planner and, 197; Google SERP dictionary definitions of, 192–96; Internet and, 2–3, 13; Lexico definition, 105; in online dictionaries, 192–93; PAA widget on, 188–90, *189*, *190*, 231n62; Prince opposition to, 179; as umbrella identity category, 97
transgender community: class and, 5–6, 24; "gay market" and, 57; Internet and, 2–3, 13; modern lexicon for, 179–84; movement history, 4–7; positive media coverage of trans individuals, 201; transgender platform era, 173; trans individuals in mass media, 127–28. *See also* gender community; terminology; *specific topics*
Transgender Community Forum (TCF), 74, *75*, 76, *76*, 79; Blake writings in, 193; GEA website hosting, 122. *See also* Transgender Gazebo
Transgendered Teens Web Directory, 171
Transgender Forum (TG Forum), 121, *121*, 122–23
Transgender Fund, 166–67
Transgender Gazebo, 80, 171
transgenderist (TG), 9, *9*, 24
TransgenderNet (TGNet), 38
Transgender Tapestry, 103, 171, 182; final issue, 174; Internet and education level discussed in, 151; on "transgender," 97; trans youth content featured by, 167–68; youth study announced in, 159
transition: memoirs, 127–28, 129–30, 129–31; 1980s information resources on, 117; youth, 163–64
trans memoirs, 127–28, 129–31; home page vs., 131
"trans pride," ads linked with, 197
transsexual (TS), 9, 9–10; banning of term by AOL, 26–27; Blake on, 111, 223n67; crossdresser term and, 12; definition flame wars between, 91; Google definitions of, 193, *193*; name changes as "rebirth," 47; "real," 130; "transexual" spelling of, 10, 213n15; "transsexual fantasies" in search engines, 193, *193*, 196
"transtrenders," 91
Transvestia, 5, 30
transvestite (TV), 9, *9*, 9–10; AOLGG divisions and, 72–73; terminology and, 8; "TV Chat" and, 67, 68, 71

trans youth: home pages, 144–45, 163–65; on Instagram, 18; Internet lifeline for, 2, 28; Internet use by, 160–65; local groups limited access for, 28. *See also* youth, issues for queer and trans

Trans-Youth Services (TYS), 165–66

Tri-Ess, 5, 23–24, 31, 170; cross-dressing text promoted by, 112; library card system of, 51–52; membership, 6; 1990s, 146; sorority model, 135; terminology of 1990s and, 9, *11*; youth chapter of, 158

TS. *See* transsexual

Tumblr, 174–77; "adult content" ban on, 199–200; commodity value of queer tags on, 198, 232n85; generation gap and, 204; pornography, tags and, 198; scholarship, 198

TV. *See* transvestite

Twitter, 81, 91, 204

TYS. *See* Trans-Youth Services

United Sisterhood of Transsexual Outreach Organizations (US TOO), 42–46, *44*, 217n56

Urban Dictionary, 192

Usenet, 24, 27, 82, 179, 209; affordances, 110; as anarchic and decentralized, 81, 83–86, 92–93; Blake "cisgender ideal" posts on, 103–13, *108*, *109*; "cisgender" as originating on, 93, 95, 114; e-zine survey of posters, 88–89, 221n27; flaming on, 86, 89–90, 91, 92; negative image of, 89–90, 92–93, 222n47; network of posts with "cisgender" and variants, *99*, *100*; newsgroup topics, 88; posts using "cisgender" and variants, *99*, *100*, *101*; quoting use, *98*, 100; spam and, 83–84; trans activism debate on, 97; transgender newsgroups on, 84, 87–93, *88*; as unregulated, 83, 84; user arguments, 90

users, Internet: agency, 28; channel model and, 80; gender community active, 16; gender community occupations, 16–17; names of, 4; net history range of, 4; 1990s commercial services and, 56–57; percentages, 16; rising number of, 16. *See also specific platforms*

US TOO. *See* United Sisterhood of Transsexual Outreach Organizations

Vanity Club, 135–36

walled gardens, 57, 80, 116, 206

Washington Post, 67

Web histories; method and resources, 19–26

webrings, 133–35, 148, 163

websites: archived, 204; graphics addition to WWW and, 120–21; group, 123–24; hotline *vs.*, 123–24; 1990s features of, 124–25; 1995 launch of notable, *120*, *121*, *121*, *122*; 1996 rise in, *122*, 122–24, *124*; rating programs, 144; shift away from, 171; user ownership, 209

WELL. *See* Whole Earth 'Lectric Link

WestHollywood, 123, 135, 136, 143, 144

"What Joann Has Been Up To," 110–11

Whipping Girl (Serano), 93

whiteness: naming practices and, 150–51; white privilege, 149–50, 226n13

white supremacists, BBS use by, 39, 40

Whole Earth 'Lectric Link (WELL), 42

Wikipedia, 189–90; cisgender page on, 95–96, 105

Wilchins, Riki, 7, 168, 213n6; discrimination and, 149–50, 226n14; "genderqueer" use by, 214n23; political activism and, 13; profession of, 17; "transexual" spelling campaign of, 10, 213n15

Women's Studies Listserv (WMST-L), 96

"woodworking," 36

264 | INDEX

World Wide Web (WWW), 15, 17; advantages of, 119; AOL access to, 115–16; appeal of surfing on, 116; archives, 202–3, 204; children's access to, 137, 139; "cisgender" adoption and, 27; clearing house model compared to, 118–19; concerns over minors' access to, 116; digital citizenship concerns on, 136–45; early, 205; getting online in 1990s, 120–22; information seeking transformed by, 116–20; method and resources for studying histories, 19–26; prior self-representation formats vs., 127–28; site-rating programs, 144; "structure of feeling" surrounding early, 128. *See also* home page; websites

Xerox machine, 31
X-Stop, 141–42

Yahoo Groups, 206
YAO. *See* Youth Action Online
youth, issues for queer and trans, 171; community-group access, 159–60, 166, 167; institutional connections and, 165–70; Internet use and, 160–65; parental consent and, 159–60; risk of youth outreach, 158
Youth Action Online (YAO), 162–63
YouthArts, 161
Youth Assistance Organization. *See* Youth Action Online

ABOUT THE AUTHOR

AVERY DAME-GRIFF is a Lecturer of Women's and Gender Studies at Gonzaga University. He founded and curates the Queer Digital History Project (queerdigital.com), an independent digital history project documenting pre-2010 LGBTQ digital spaces online.

www.ingramcontent.com/pod-product-compliance
Lightning Source LLC
Chambersburg PA
CBHW020249030426
42336CB00010B/684